Mel Bay Presents

FLATPICKING THE RAGS AND POLKAS

(plus other 3, 4 and 5 part tunes)

BY
Steve Kaufman

1 2 3 4 5 6 7 8 9 0

Visit us on the Web at www.melbay.com — E-mail us at email@melbay.com

Table of Contents

Introduction

Welcome to my collection of favorite rags, polkas and other multi-sectional pieces. I wanted to bring this type of project to you not only to illustrate how I play and perform these great pieces, but also to help you to develop a better sense of musical concentration. When playing a two-part fiddle tune or a ballad of some kind, one is permitted to think of other things while playing. When played at full speed, a two-part tune is usually completed in 30-40 seconds. This is a short burst of concentration. If you are then going into improvising on the theme, the concentration degree also changes. In order for thoughts to flow in improvisational modes, the mind must be free. Most players look as if they are in a trance at this point. This type of thinking is called the left/right brain crossover.

Something else you will develop through this book of great pieces is musical stamina. You will develop the ability to play longer at a sitting. Most of these pieces take four to five minutes to play. One even takes up to seven and a half minutes. It is difficult mentally and physically to play these pieces in the beginning, so do not be discouraged if you "blank out" on sections, forgetting where in the piece you are supposed to be. This is normal. This is just another stage in your guitar playing that needs to be developed.

Two of the pieces in this collection are very special to me. I was looking for a tune to play in the National Flatpicking Championships in 1984. Tunes that no other flatpicking guitarist were working on. A student of mine brought in a cheap blue cassette filled with original piano rolls. He recorded them onto a cheap little tape recorder directly from his player piano in his living room. I do not know what has happened to this cassette (did I mention it was cheap?), but I kept up with it long enough to learn two special tunes. *Temptation Rag* was one tune, and I believe I captured the tune as the artist would have wanted, including the crescendos in measures 85-92. This is a classic ragtime piano move where they play octaves in both the right and left hand. On piano, they alternate the thumb note to the little finger notes as sixteenth notes in octaves with both hands and slowly bring them from an arms length stretch towards each other.

The other special piece was *Black and White Rag.* I learned it from a combination of sources, one being the aforementioned blue cassette. Both of these tunes were played very similarly to the way I've transcribed them in this collection. What happened at the Nationals? The contest rules state that each contestant must be prepared to play two tunes of their choice in the preliminary round. I played *Redwing* in three different keys, as well as the *Temptation Rag.* I was lucky enough to move to the final rounds, but the stage manager came up to all of us and said that they were running late, and each of us could only play one tune. That made the round like a sudden-death match. I chose *Black and White Rag* as my piece. I don't even remember what the other tune I had ready was, but I remember *Black and White Rag* bringing me to the winners circle.

I hope you enjoy all of the transcriptions in this collection and as always if you have questions regarding these pieces feel free to contact me at:

Steve Kaufman
P.O. Box 1020
Alcoa, TN 37701

Or email me at: **steve@flatpik.com** (probably the quickest route).

Best always, and keep pickin'.

Understanding the Notes and Tablature System

Tablature:

Tablature (for you note readers) is the "paint by number" method of learning a stringed instrument.

Example 1. **The numbers represent the frets.** If you use a "1" on a line, you are being instructed to hold down the first fret. A "0" (zero) represents an open string.

Example 2. **The lines represent the strings.** You have six horizontal lines written directly under the staff lines. The top line represents the first string. The second line represents the second string and the last line, lowest in the tab system, represents the sixth string. When you see a number on a line, first understand that the number is telling you which fret to hold down, and then count down from top to bottom to the line that the number is written on. This will tell you which string the fretted note is on.

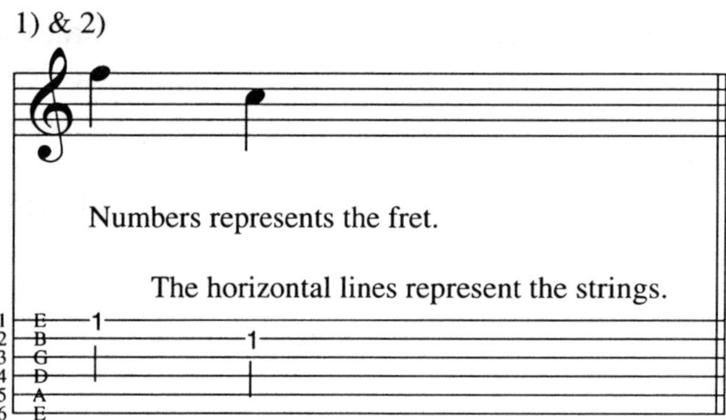

Example 3. **The numbers between the standard notation and the tablature lines represent the fretting fingers of the left hand.** The first set of notes that you see are called *Quarter Notes* (see example 3). After they are hit, each are to last for a whole beat. They are called quarter notes, because it takes four of these notes, or four quarters, to make a whole measure in 4/4 time.

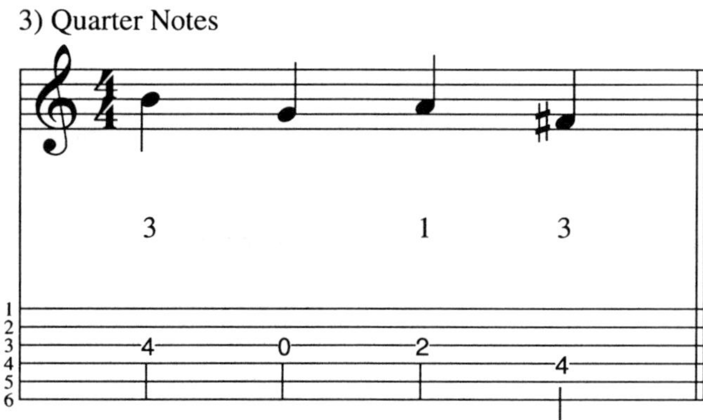

Example 4. The next set of notes/tab are called *Eighth Notes* (see example 4). They are equal to **1/2 of a beat** each. It takes two eighth notes to equal the length of time that a quarter note would get. **Eight eighth notes would fill up a whole measure in 4/4 time.** Six eighth notes would fill up a whole measure in 3/4 time. **Eighth notes** that are beamed together at the top or bottom are always hit **down first—then up.** The first eighth note beamed is always down, the next one is up. The first one is down, and the last one is up. If you have a full measure of eighth notes, the the first one in the measure is hit down and the last one is hit up. When you finish a measure like this, stop and check to see if you have hit the last note on an up swing.

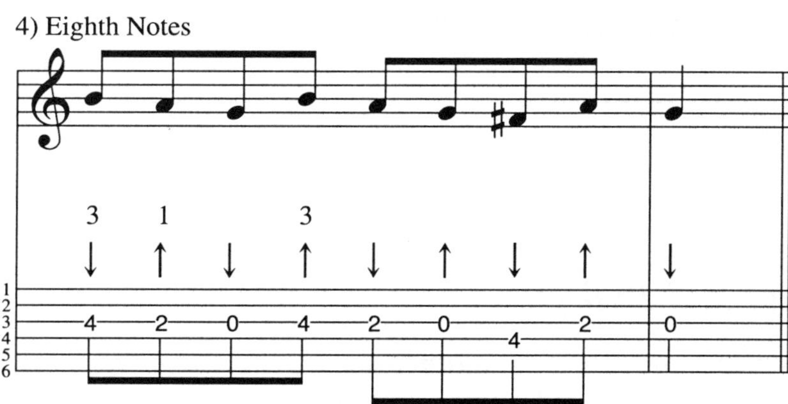

Example 5. **An illustration of other types of timing.** The first measure represents two *Half Notes.* They are called half notes because each one eats up half of a measure in 4/4 time. They last two beats each. In tablature, a half note looks just like a quarter note. This may seem a little confusing at first, but if you look at the standard notation, you will know to hold the note for two beats. Sometimes, tablature is written without stems, but in this book we have included them to show how long you should sustain the notes. In the next measure is a *Dotted Half Note.* It receives three beats. Like the half note, it has a single stem. This measure ends with a 1-beat rest.

The next measure has a whole note in it. The note lasts for four beats, and takes up the whole measure (hence the name whole note). In the tab system, it is written as a number without a stem, probably because there is no stem in the standard notation. As with any note, be sure to keep the pressure down on the fret as long as possible. This will ensure that the note is lasting the proper amount of time and that you won't sound choppy.

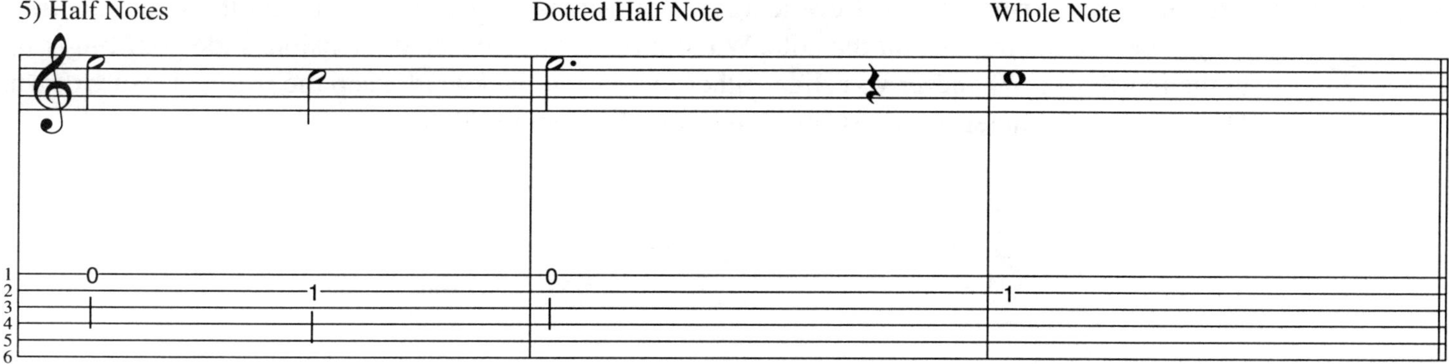

Example 6. **This example is made up of different types of rests.** One-beat, two-beat and four beat-rests.

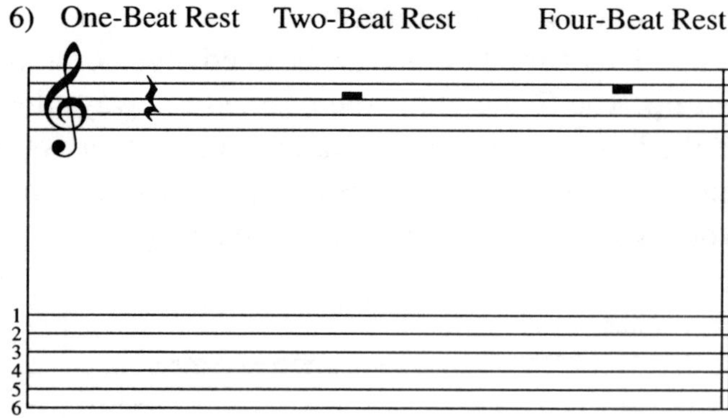

Hammer-Ons, Slides and Pull-Offs

Example 7. **Example seven represents the hammer-on.** These are eight note hammer-ons. Hit the first note and then propel your left hand's finger onto the fret that is marked. You must attack the hammered note. You don't want to push your finger onto the string—you must shoot it onto the string. The more attack you have, the clearer the hammer-on will be.

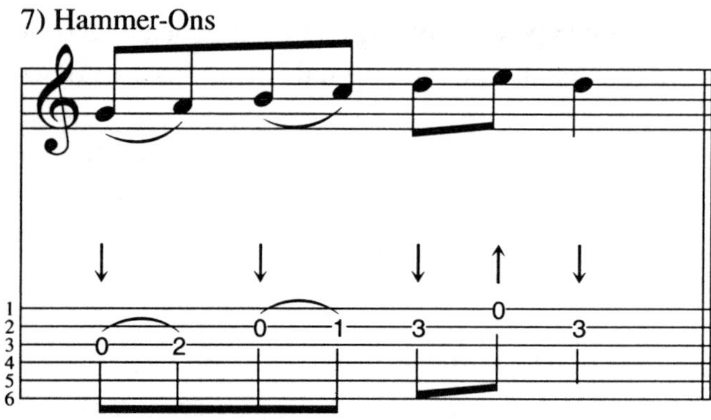

Example 8. **The slides are written two different ways.** Both slides written here represent the same function. Finger the second fret and hit the note. Without releasing the fret and tension, slide your finger up to the fourth fret. Whenever you slide, either forward or backward, keep the string pressure down. Don't take your finger off the string or the sounding note will go away.

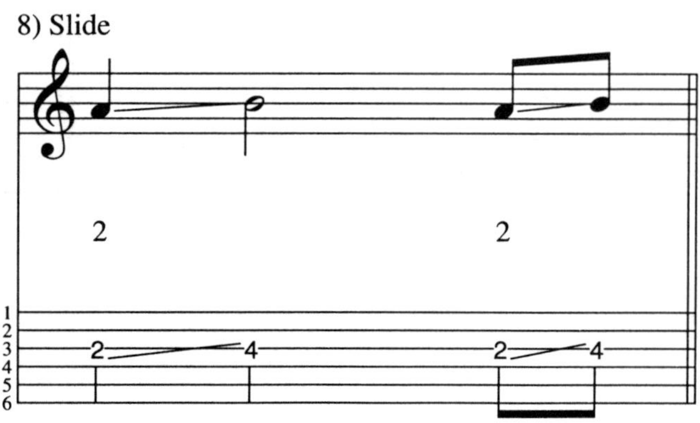

Example 9. **Pull-offs are the opposite of the Hammer-ons.** Hit the fretted note as you normally would. Then, dig your finger under the string and pull it down and off. By digging your left hand's finger under the string you will in essence be plucking the string with the left hand. This will produce the pull-off effect and you will get two notes heard with one note hit.

Hammer-ons, pull-offs and slides do not have to be labeled with letters as such. There is only one way to do a slide, one way to hammer on, and one way to pull off.

Watch out for your down/up picking as you perform these techniques. The explanations and diagrams are marked throughout the book. But be careful, if you get your down ups mixed up then a picking crash is inevitable. You may just knock the bark off the tree, but none the less it will cause a break in timing or stumble of some kind.

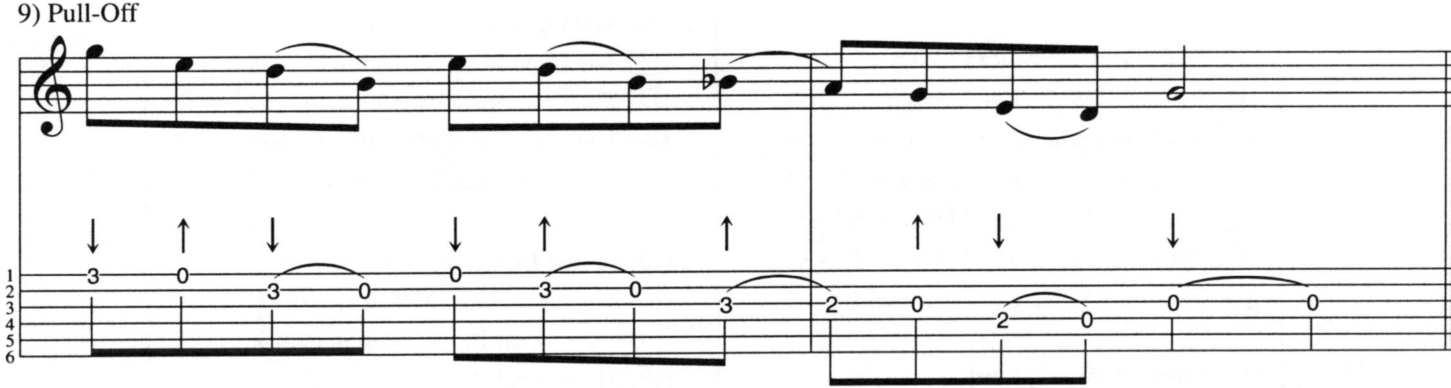

CD Tracks – Disc 1

1 Bethena [7:27]
2 Bethena Intro Measures 1 – 8
3 Bethena Measures 9 – 28
4 Bethena Measures 29 – 52
5 Bethena Measures 53 – 68
6 Bethena Measures 69 – 76
7 Bethena Measures 77 – 112
8 Bethena Measures 113 – 129
9 Bethena Measures 130 – 151
10 Bethena Measures 152 – 176

11 Black and White Rag [3:00]
12 Black and White Rag Measures 1 – 18
13 Black and White Rag Measures 19 – 50
14 Black and White Rag Measures 51 – 66
15 Black and White Rag Measures 67 – 83
16 Black and White Rag Measures 84 – 99
17 Black and White Rag Measures 100 – 107

18 Clarinet Polka [2:29]
19 Clarinet Polka Measures 1 – 18
20 Clarinet Polka Measures 19 – 34
21 Clarinet Polka Measures 35 – 50
22 Clarinet Polka Measures 51 – 67
23 Clarinet Polka Measures 68 – 85

24 East Tennessee Rag [1:18]
25 East Tennessee Rag Measures 1 – 17
26 East Tennessee Rag Measures 18 – 33
27 East Tennessee Rag Measures 34 – 50
28 East Tennessee Rag Measures 51 – 66

29 Jesse Polka [5:29]
30 Jesse Polka Measures 1 – 5
31 Jesse Polka Measures 6 – 38
32 Jesse Polka Measures 39 – 54
33 Jesse Polka Measures 55 – 63
34 Jesse Polka Measures 64 – 80
35 Jesse Polka Measures 81 – 96
36 Jesse Polka Measures 97 – 129
37 Jesse Polka Measures 130 – 145
38 Jesse Polka Measures 146 – 155
39 Jesse Polka Measures 156 – 172
40 Jesse Polka Measures 173 – 188
41 Jesse Polka Measures 189 – 198

CD Tracks – Disc 2

1 Lady's Fancy [3:11]
2 Lady's Fancy Measures 1 – 9
3 Lady's Fancy Measures 10 – 18
4 Lady's Fancy Measures 19 – 26
5 Lady's Fancy Measures 27 – 34
6 Lady's Fancy Measures 35 – 42

7 The Lime Rock [4:53]
8 The Lime Rock Measures 1 – 10
9 The Lime Rock Measures 11 – 28
10 The Lime Rock Measures 29 – 36
11 The Lime Rock Measures 37 – 45
12 The Lime Rock Measures 46 – 54
13 The Lime Rock Measures 55 – 63
14 The Lime Rock Measures 64 – 72

15 Maple Leaf Rag [3:17]
16 Maple Leaf Rag Measures 1 – 18
17 Maple Leaf Rag Measures 19 – 50
18 Maple Leaf Rag Measures 51 – 66
19 Maple Leaf Rag Measures 67 – 83
20 Maple Leaf Rag Measures 84 – 100

21 Temptation Rag [4:06]
22 Temptation Rag Measures 1 – 1
23 Temptation Rag Measures 5 – 23
24 Temptation Rag Measures 24 – 43
25 Temptation Rag Measures 44 – 59
26 Temptation Rag Measures 60 – 68
27 Temptation Rag Measures 69 – 84
28 Temptation Rag Measures 85 – 92
29 Temptation Rag Measures 93 – 112
30 Temptation Rag Measures 113 – 144
31 Temptation Rag Measures 145 – 148

32 Tico Taco No Fuba [3:45]
33 Tico Taco No Fuba Measures 1 – 7
34 Tico Taco No Fuba Measures 8 – 39
35 Tico Taco No Fuba Measures 40 – 55
36 Tico Taco No Fuba Measures 56 – 71
37 Tico Taco No Fuba Measures 72 – 87
38 Tico Taco No Fuba Measures 88 – 103
39 Tico Taco No Fuba Measures 104 – 119
40 Tico Taco No Fuba Measures 120 – 135
41 Tico Taco No Fuba Measures 136 – 151
42 Tico Taco No Fuba Measures 152 – 167
43 Tico Taco No Fuba Measures 168 – 175

Bethena

Scott Joplin

Arr. by Steve Kaufman

C
G
A7
D7
G
21
B7
B7
A7
F7
25
B
B♭
B♭
F7
B♭
29
E♭
B♭
G7
C7
F
33
B♭
B♭
F7
B♭
37

E♭
A♯○
B♭
G7
C7
F7
1.
B♭
41
1.
B♭
B♭
B♭
Gm
D
Dm
A7
A○
45
D○
B○
A9
Am
D7
D7
49
A
G
A7
D7
B7
Em
53
C
G
A7
D7
57

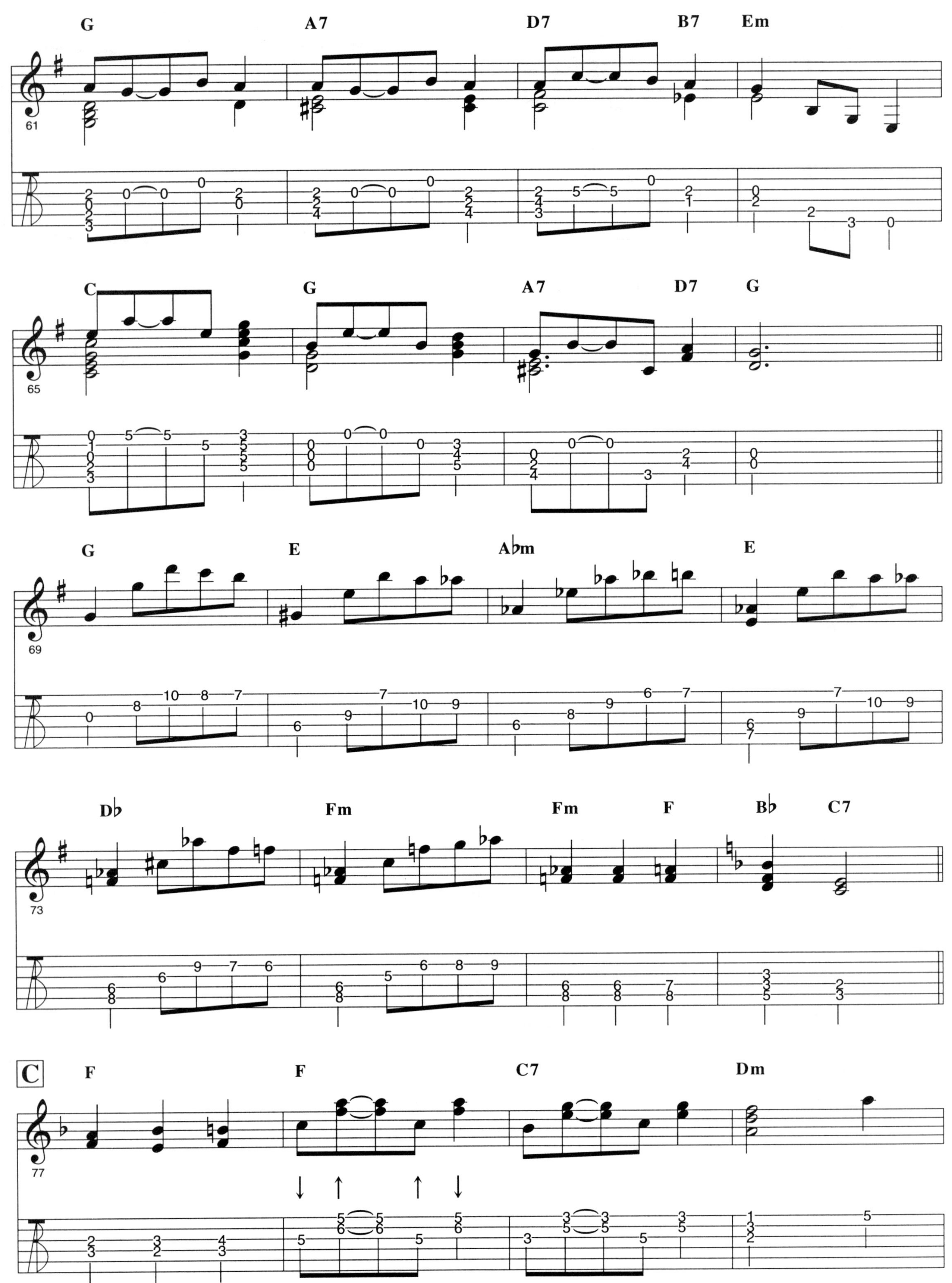

G
A7
D7
B7
Em
61
C
G
A7
D7
G
65
G
E
A♭m
E
69
D♭
Fm
Fm
F
B♭
C7
73
C
F
F
C7
Dm
77

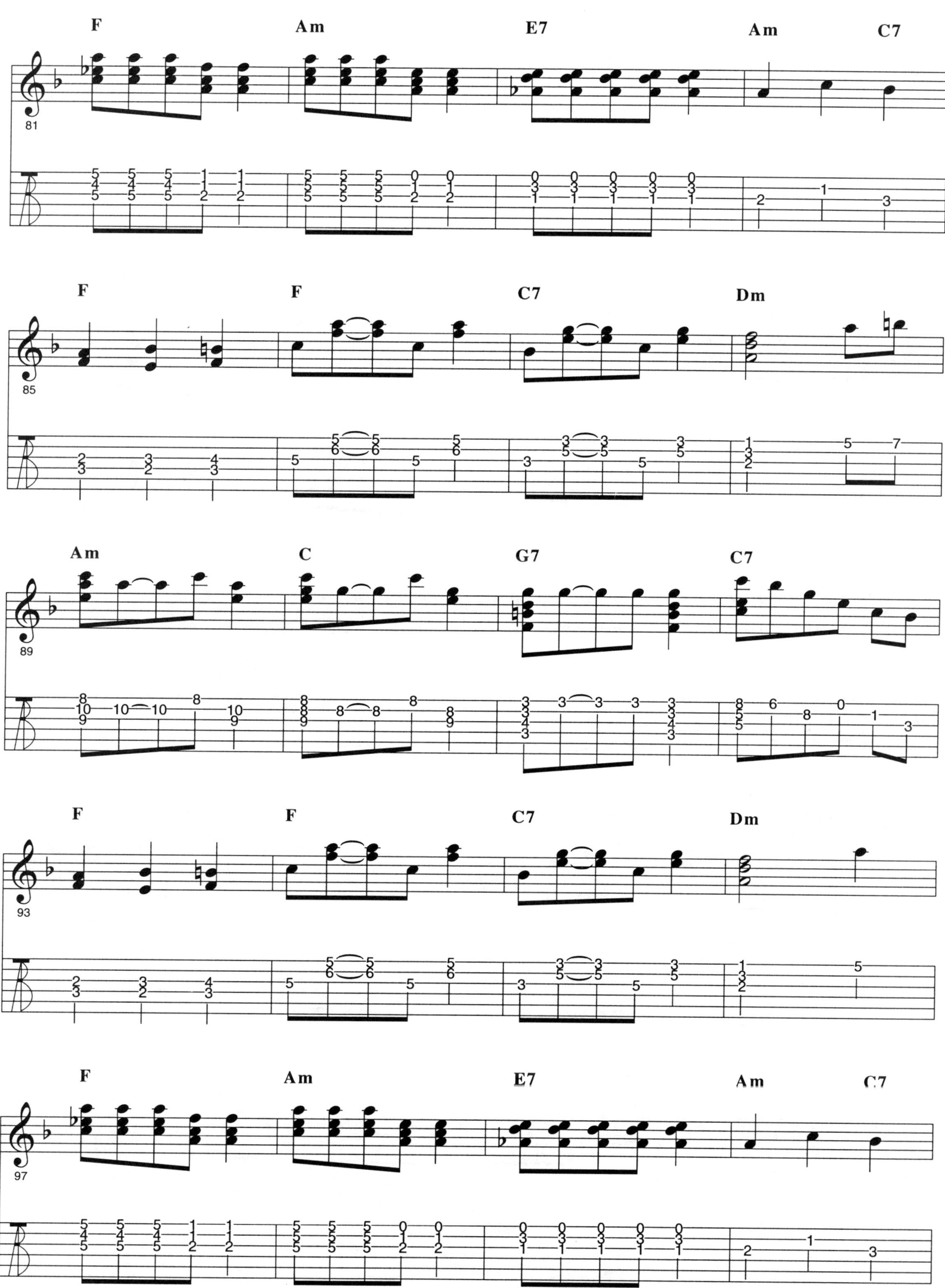
F Am E7 Am C7
81
F F C7 Dm
85
Am C G7 C7
89
F F C7 Dm
93
F Am E7 Am C7
97

F
F
C7
Dm
101
B♭
F
G9
C7
F
B♭m
105
109
D
Bm
Bm
F♯
Bm
113
Bm
Bm
G
F♯
117

Bm
Bm
F♯
Bm
121
Em
Bm
F♯
1.
Bm
125
2.
Bm
G♯○
D7
E
G
G♯○
D
A
129
D
D7
G
G♯○
D
F♯7
133
Bm
G♯○
D7
G
G♯○
D
A
137

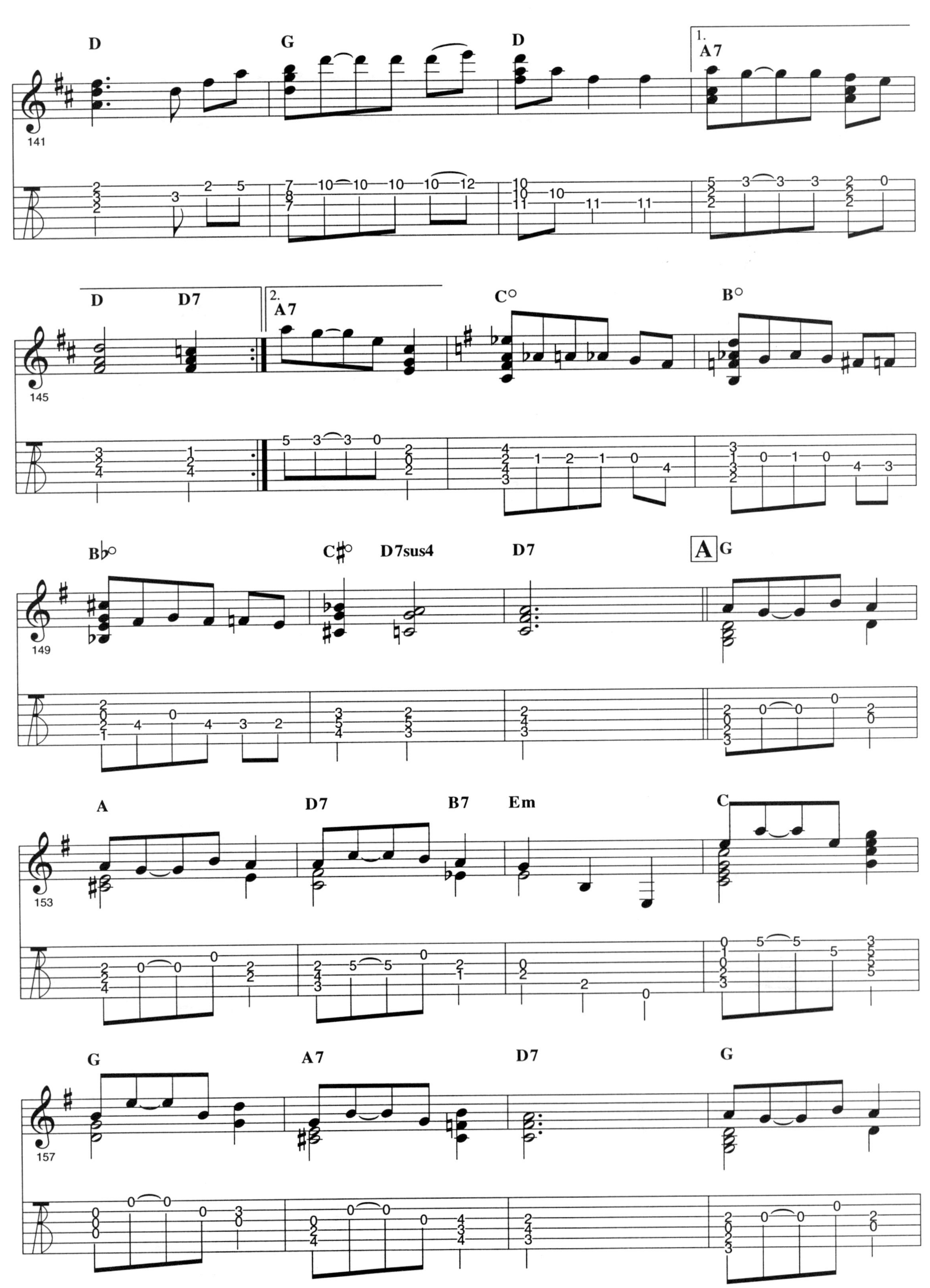

D
G
D
1.
A7
141
D
D7
2.
A7
C○
B○
145
B♭○
C♯○
D7sus4
D7
A
G
149
A
D7
B7
Em
C
153
G
A7
D7
G
157

A7
D7
B7
Em
C
161
G
A7
D7
G
G♭°
G
165
G
G♭°
G
G
G
169
G
G
E♭
G
G
173

Black and White Rag

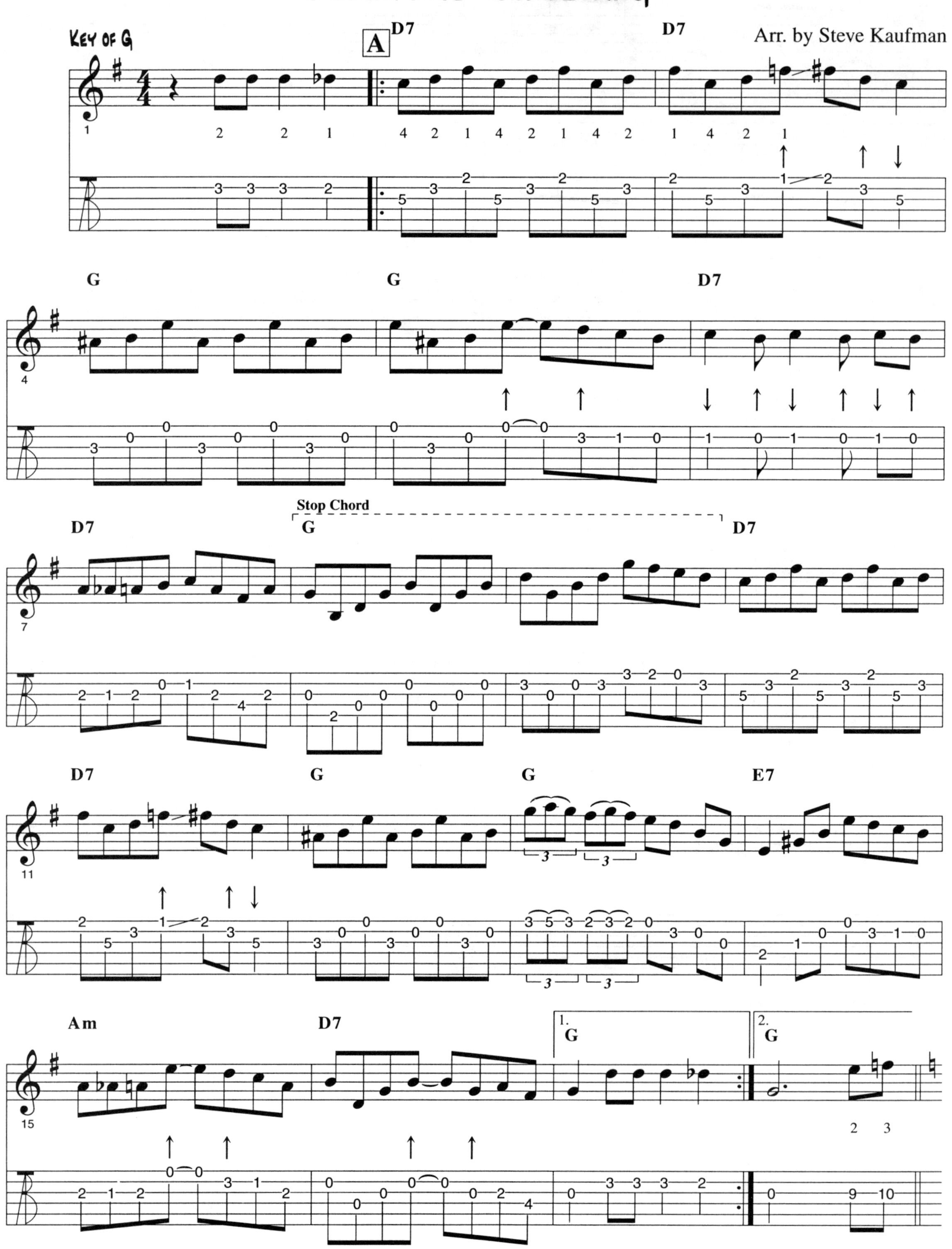

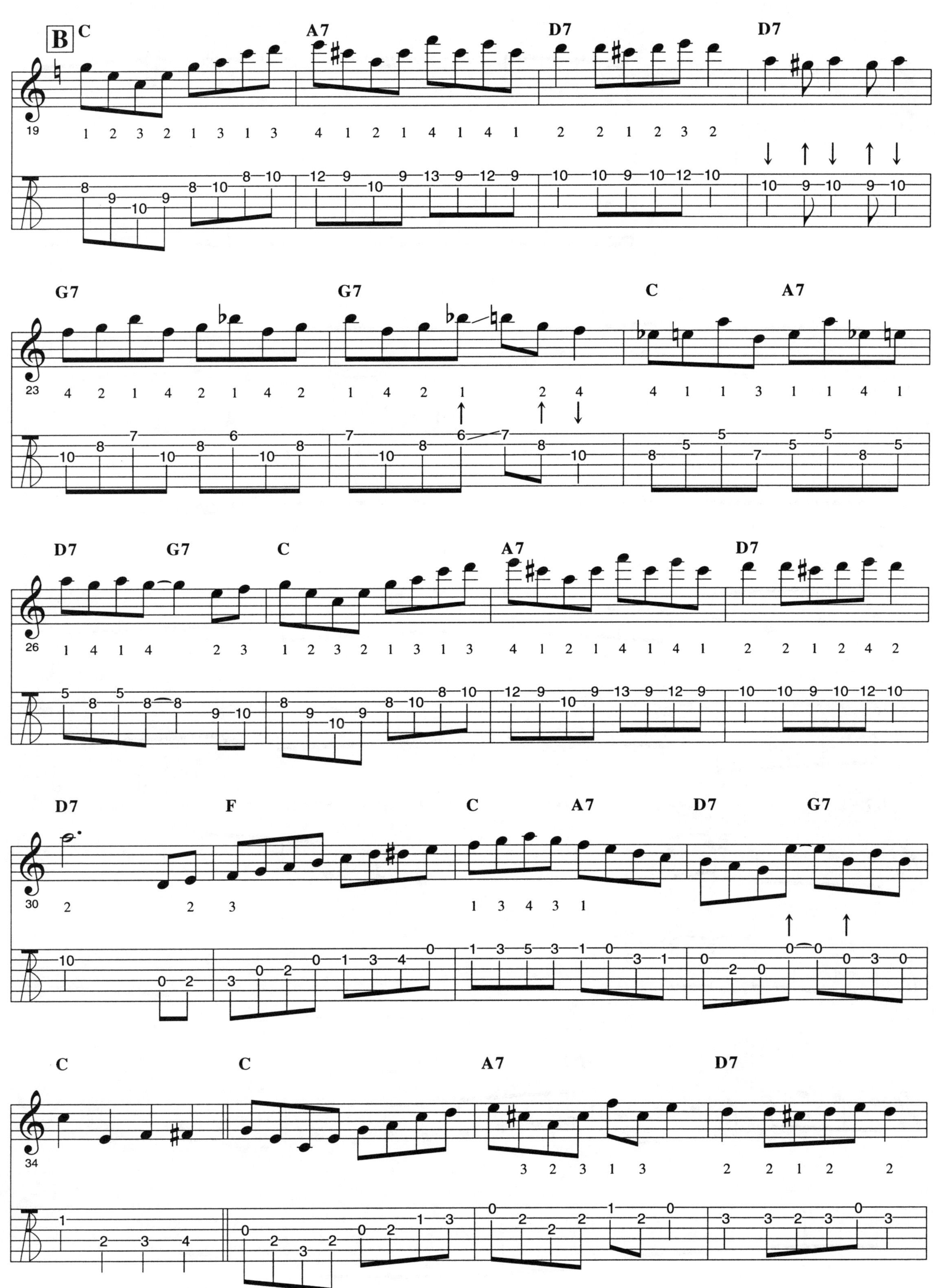
B
C A7 D7 D7
G7 G7 C A7
D7 G7 C A7 D7
D7 F C A7 D7 G7
C C A7 D7

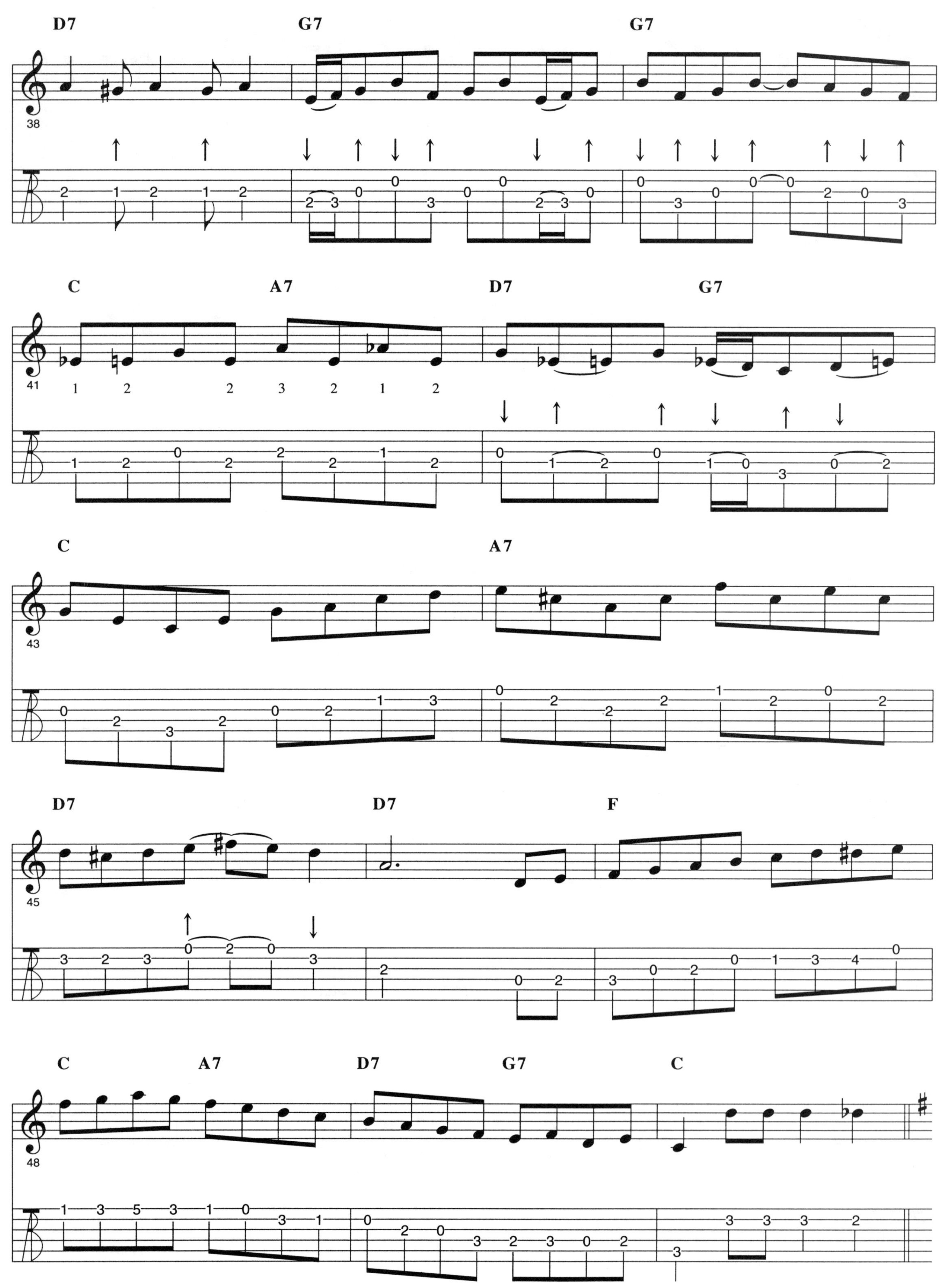
D7 G7 G7
C A7 D7 G7
C A7
D7 D7 F
C A7 D7 G7 C

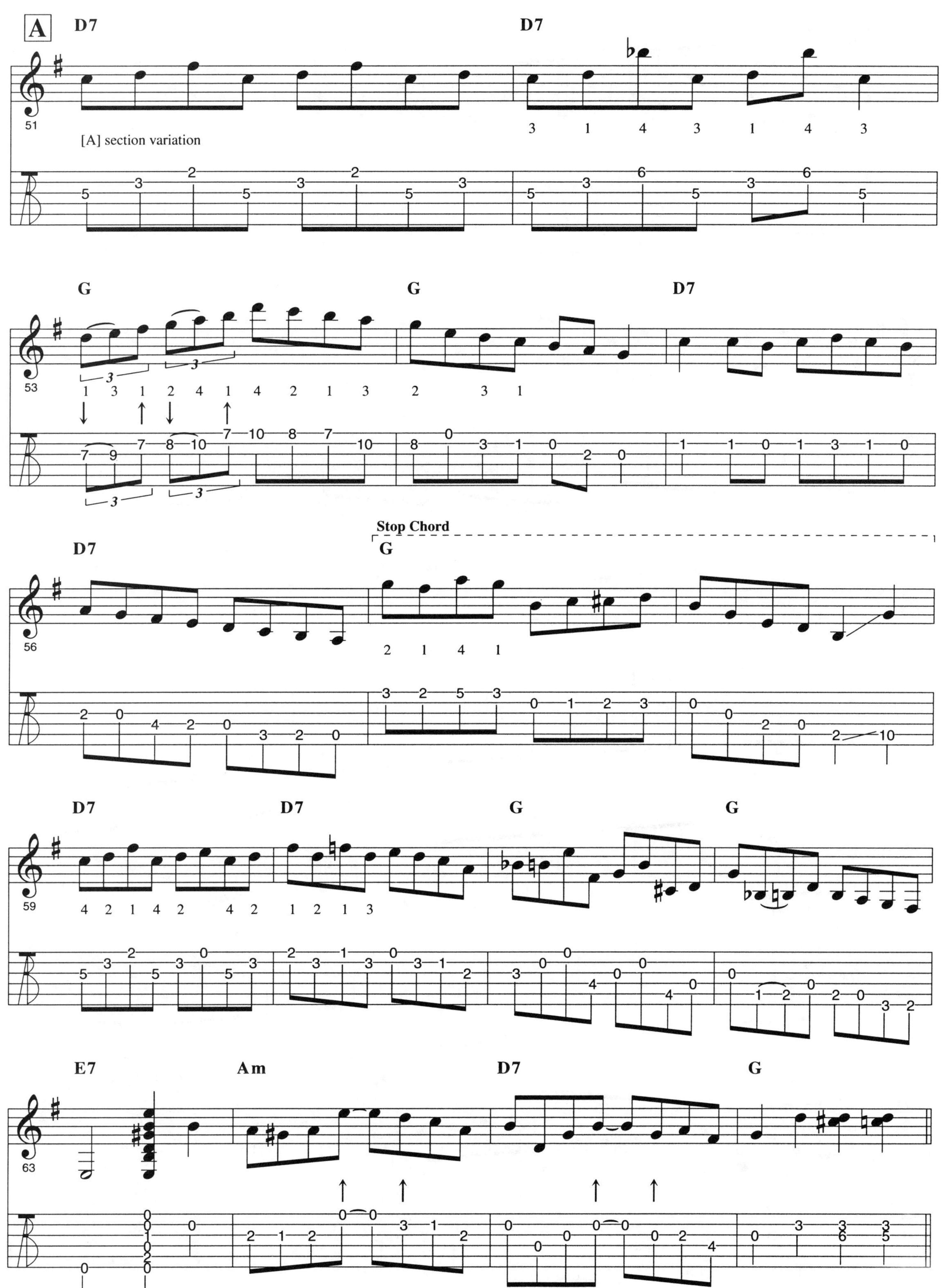
A
D7
D7
[A] section variation
G
G
D7
D7
Stop Chord
G
D7
D7
G
G
E7
Am
D7
G

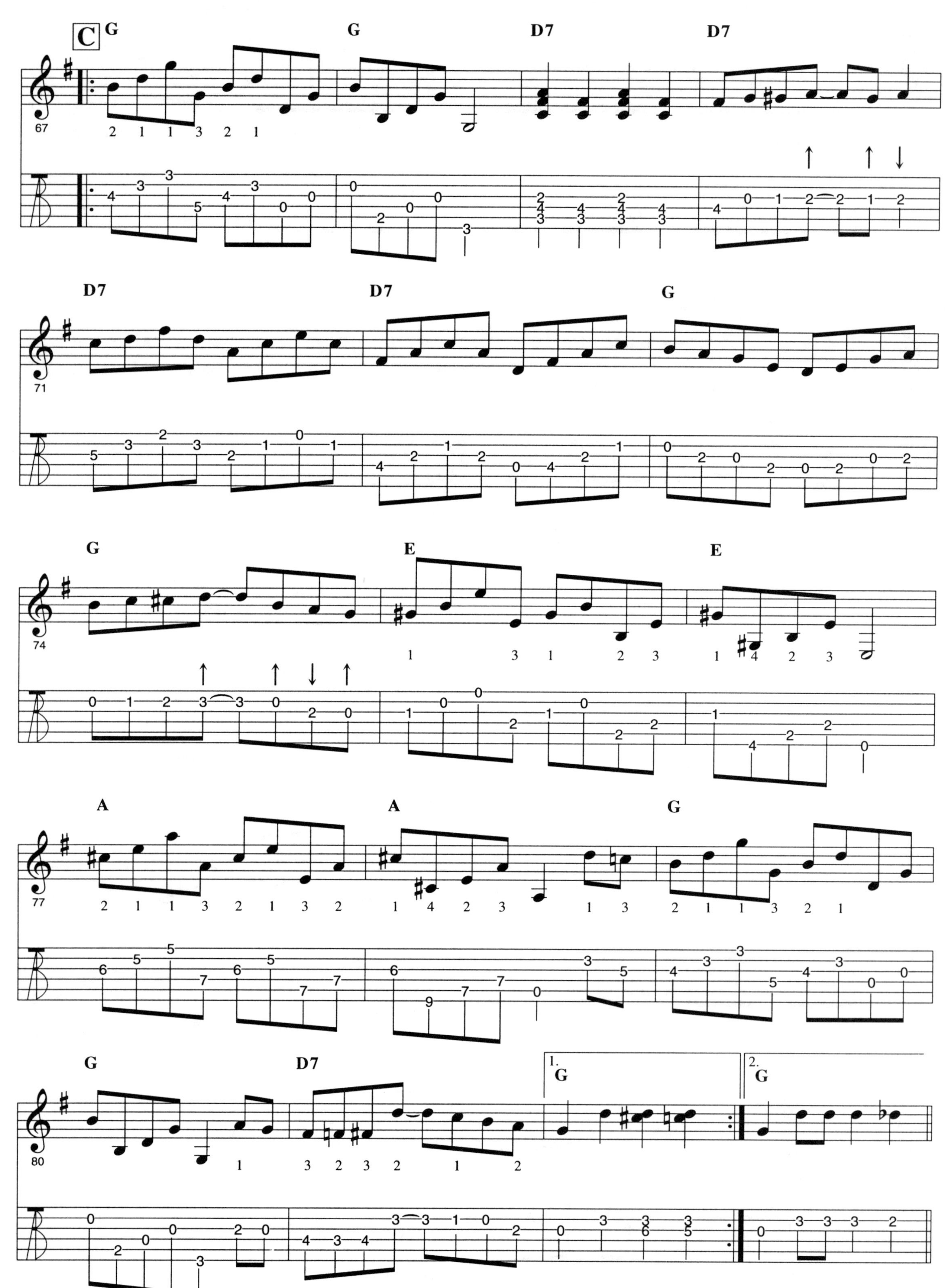
C
G
G
D7
D7
D7
D7
G
G
E
E
A
A
G
G
D7
1.
G
2.
G

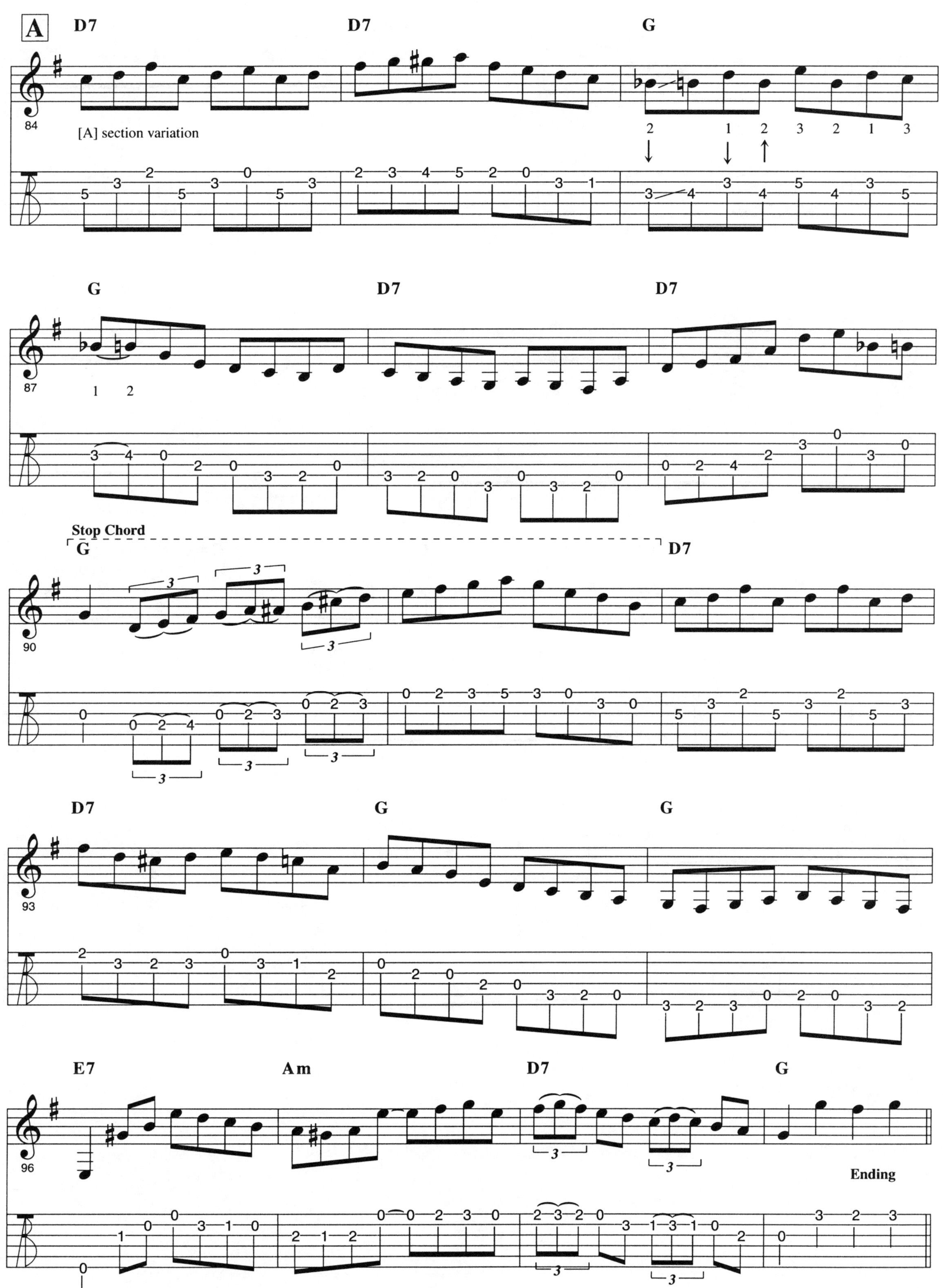
A
D7
D7
G
84
[A] section variation
G
D7
D7
87
Stop Chord
G
D7
90
D7
G
G
93
E7
Am
D7
G
96
Ending

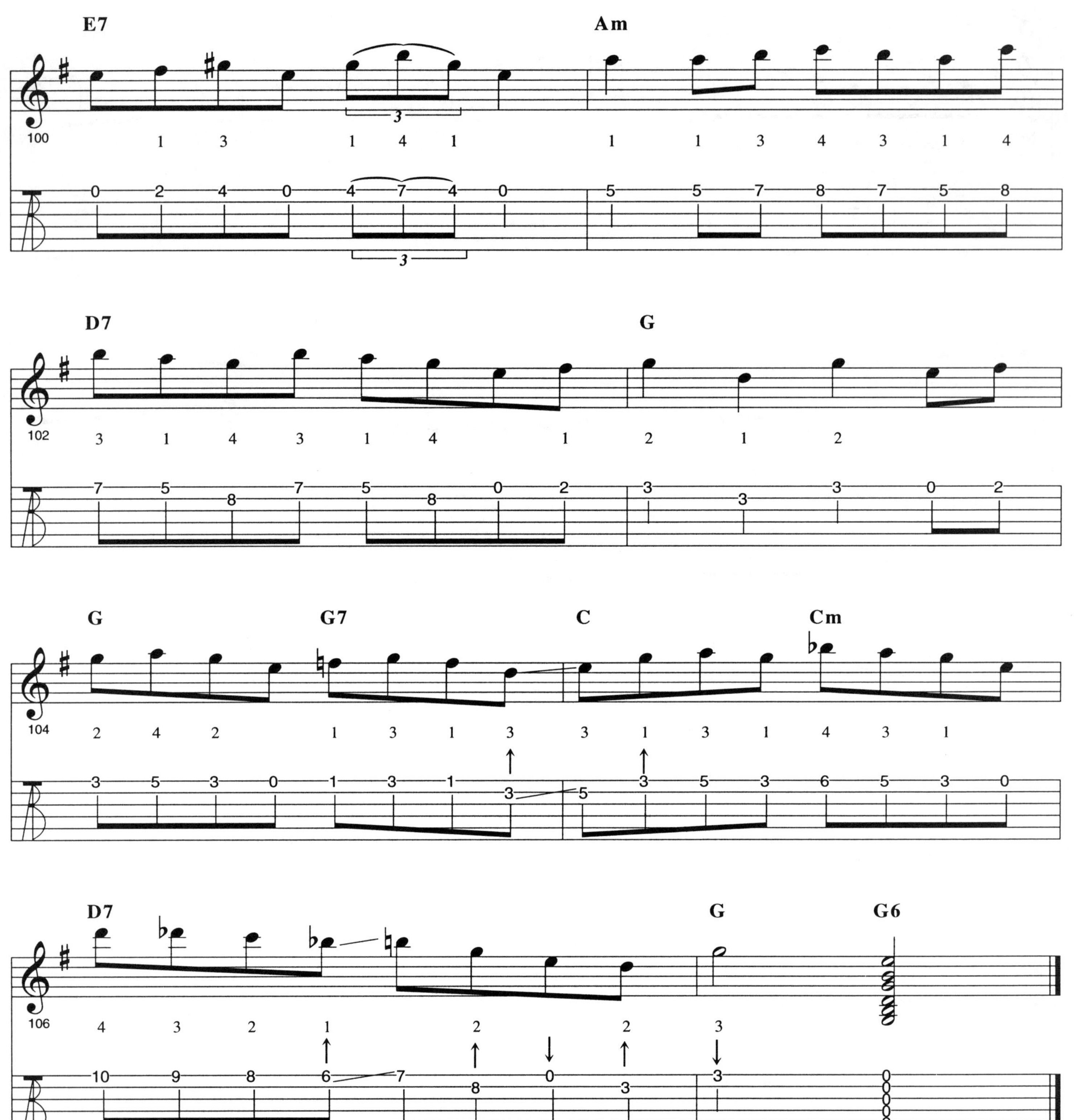
E7
Am
D7
G
G
G7
C
Cm
D7
G
G6
100
102
104
106

Clarinet Polka

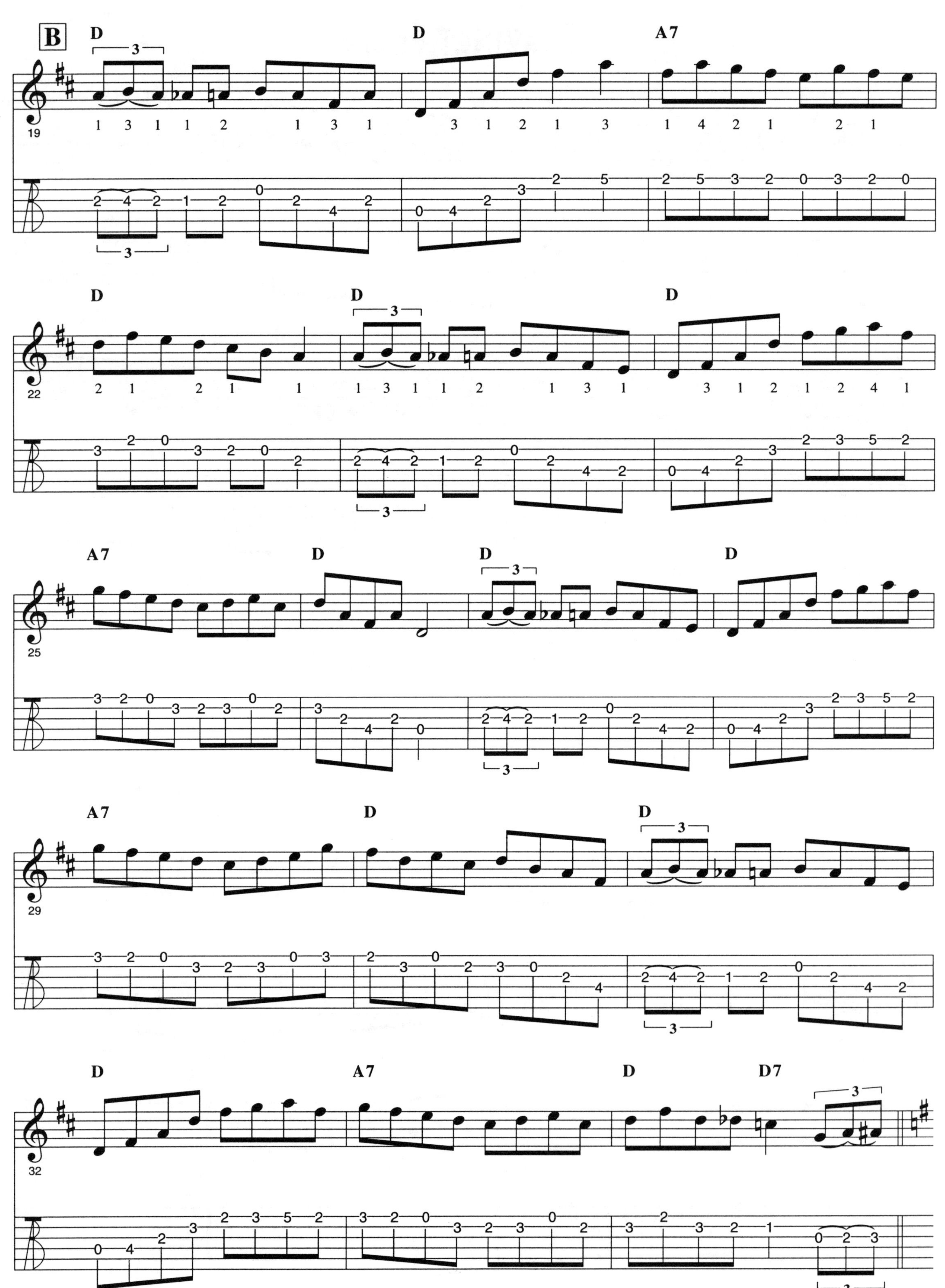
B
D
D
A7
D
D
D
A7
D
D
D
A7
D
D
D
A7
D
D7

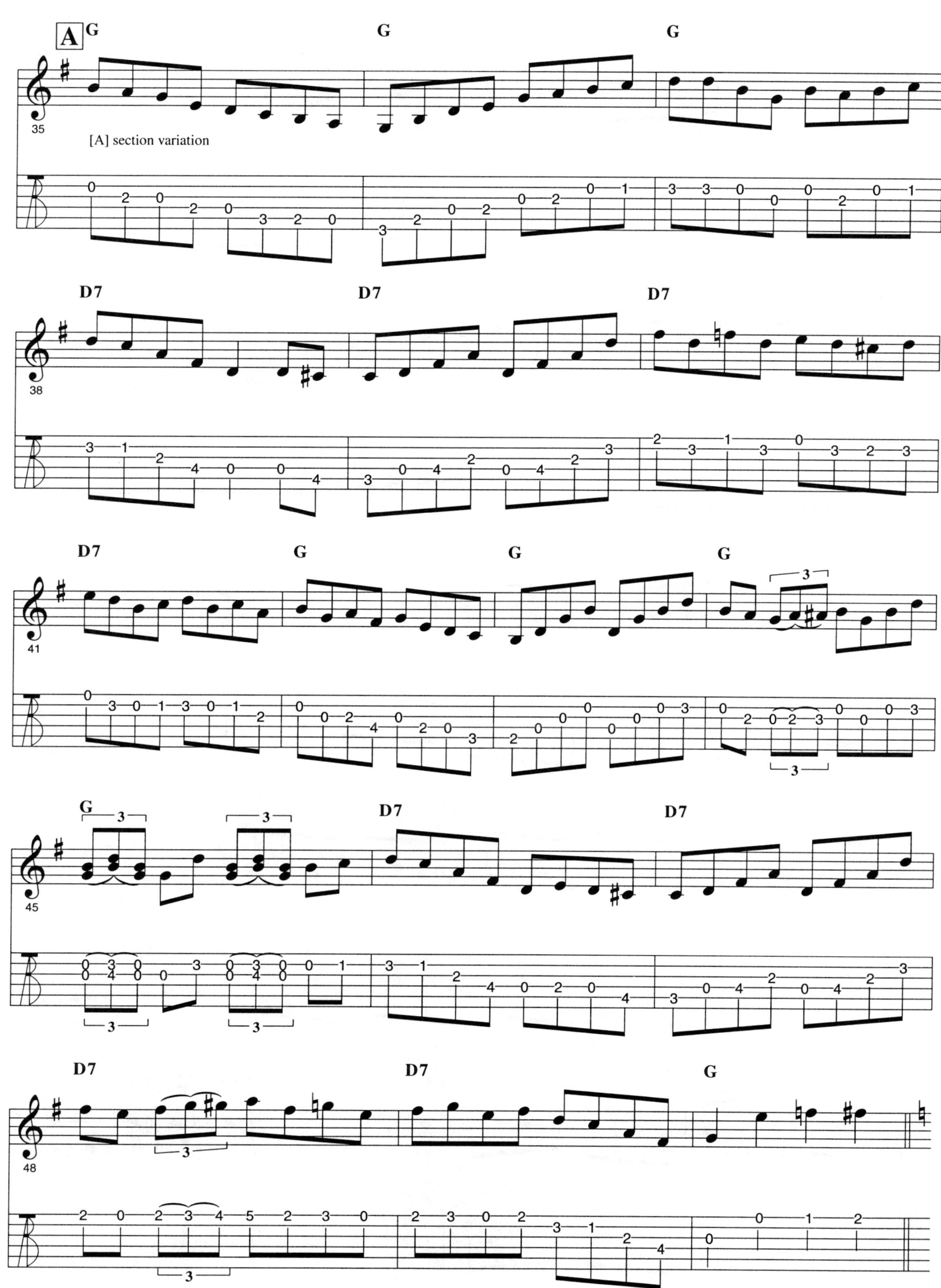
A
G
G
G
35
[A] section variation
D7
D7
D7
38
D7
G
G
G
41
G
D7
D7
45
D7
D7
G
48

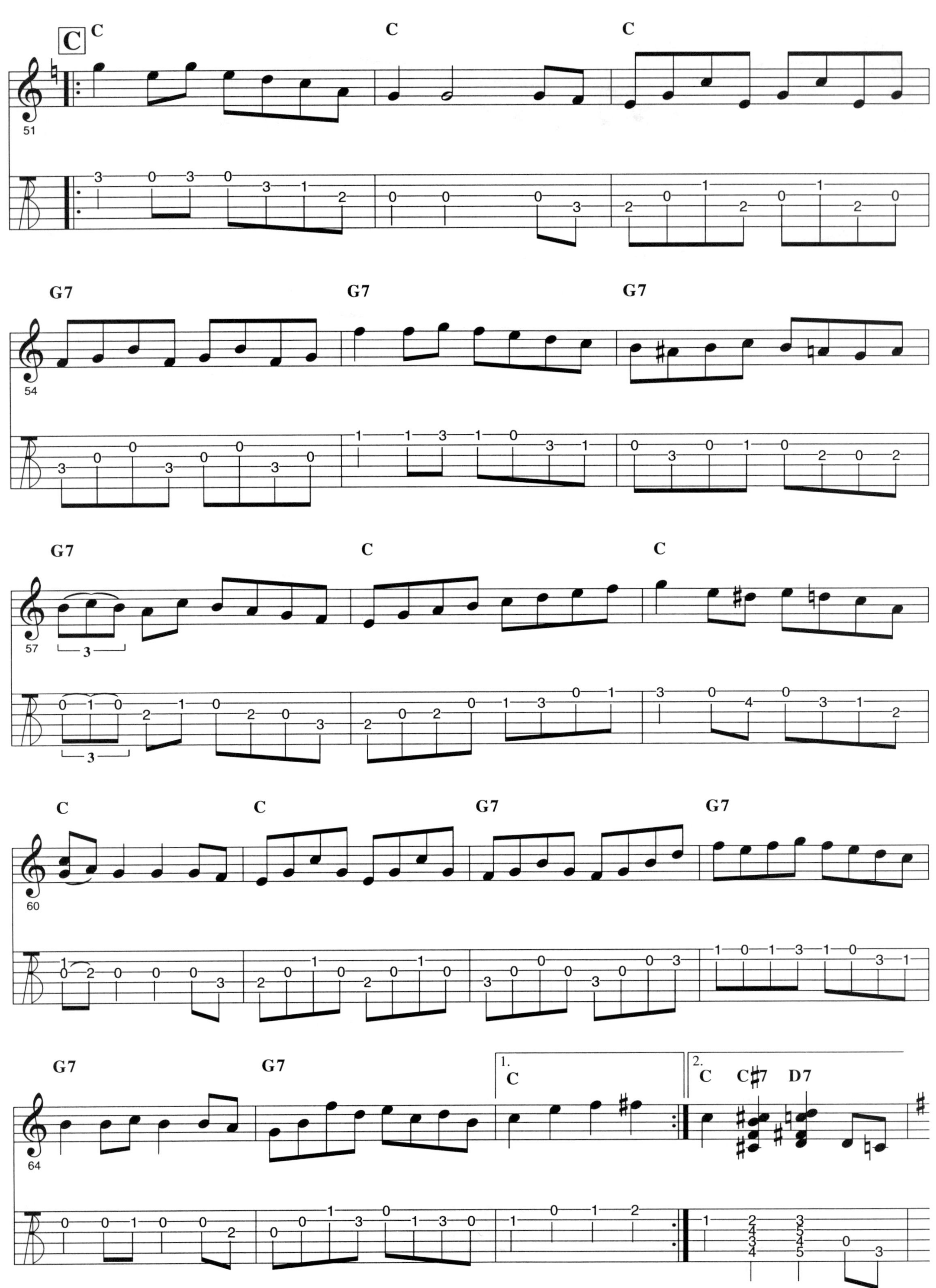
C
C
C
C
51
G7
G7
G7
54
G7
C
C
57
3
3
C
C
G7
G7
60
G7
G7
1.
C
2.
C
C#7
D7
64

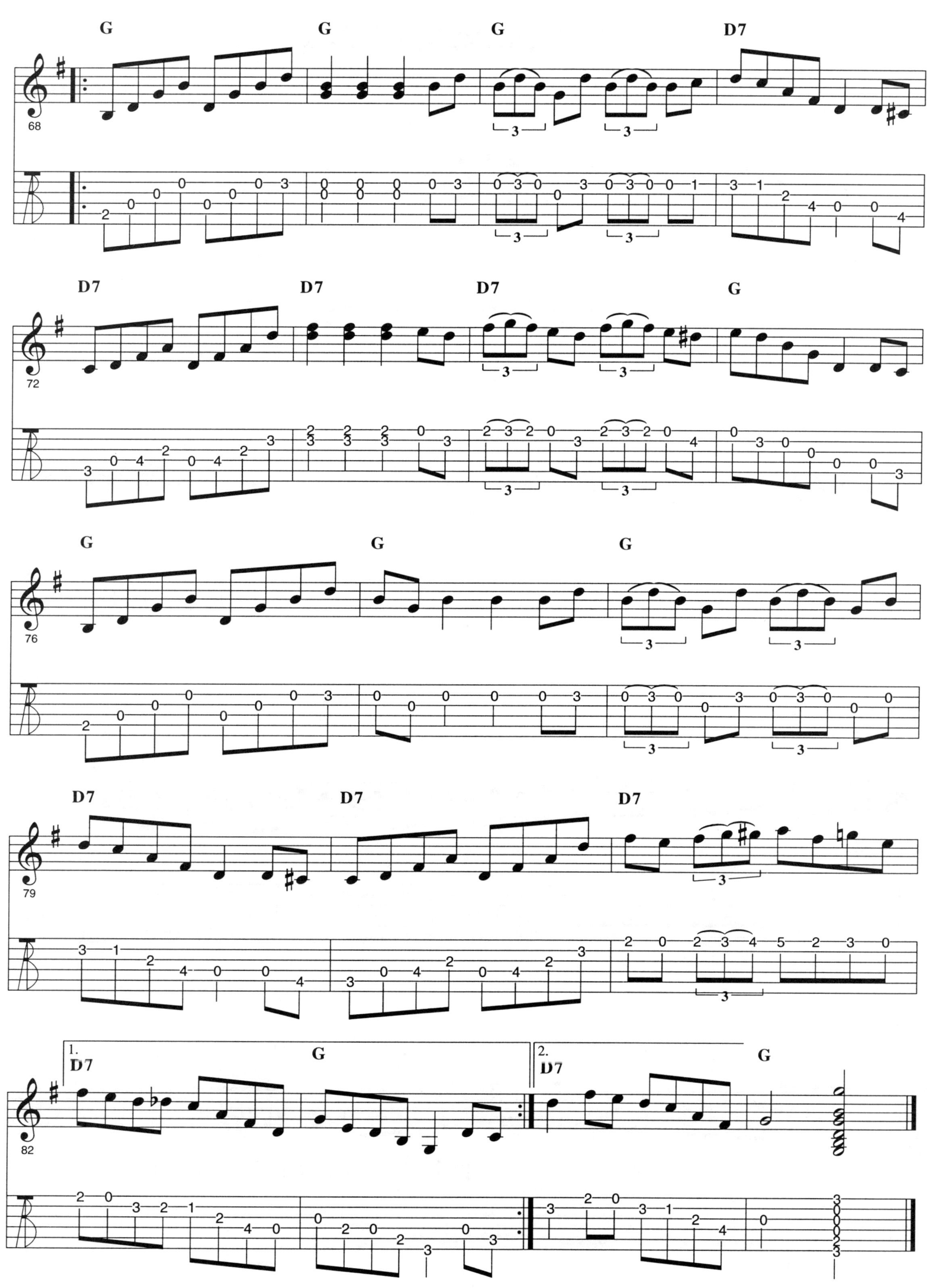
G
G
G
D7
68
D7
D7
D7
G
72
G
G
G
76
D7
D7
D7
79
1.
D7
G
2.
D7
G
82

East Tennessee Rag

Arr. by Steve Kaufman

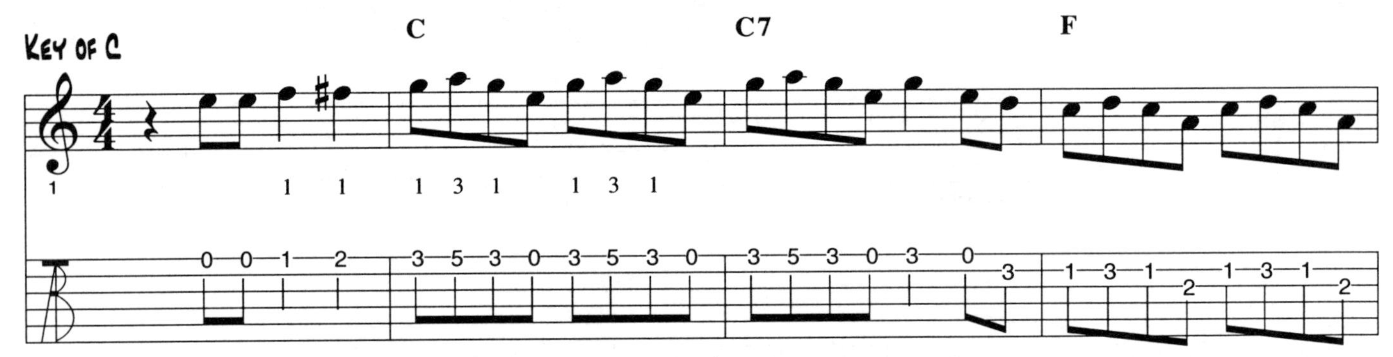

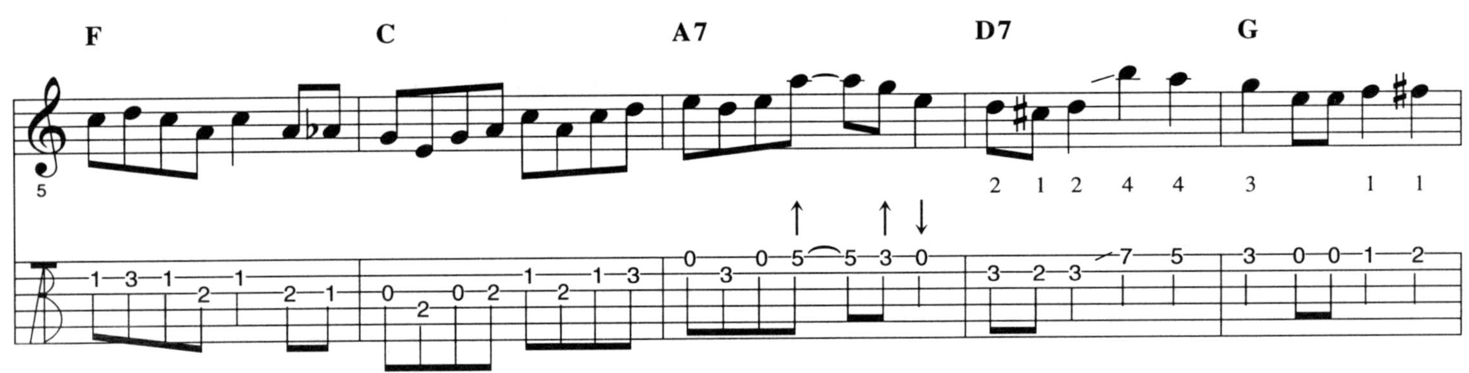

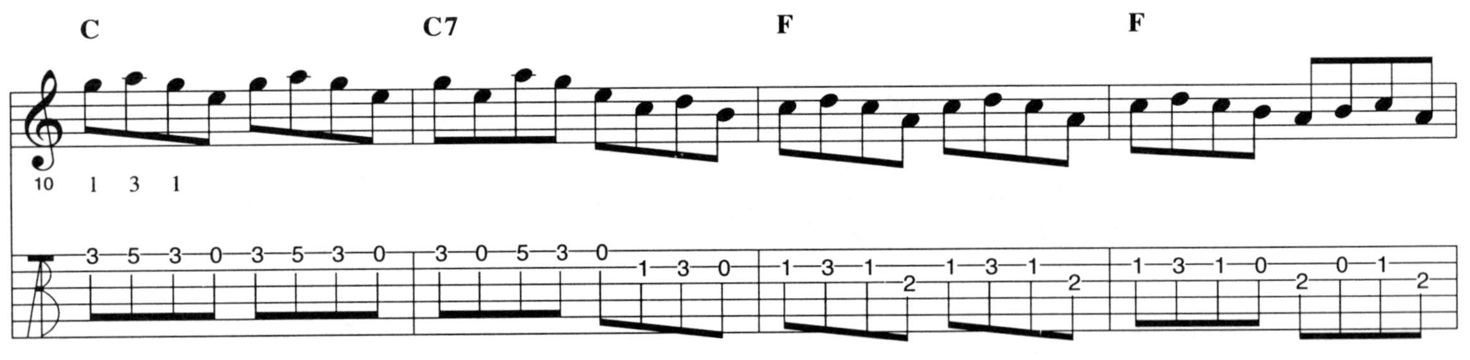

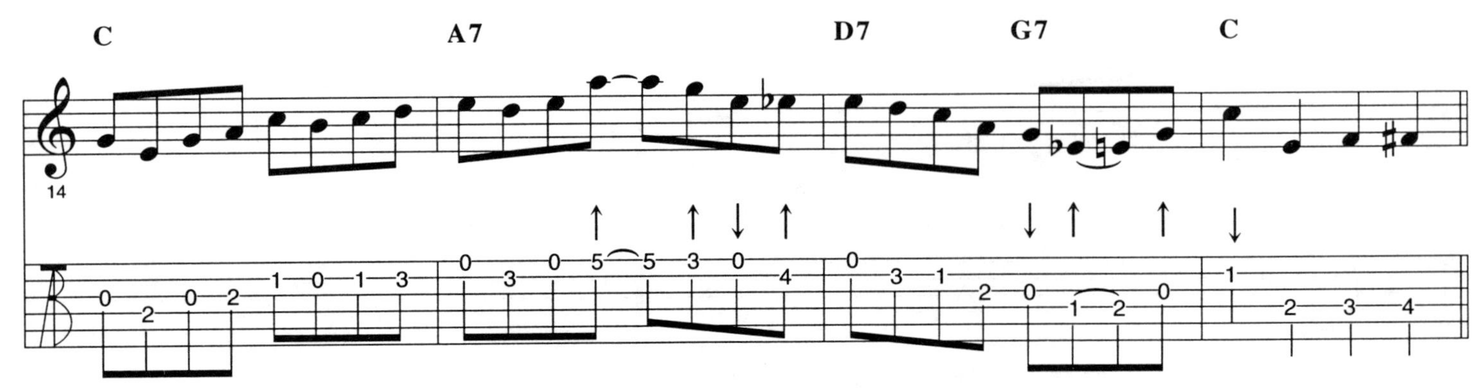

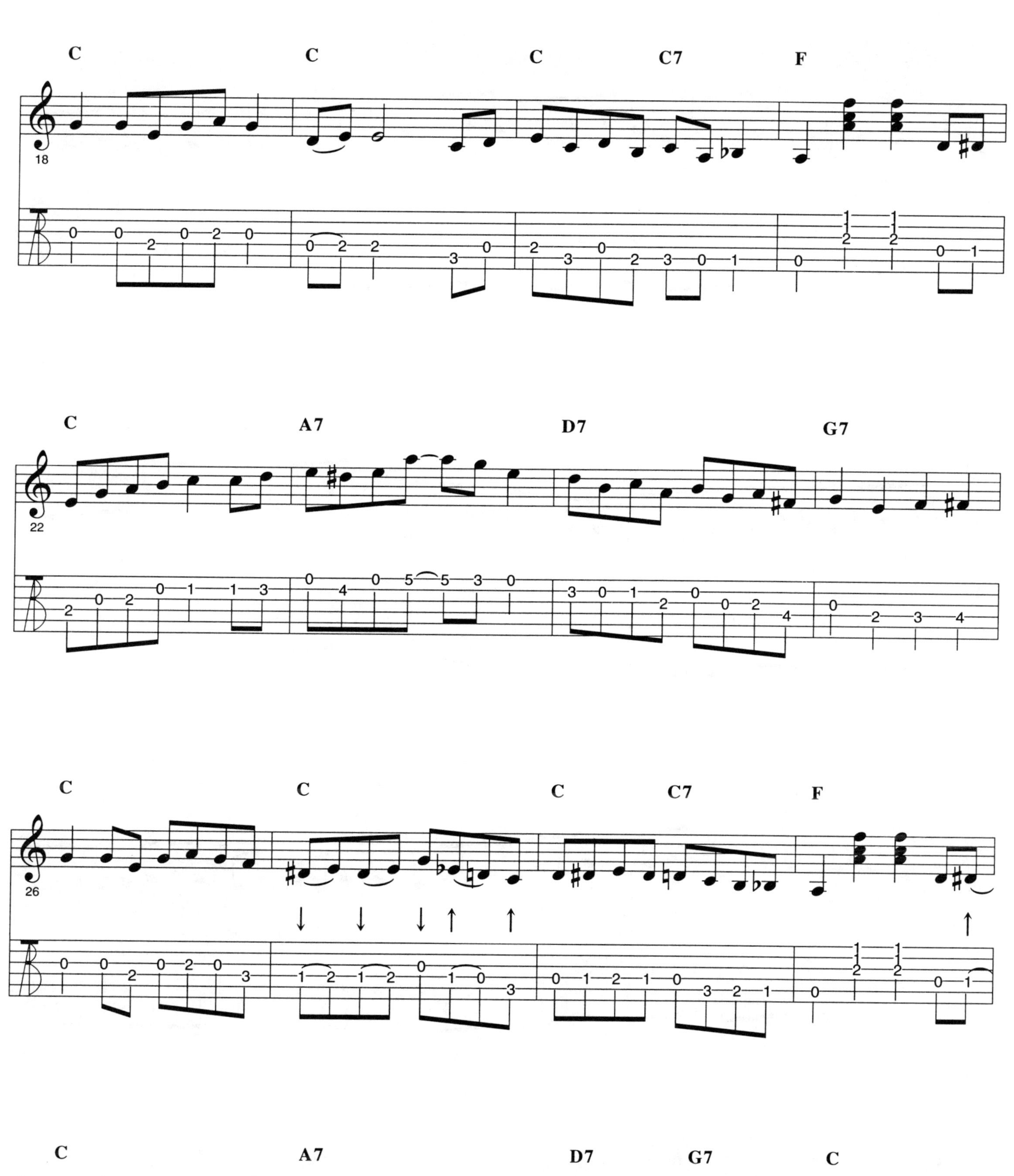
C
C
C
C7
F
18
C
A7
D7
G7
22
C
C
C
C7
F
26
C
A7
D7
G7
C
30

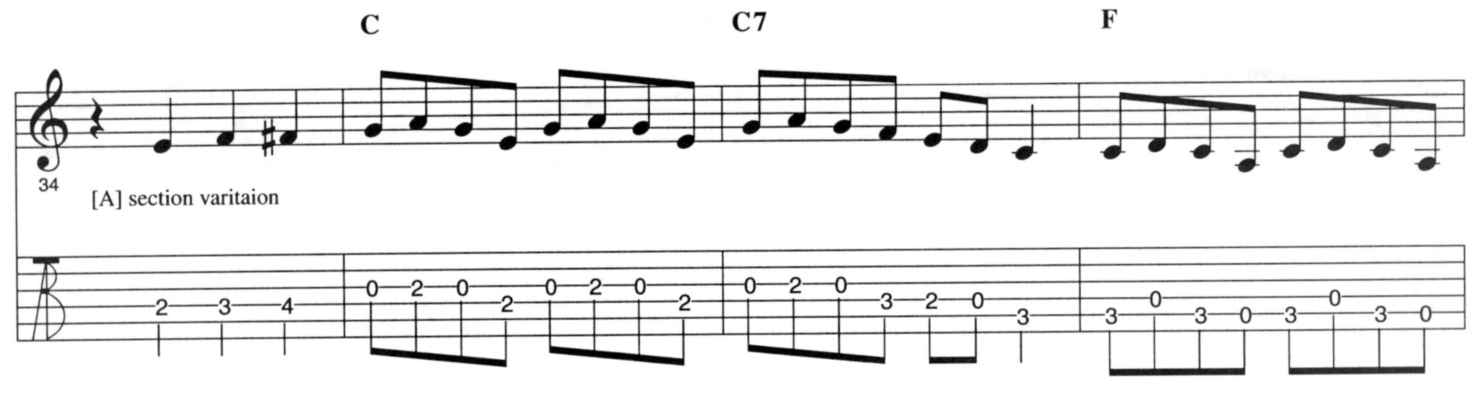
C
C7
F
34
[A] section varitaion

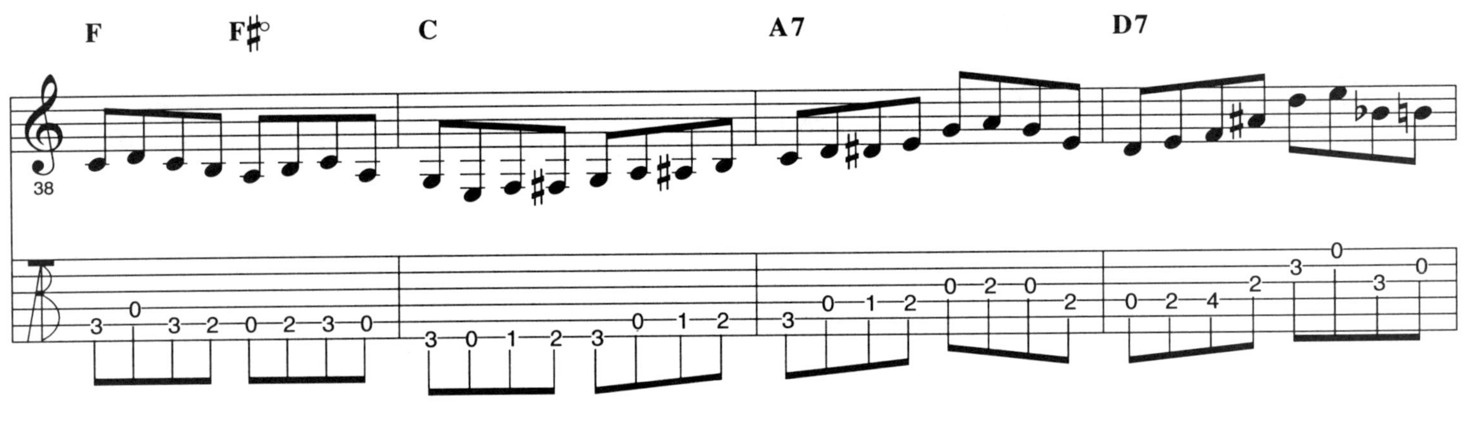
F
F♯°
C
A7
D7
38

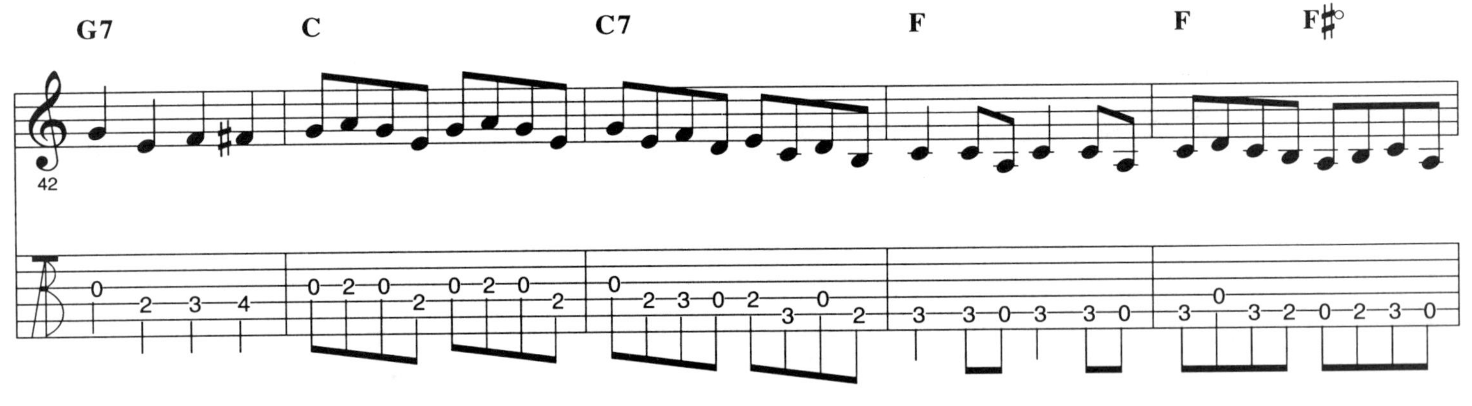
G7
C
C7
F
F
F♯°
42

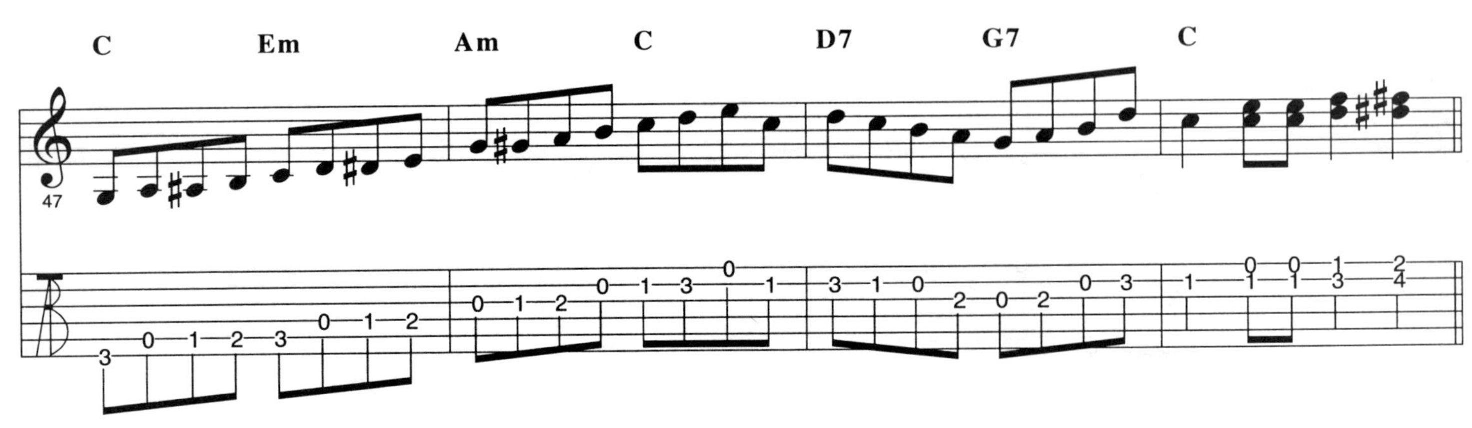
C
Em
Am
C
D7
G7
C
47

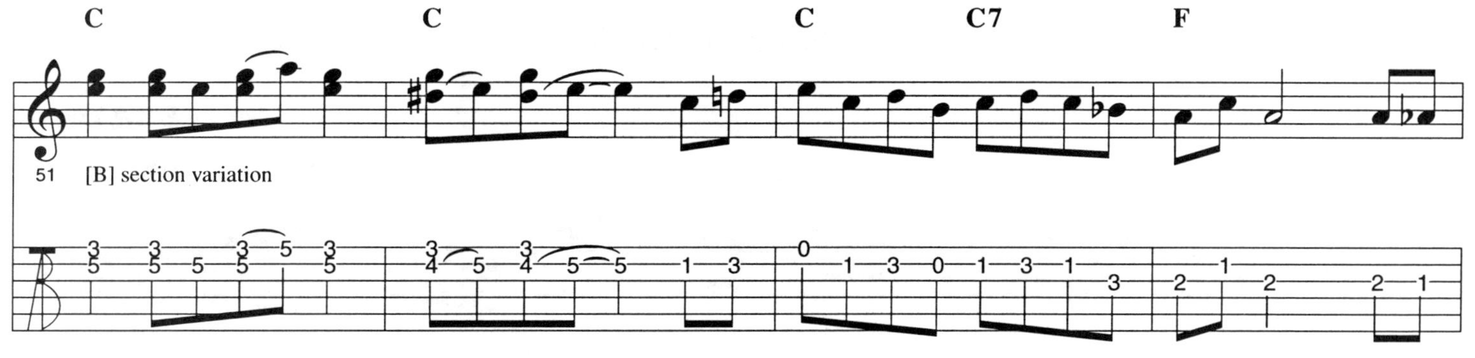
C
C
C
C7
F
51
[B] section variation

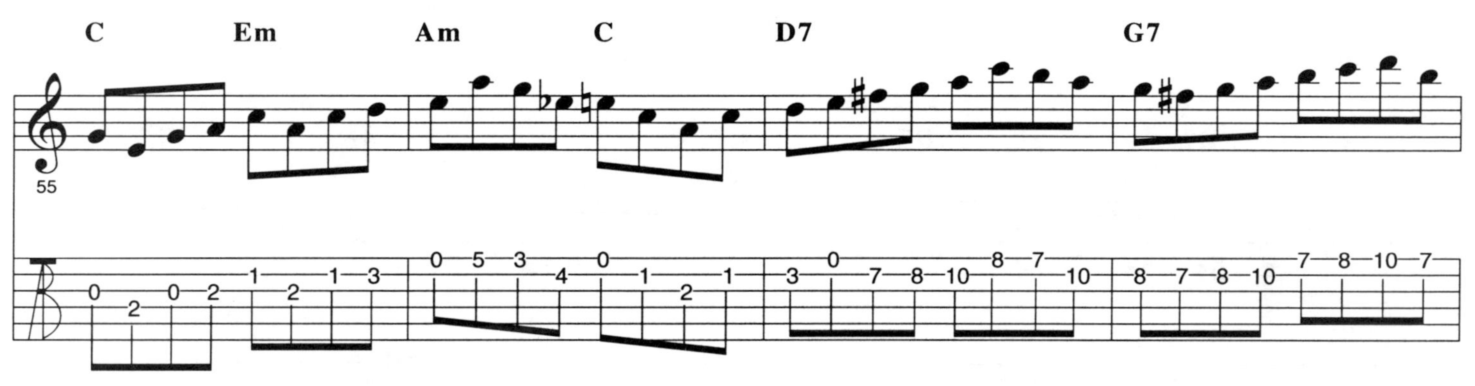
C
Em
Am
C
D7
G7
55

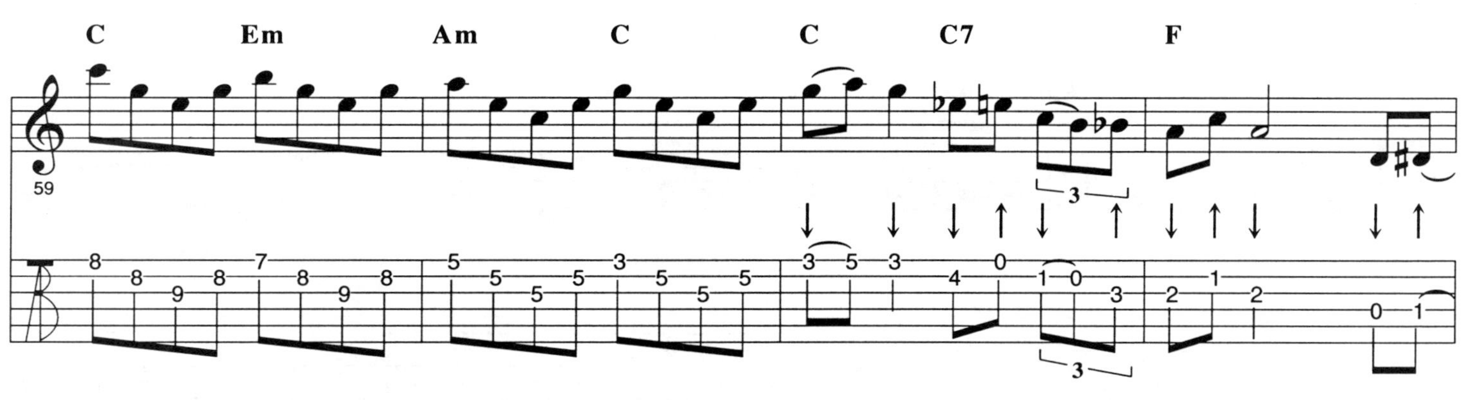
C
Em
Am
C
C
C7
F
59

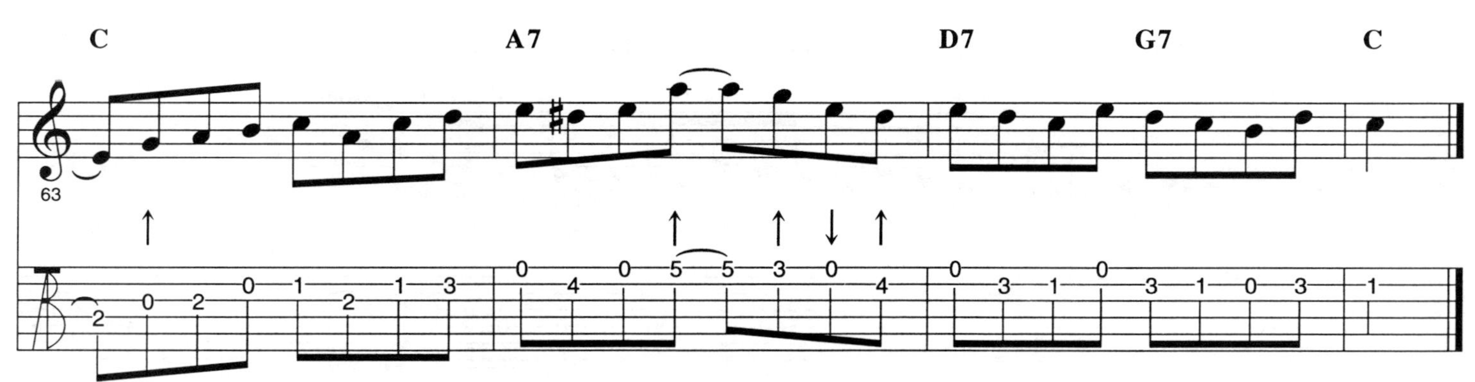
C
A7
D7
G7
C
63

Jesse Polka

Arr. by Steve Kaufman

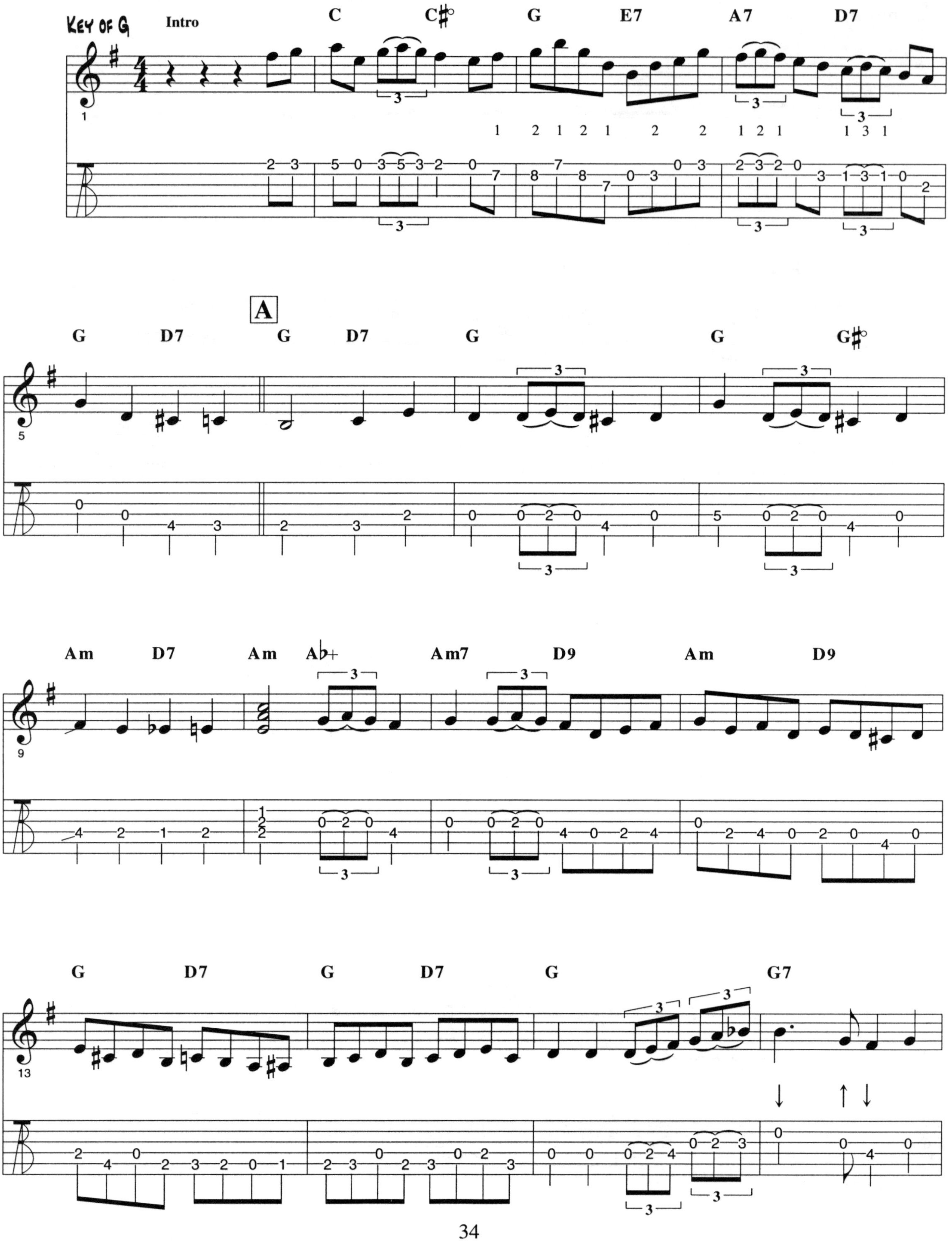

Key of G

Intro

C C#° G E7 A7 D7

A

G D7 G D7 G G G#°

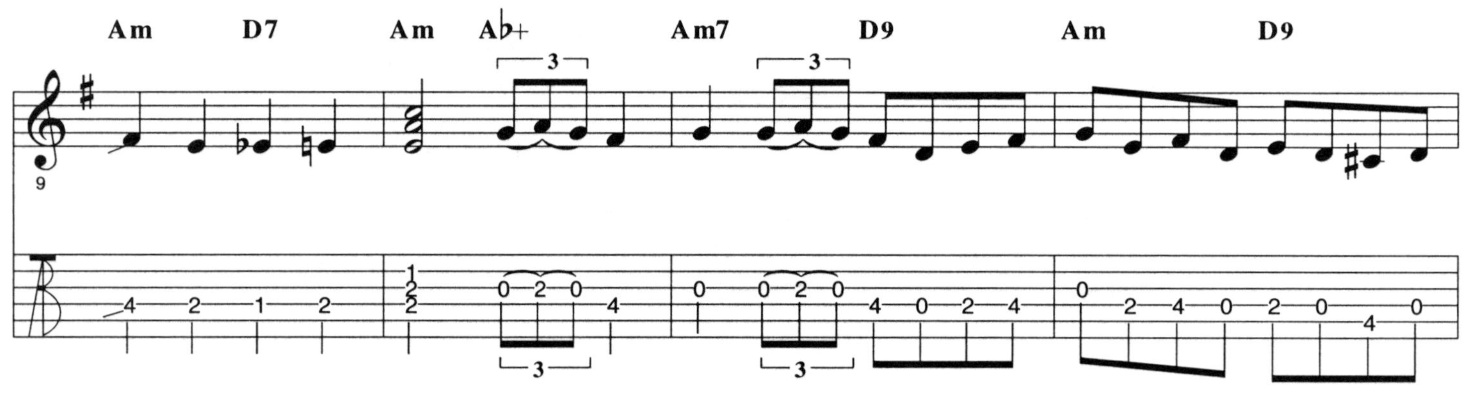

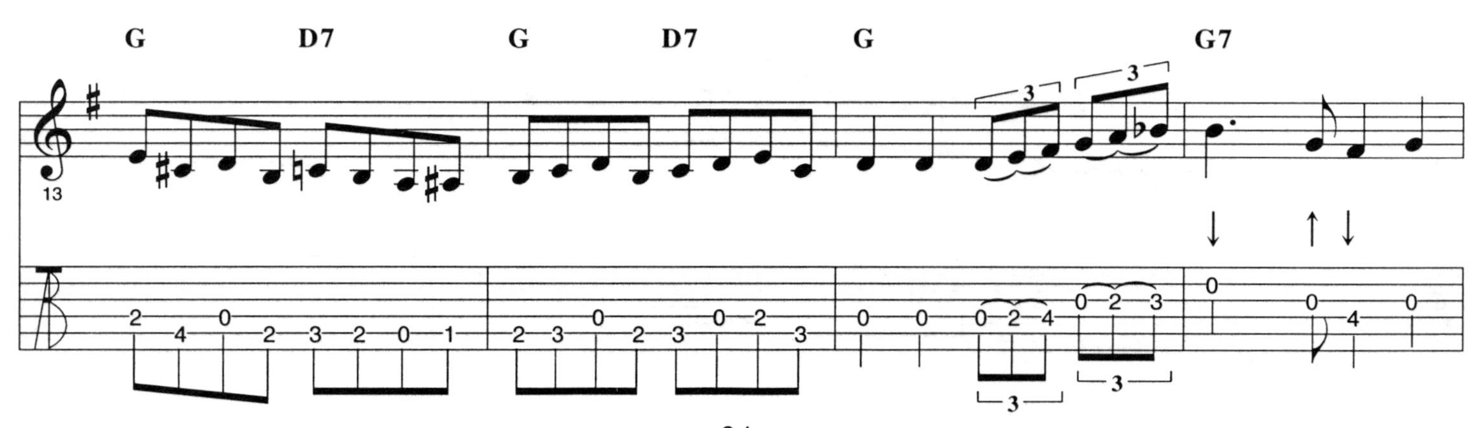

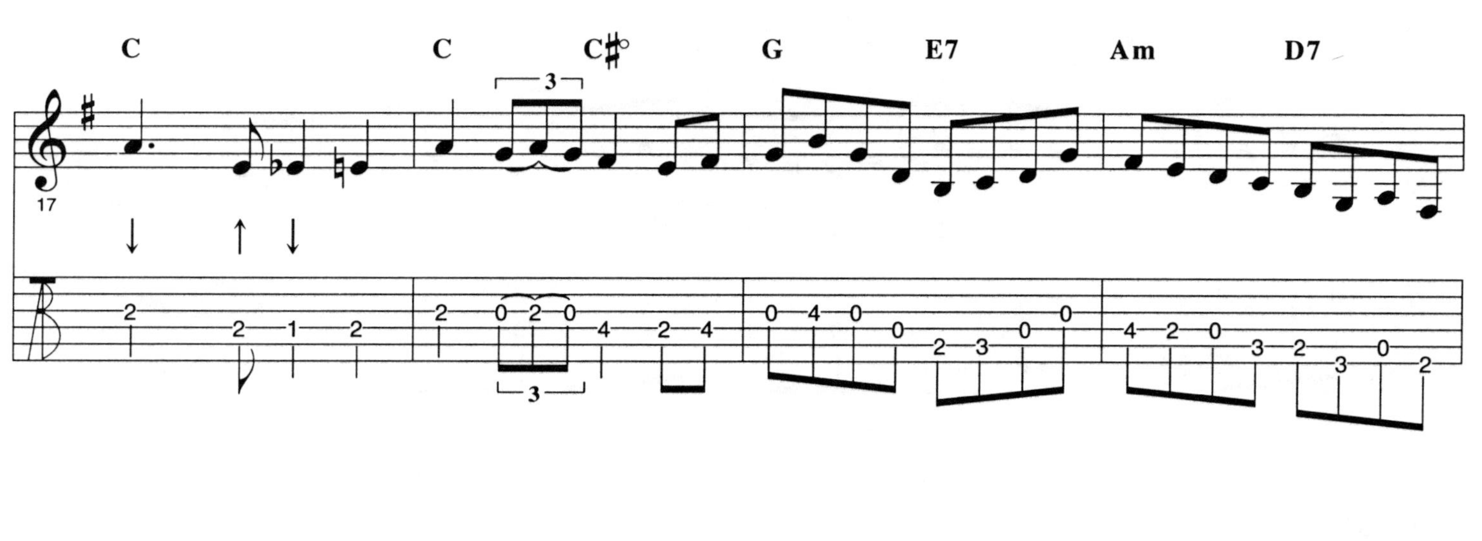
C
C
C#°
G
E7
Am
D7
17

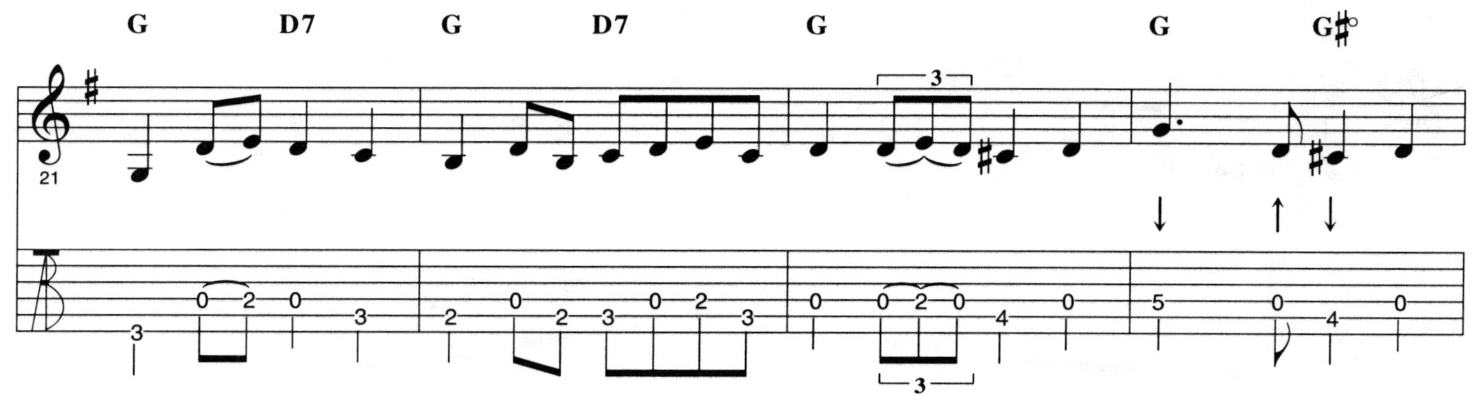
G
D7
G
D7
G
G
G#°
21

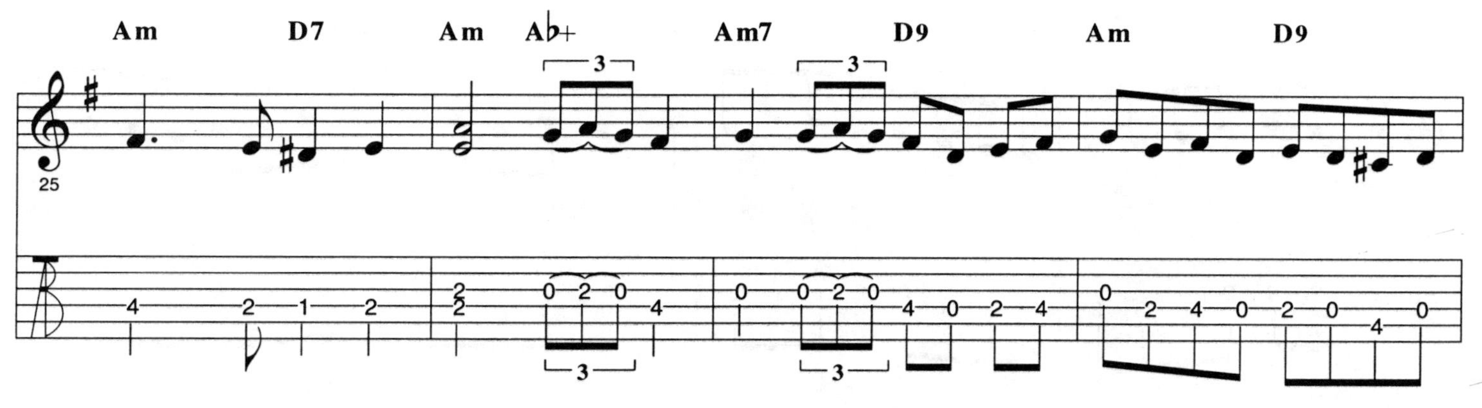
Am
D7
Am
Ab+
Am7
D9
Am
D9
25

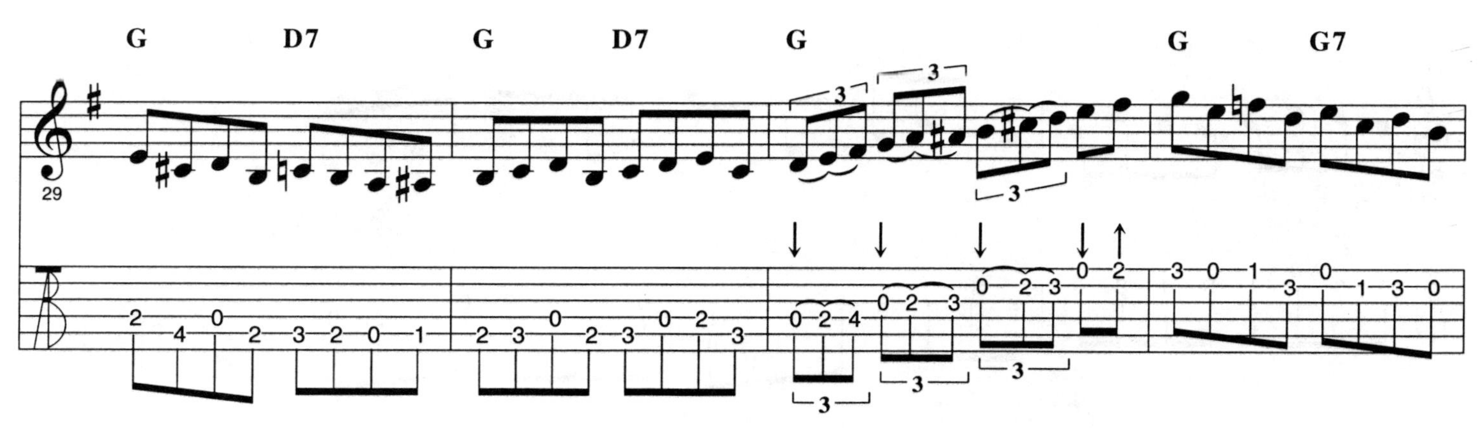
G
D7
G
D7
G
G
G7
29

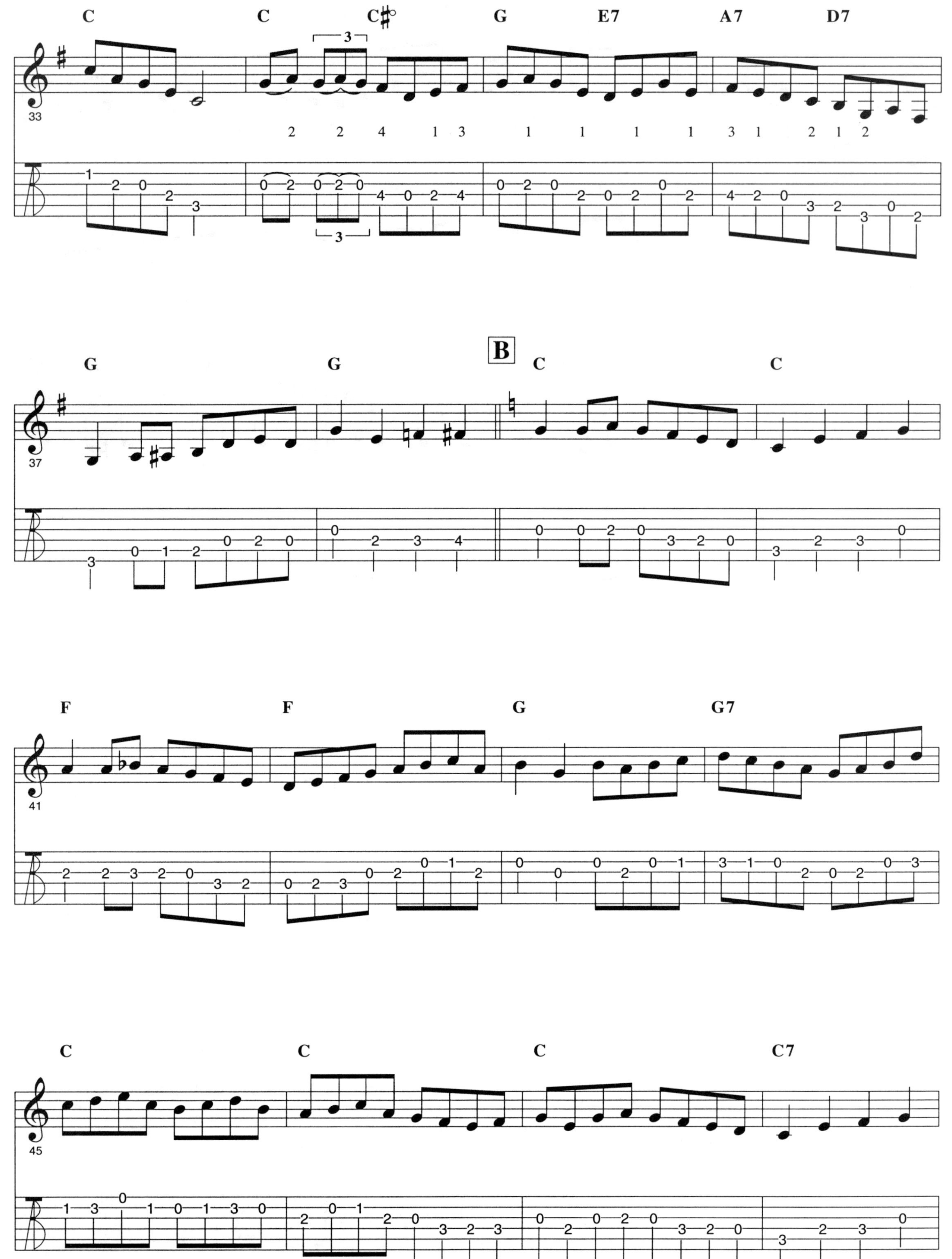
C C C♯° G E7 A7 D7
33
G G B C C
37
F F G G7
41
C C C C7
45

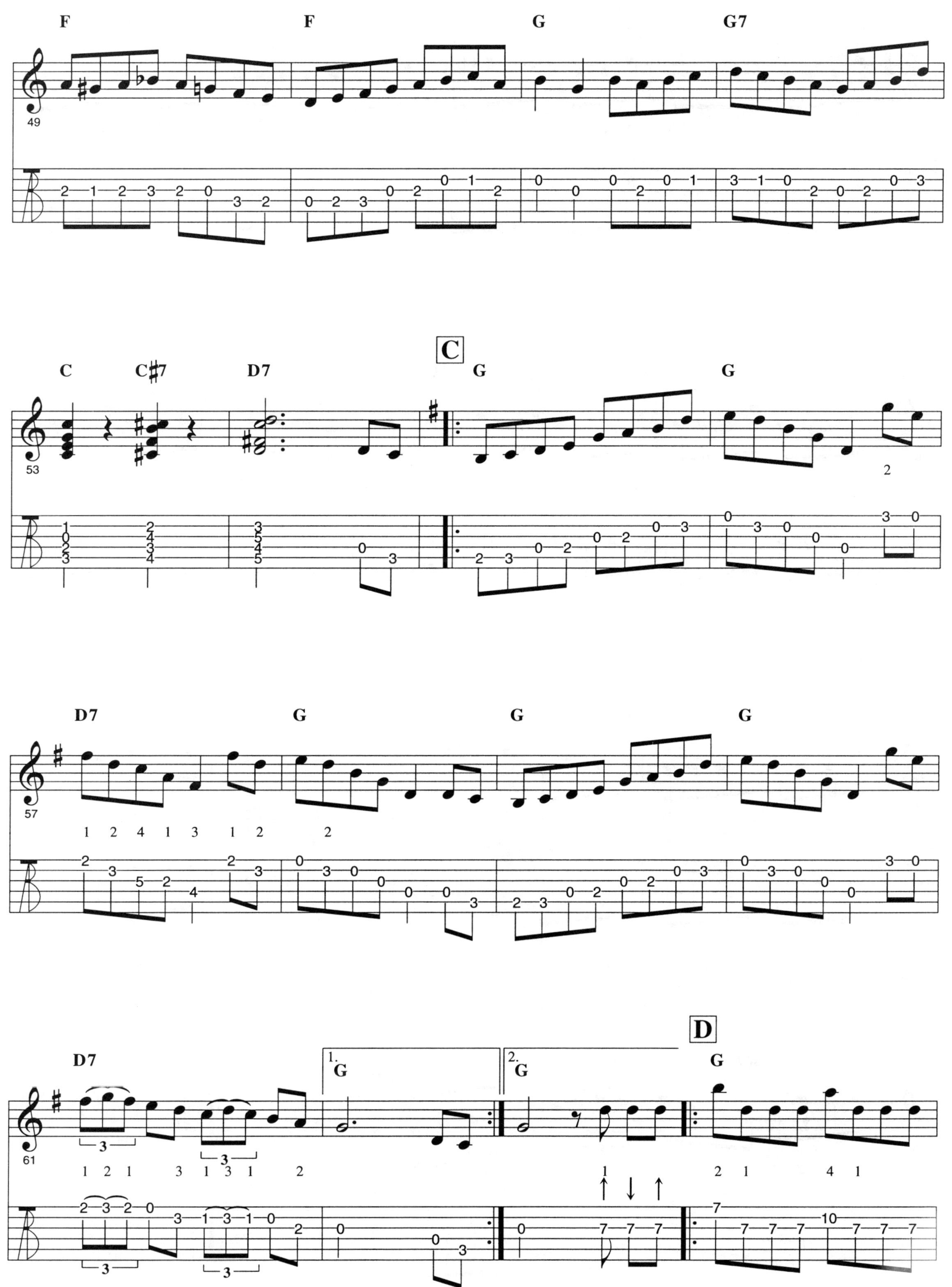
F
F
G
G7
C
C♯7
D7
C
G
G
D7
G
G
G
D7
1.
G
2.
G
D
G

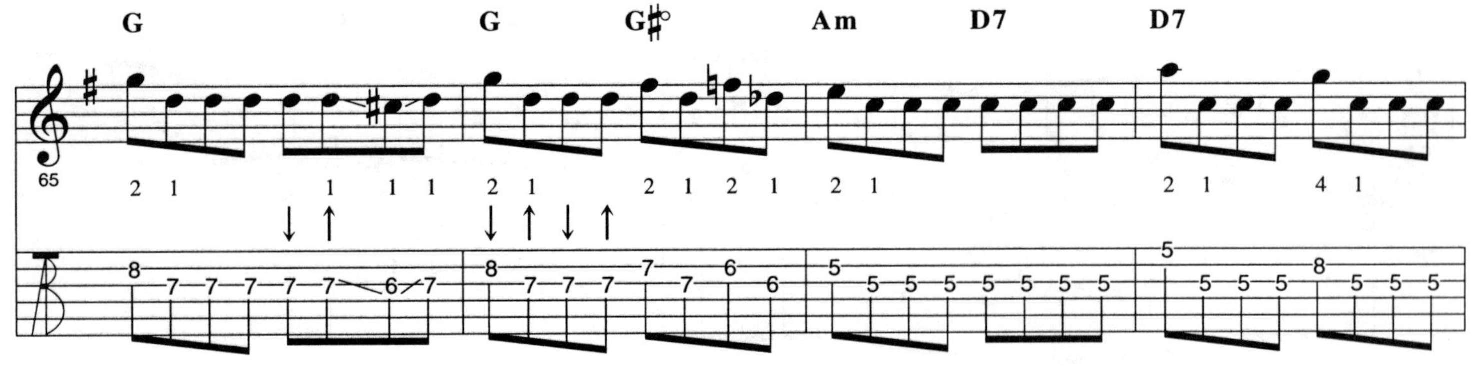
G
G
G#°
Am
D7
D7
65

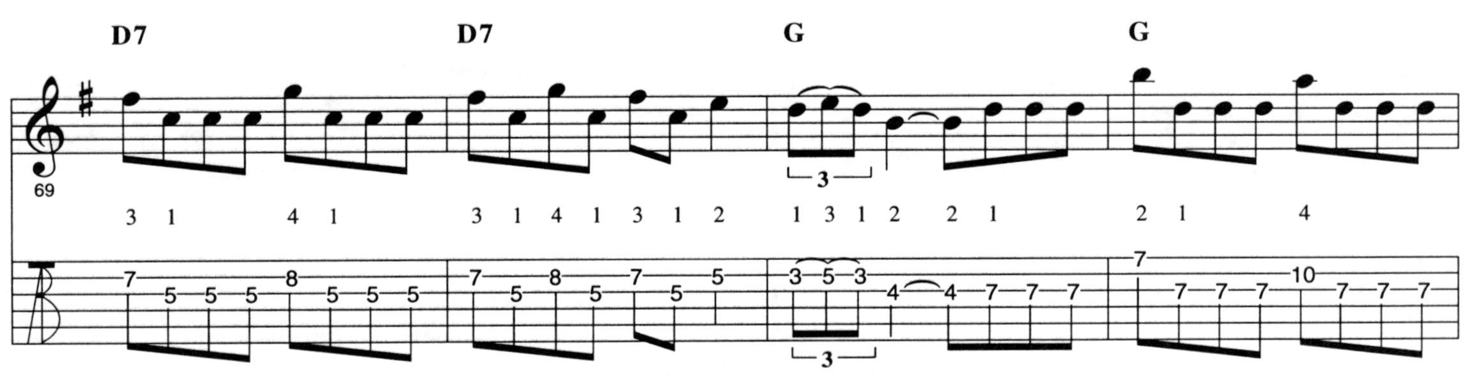
D7
D7
G
G
69

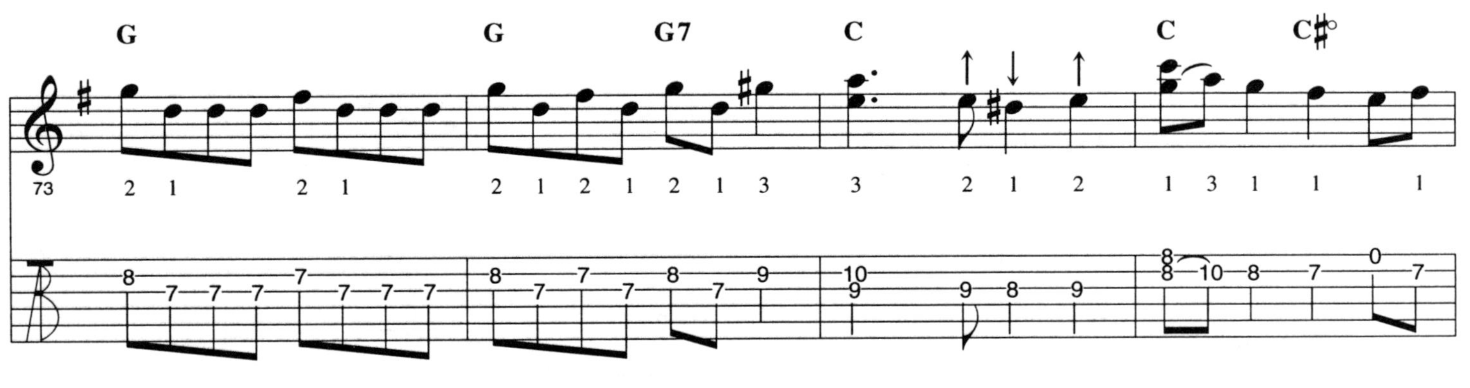
G
G
G7
C
C
C#°
73

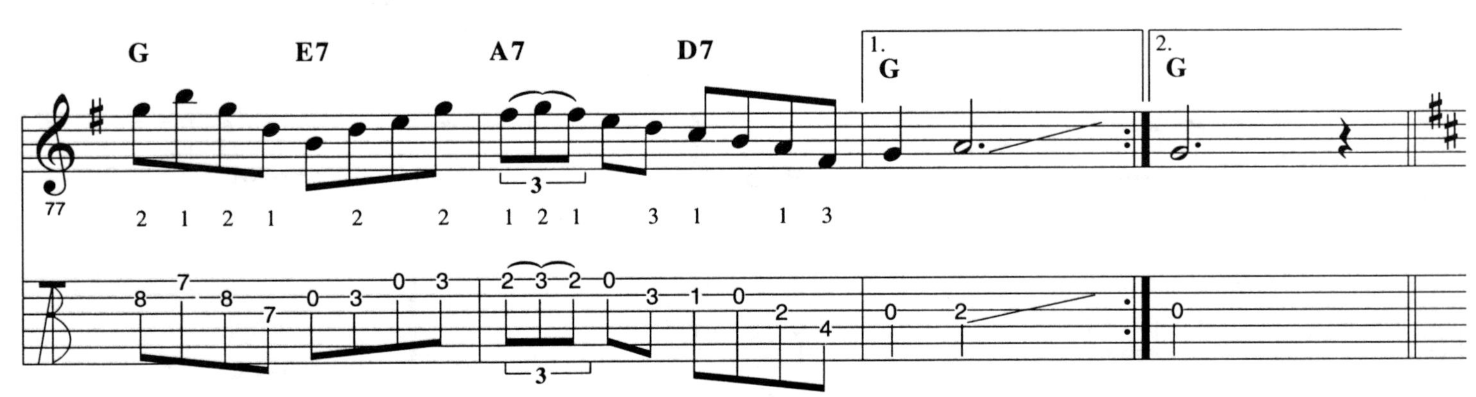
G
E7
A7
D7
1.
G
2.
G
77

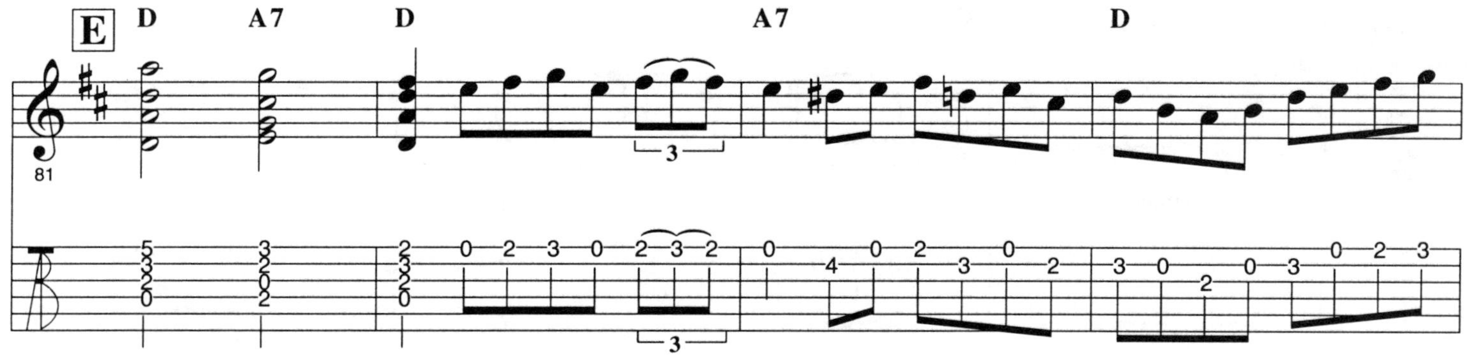
E
D
A7
D
A7
D
81

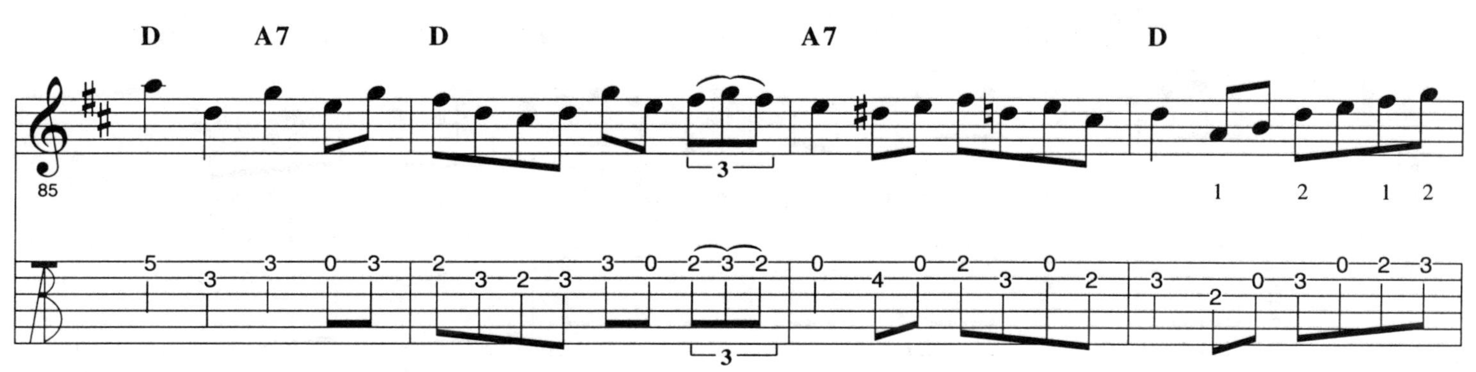
D
A7
D
A7
D
85

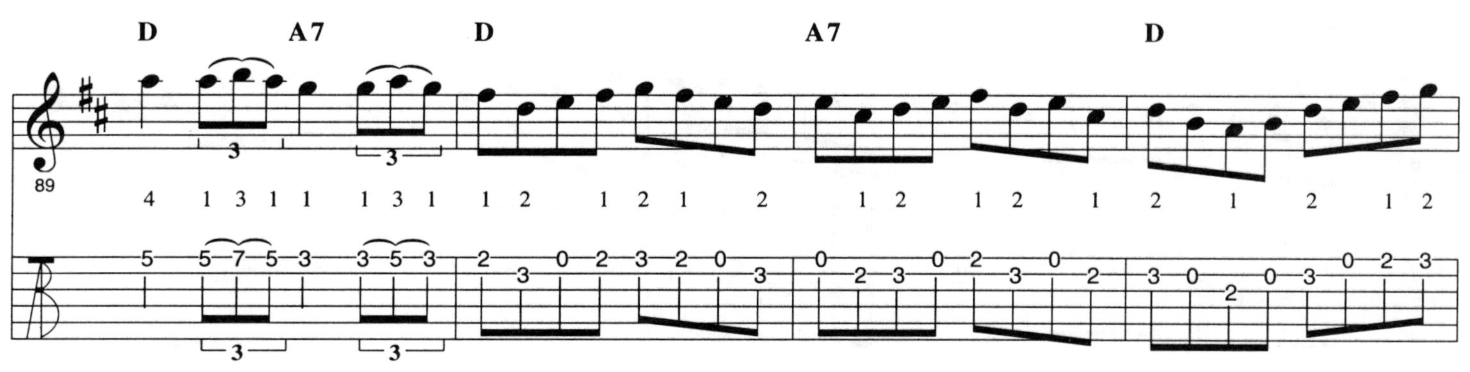
D
A7
D
A7
D
89

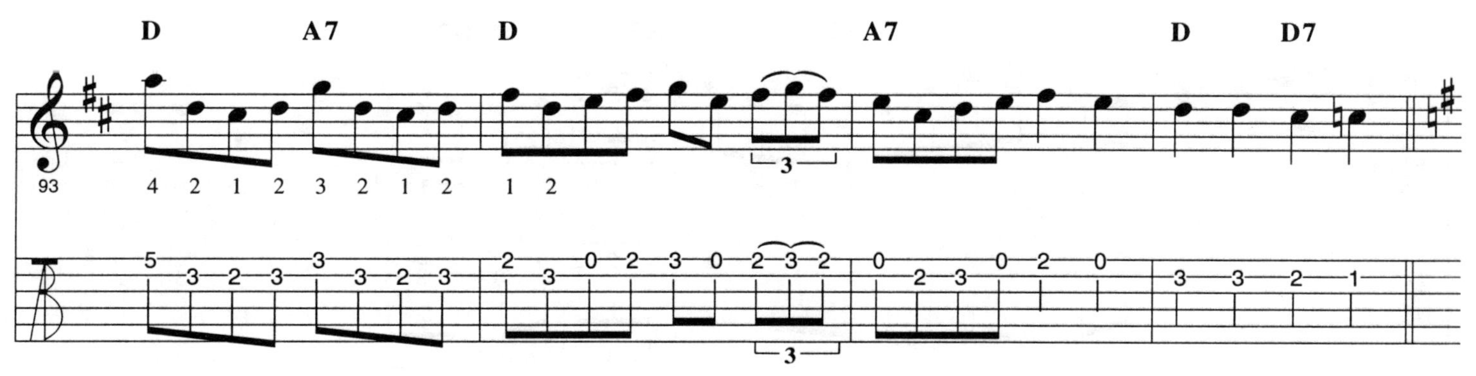
D
A7
D
A7
D
D7
93

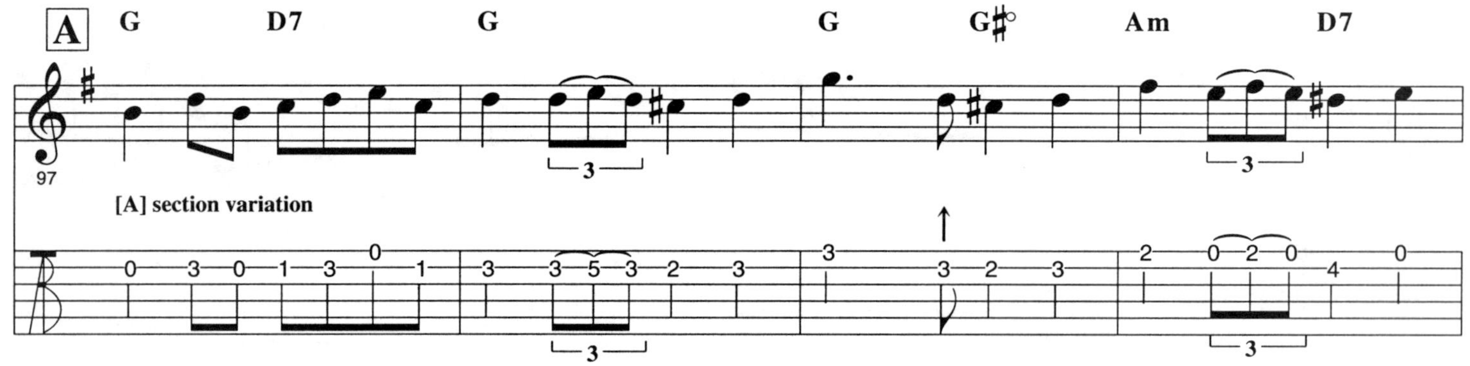
A
G D7 G G G♯° Am D7
97
[A] section variation

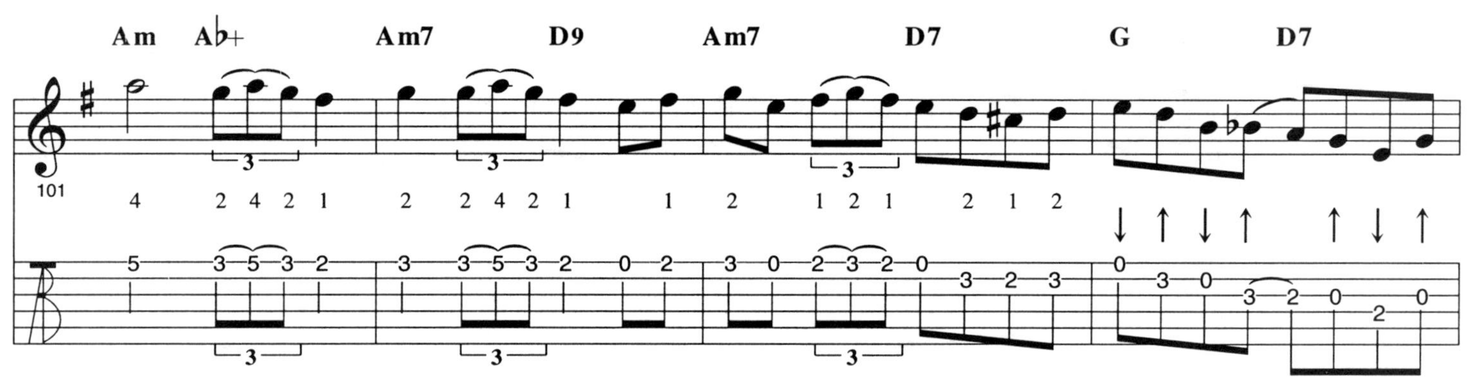
Am A♭+ Am7 D9 Am7 D7 G D7
101

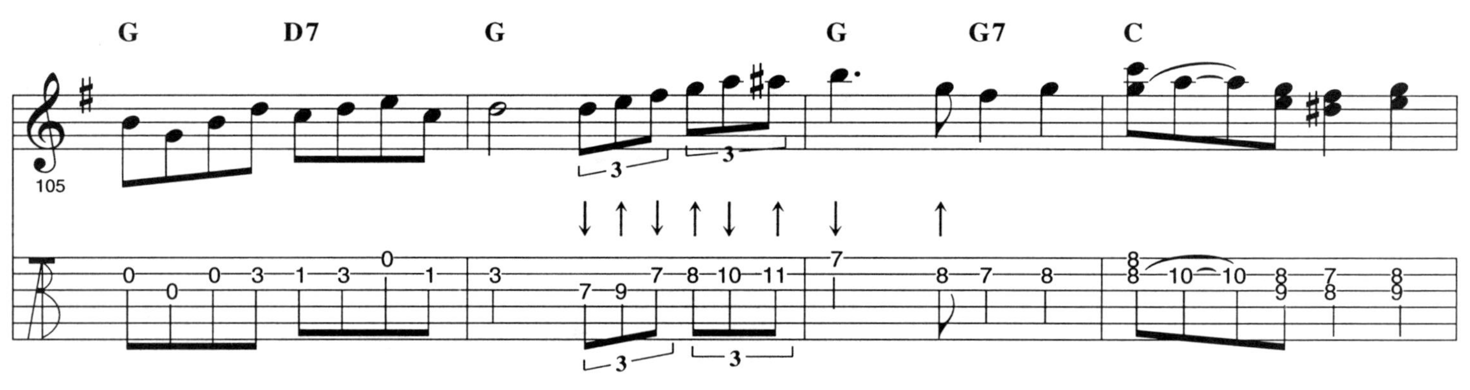
G D7 G G G7 C
105

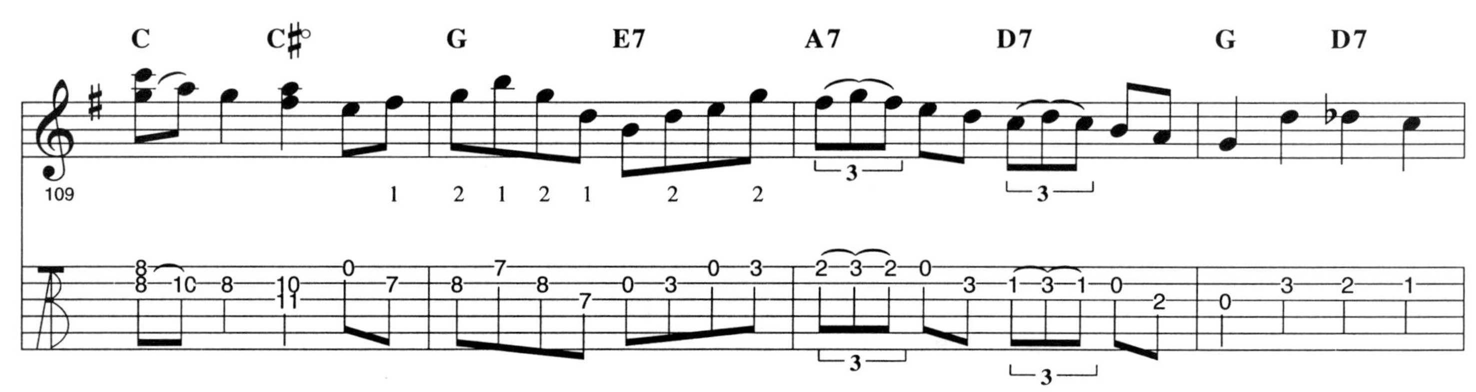
C C♯° G E7 A7 D7 G D7
109

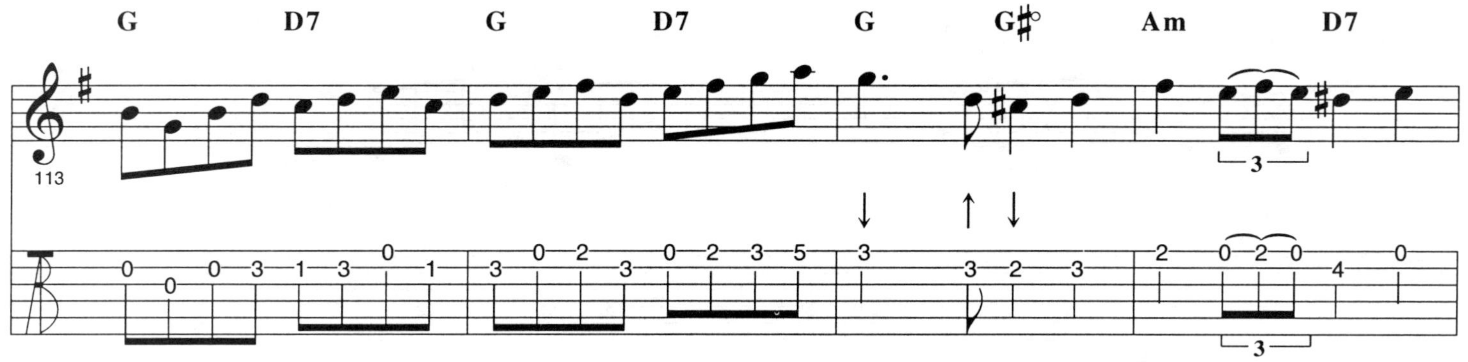
G
D7
G
D7
G
G♯°
Am
D7
113

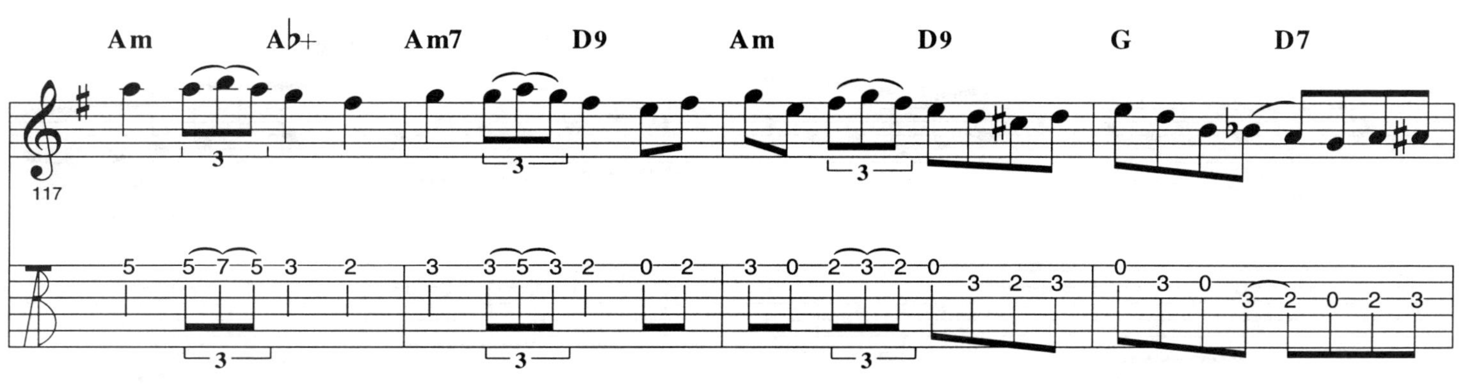
Am
A♭+
Am7
D9
Am
D9
G
D7
117

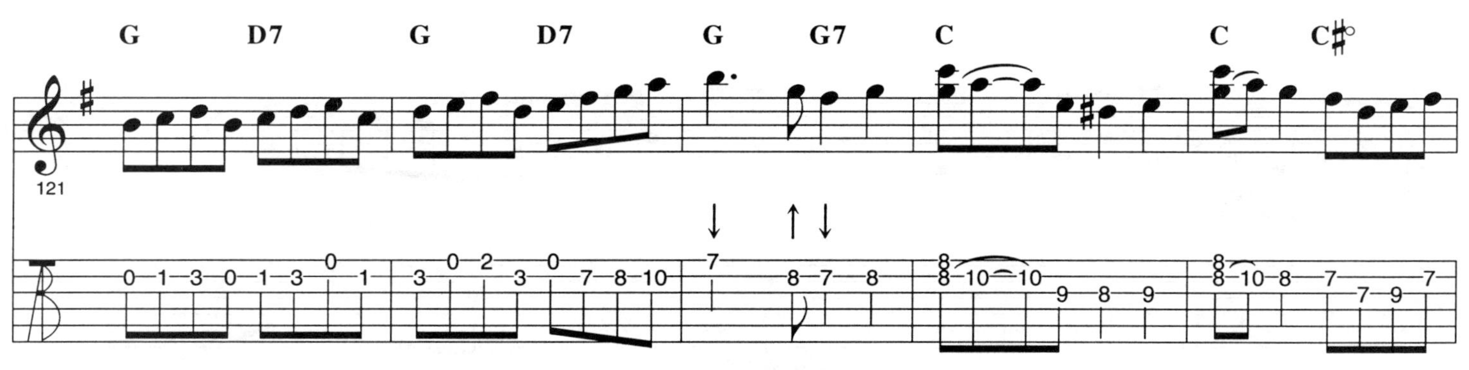
G
D7
G
D7
G
G7
C
C
C♯°
121

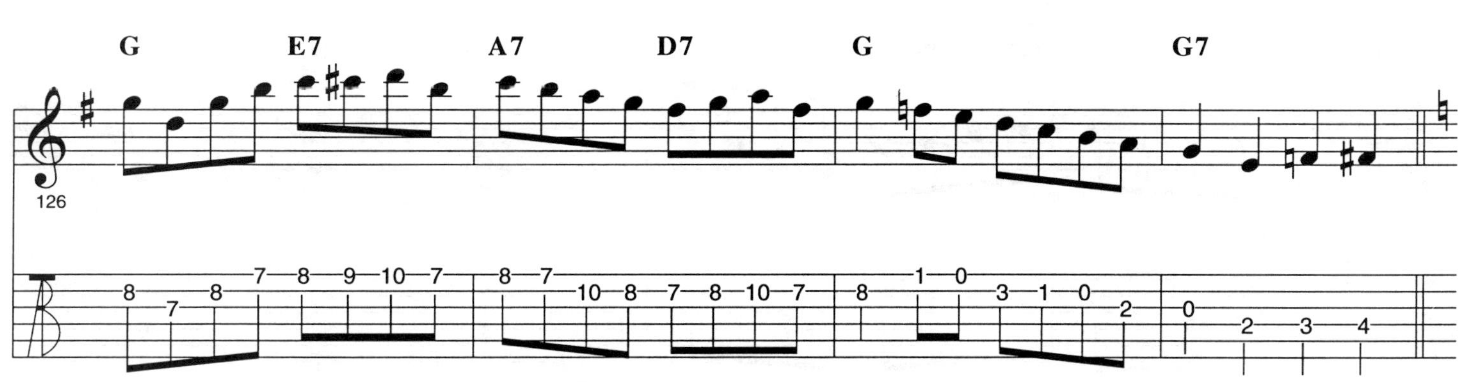
G
E7
A7
D7
G
G7
126

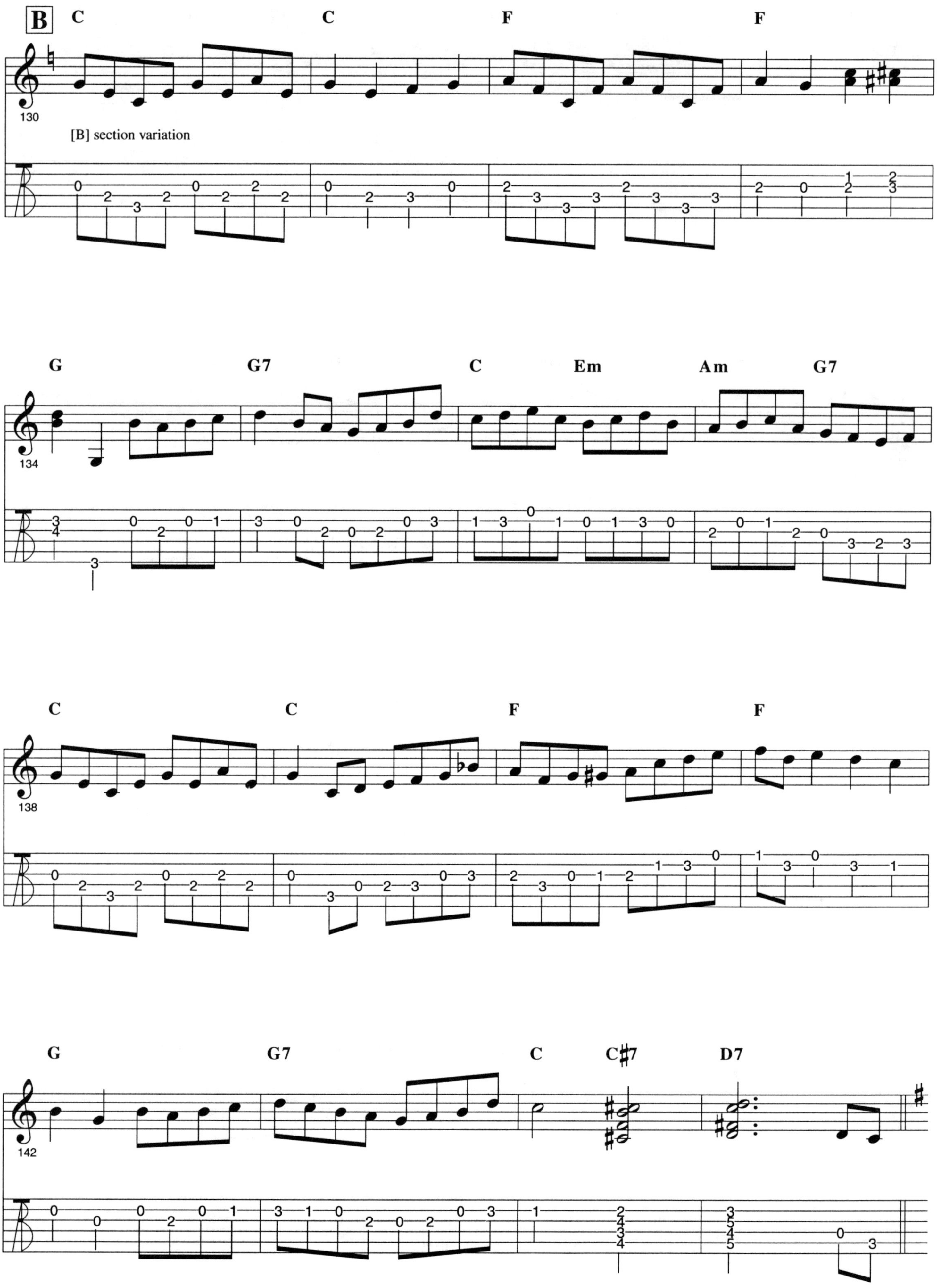

B

C C F F

130

[B] section variation

G G7 C Em Am G7

134

C C F F

138

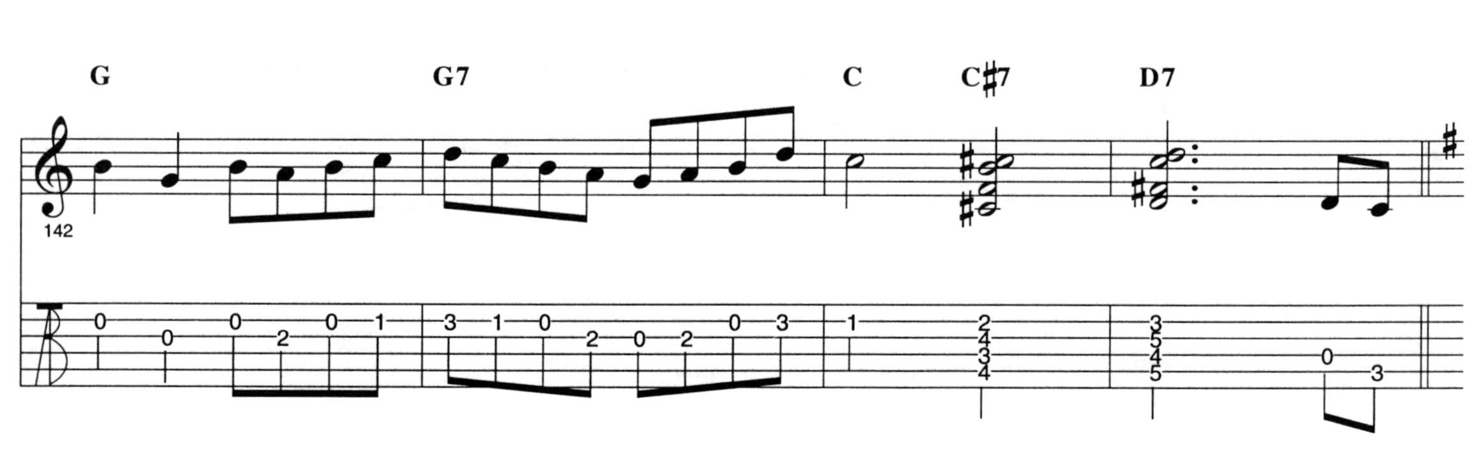

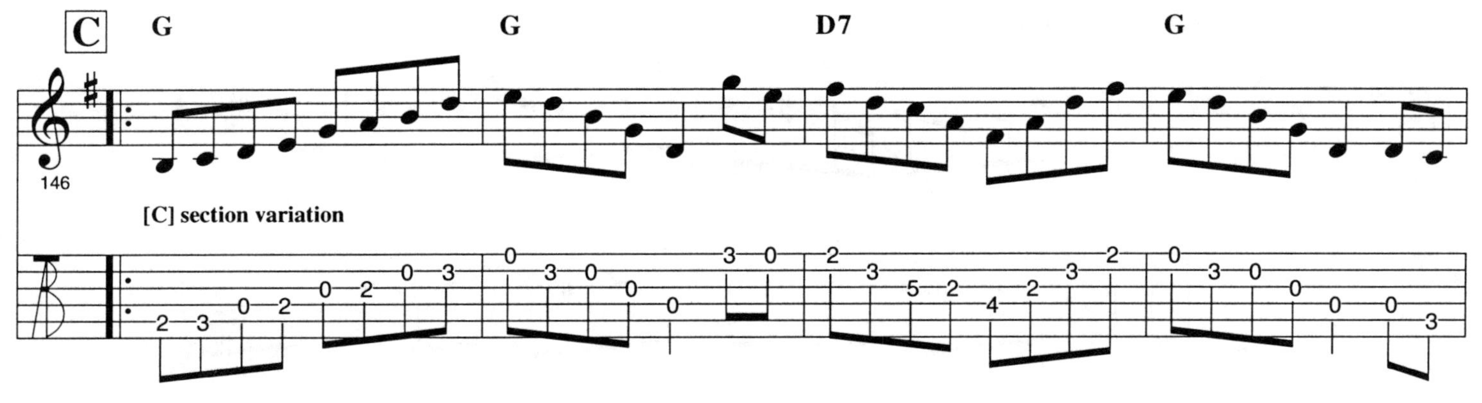
C
G
G
D7
G
146
[C] section variation

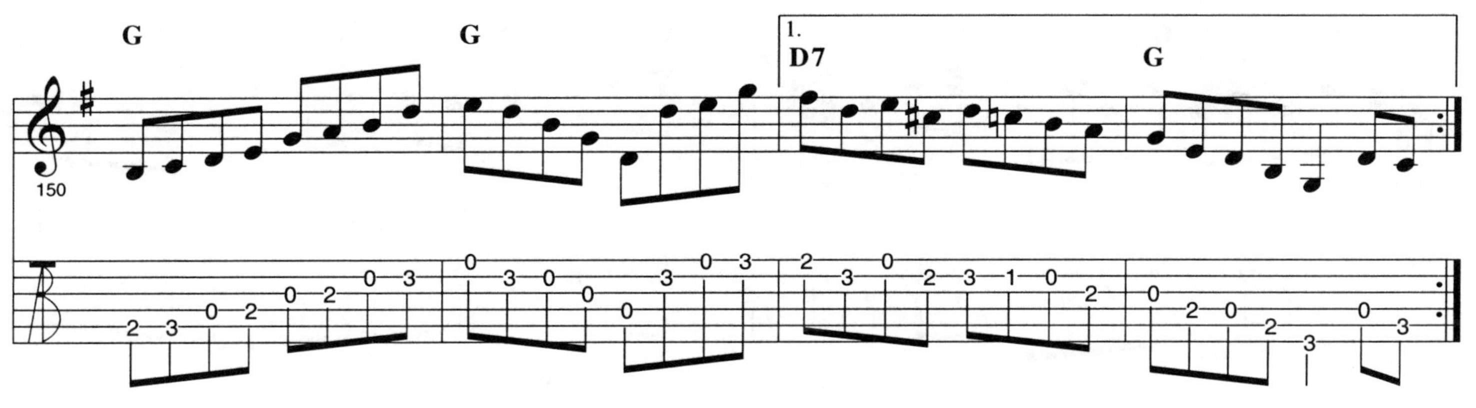
G
G
1.
D7
G
150

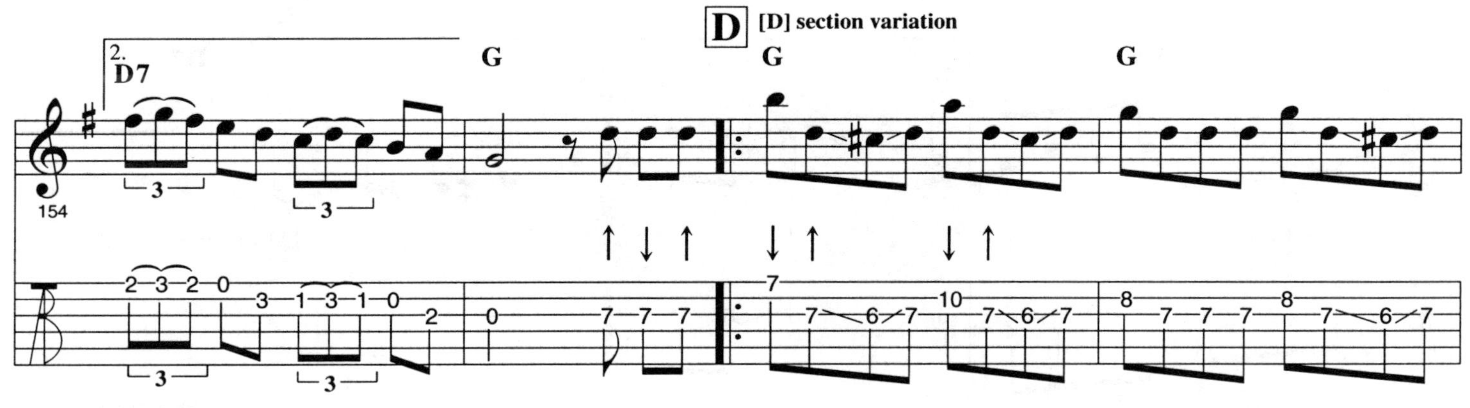
2.
D7
G
D
[D] section variation
G
G
154

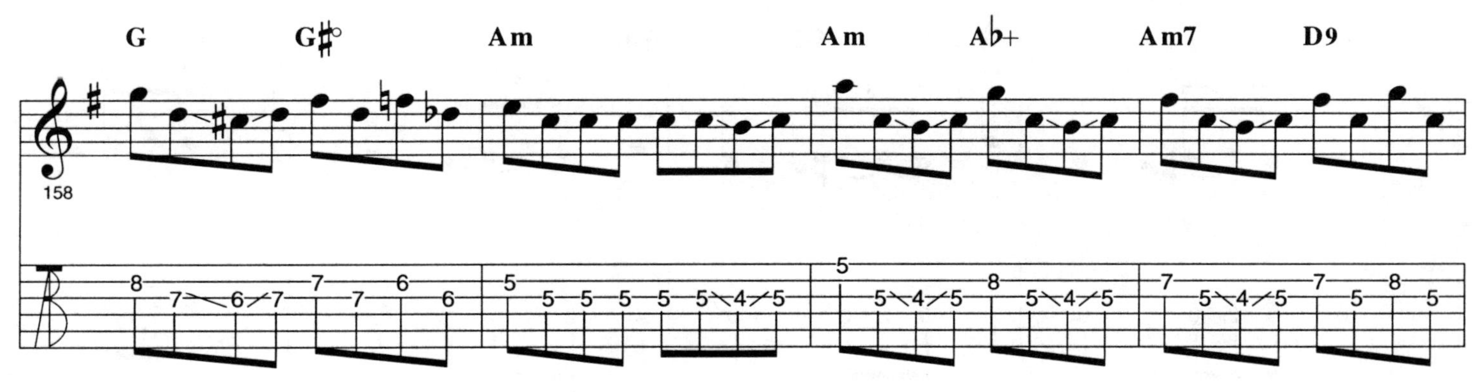
G
G#°
Am
Am
Ab+
Am7
D9
158

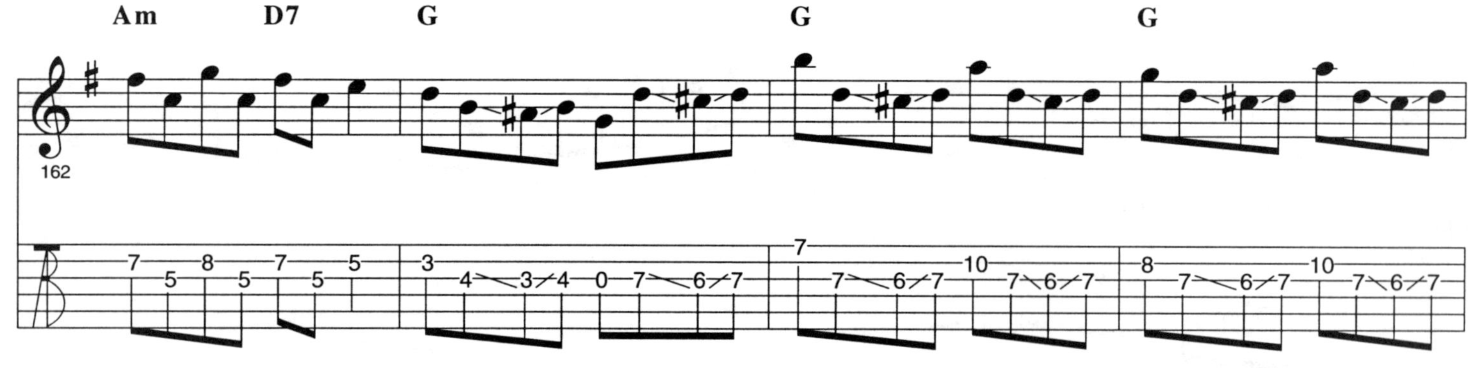
Am D7 G G G
162

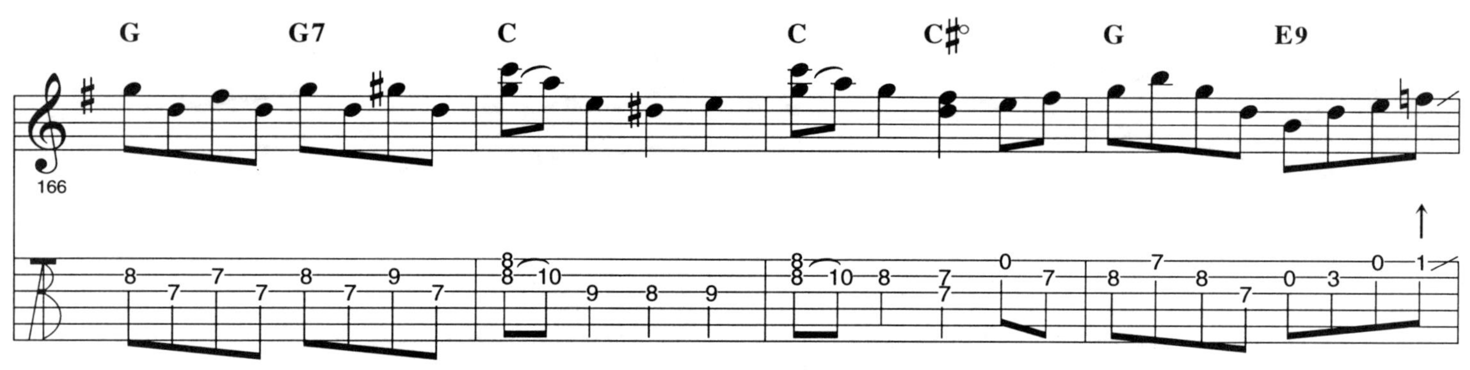
G G7 C C C♯° G E9
166

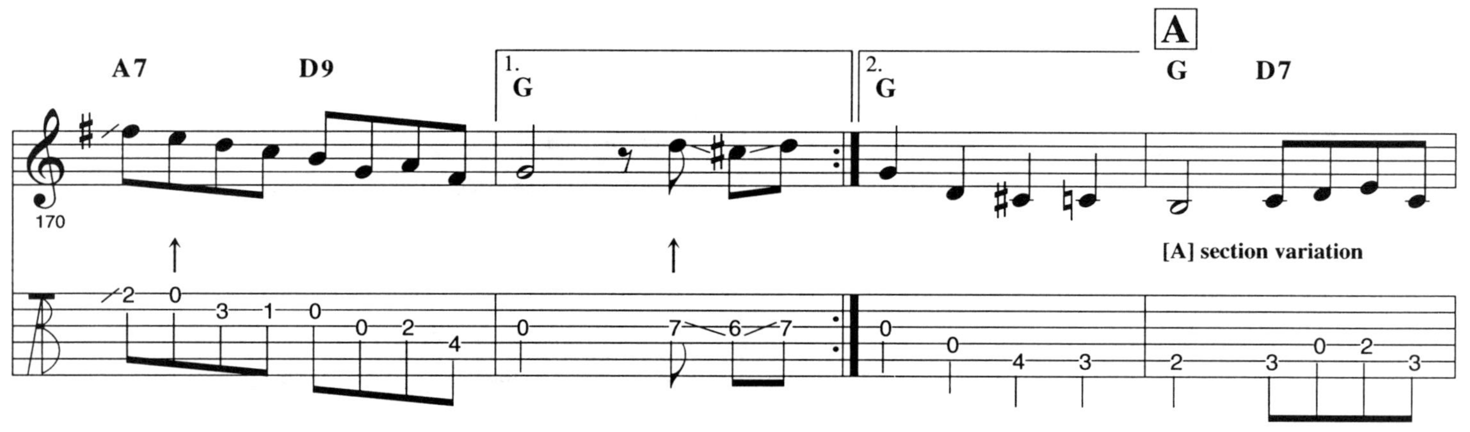
A
A7 D9 1. G 2. G G D7
170
[A] section variation

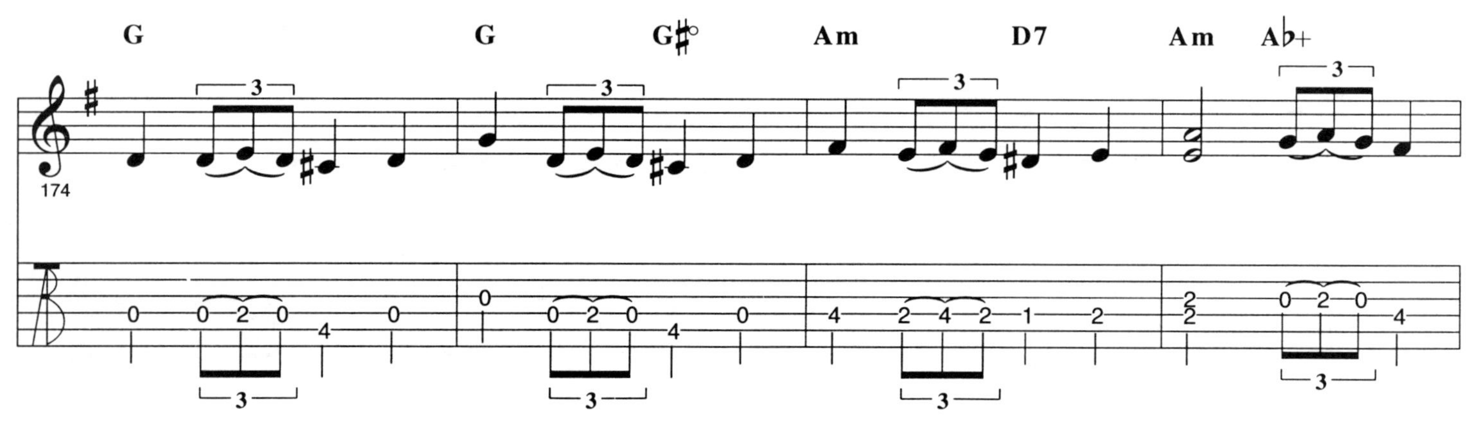
G G G♯° Am D7 Am A♭+
174

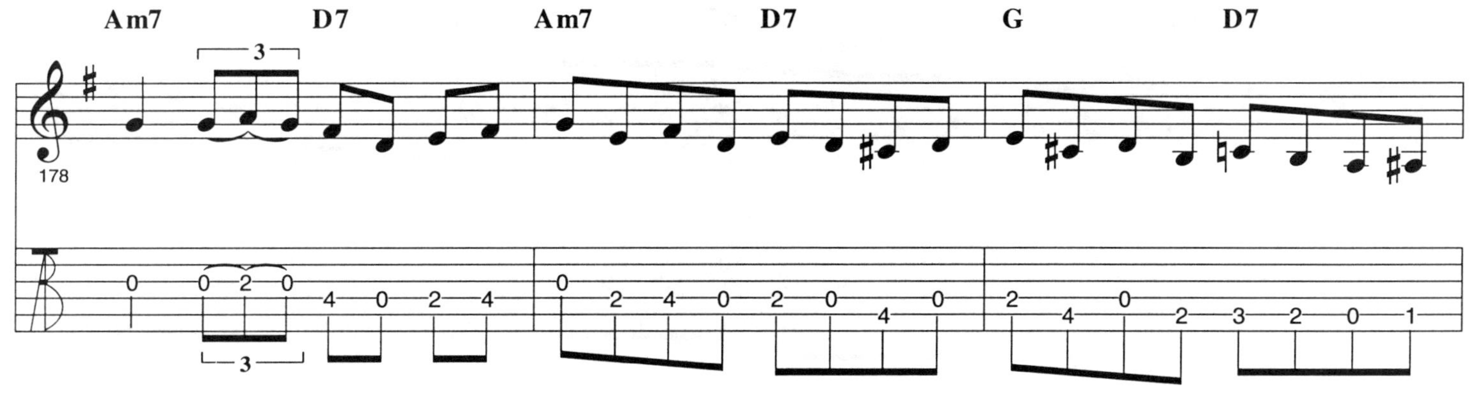
Am7
D7
Am7
D7
G
D7
178

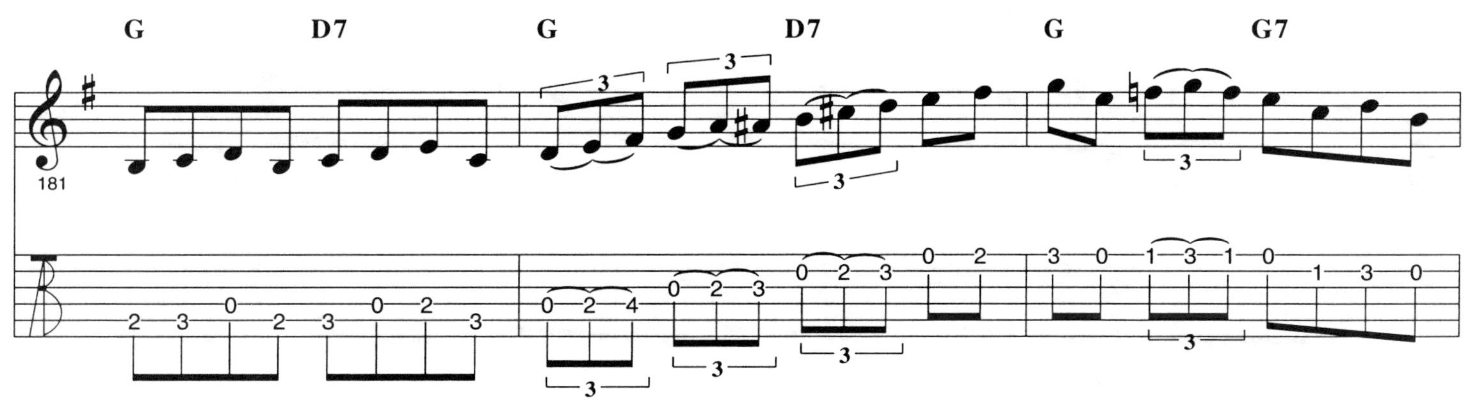
G
D7
G
D7
G
G7
181

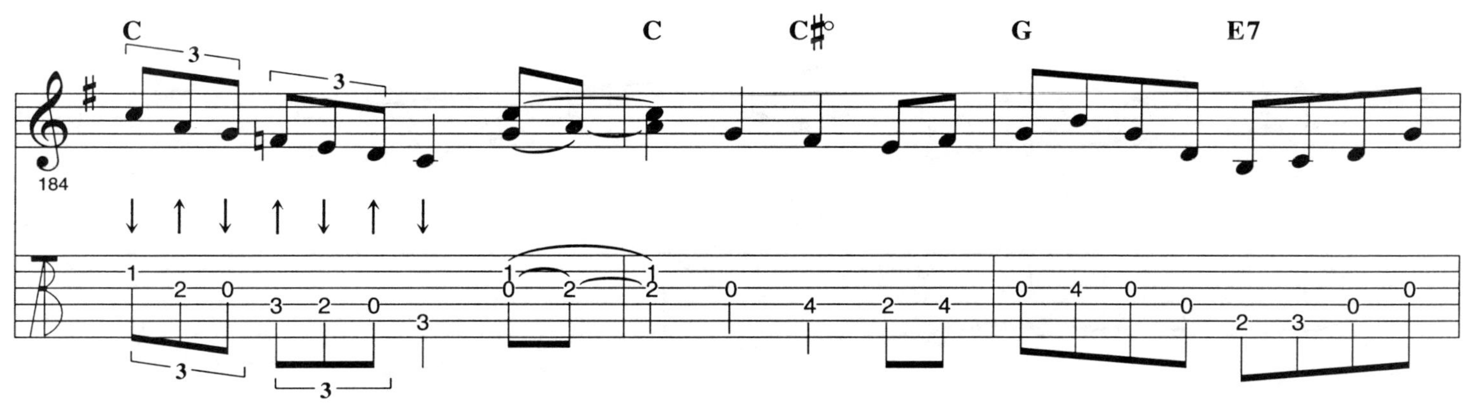
C
C
C#°
G
E7
184

A7
D7
G
Ending
187

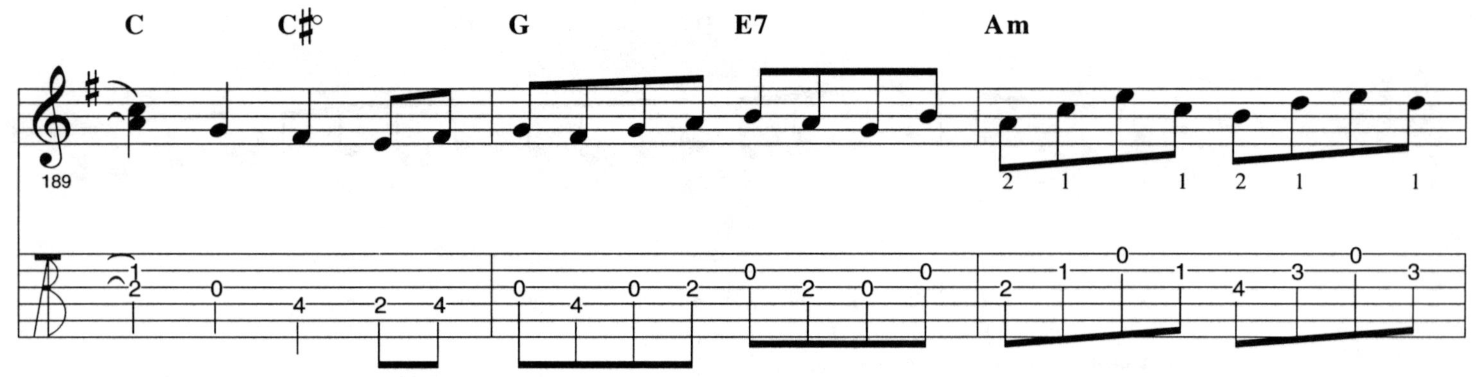
C
C♯°
G
E7
Am
189

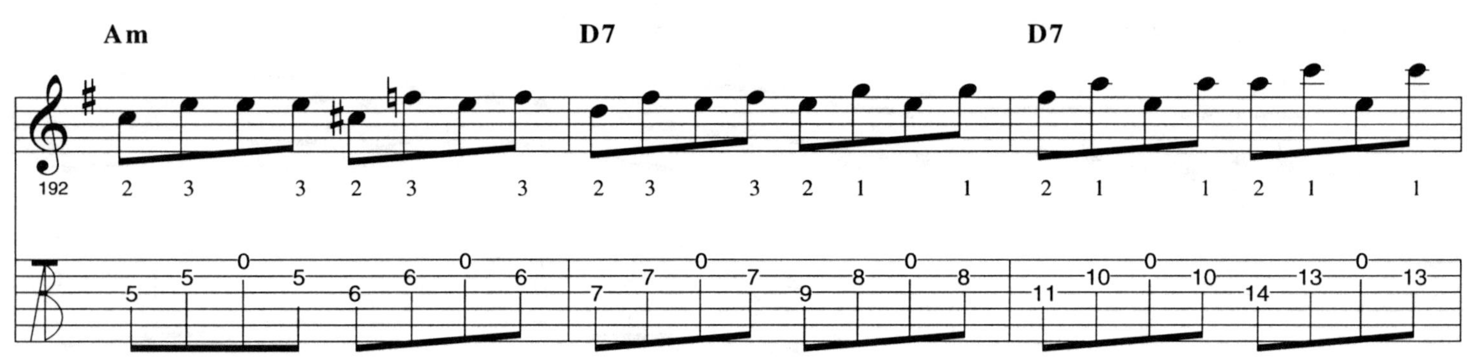
Am
D7
D7
192

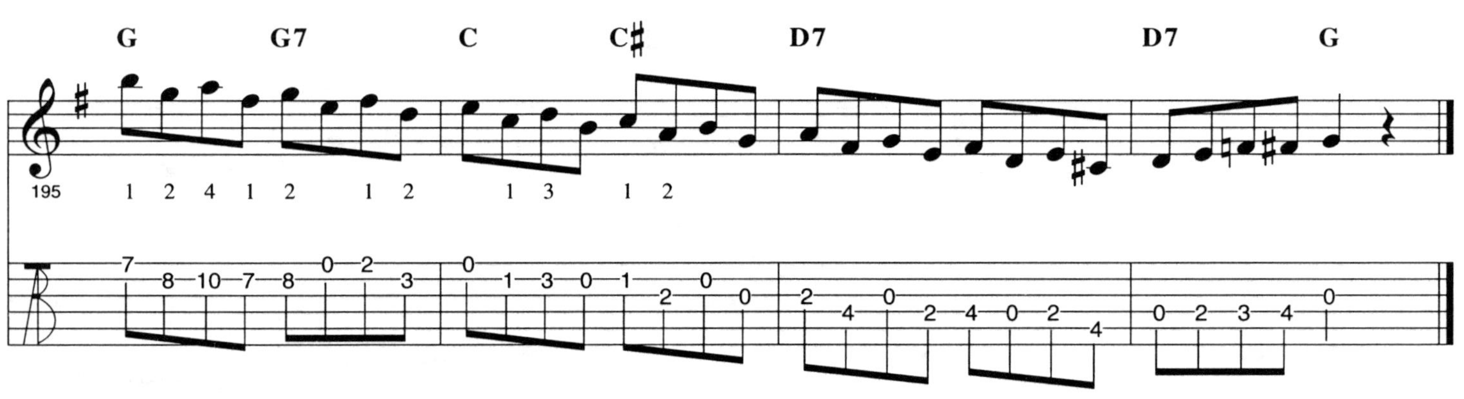
G
G7
C
C♯
D7
D7
G
195

Lady's Fancy

Key of Em — Arr. by Steve Kaufman

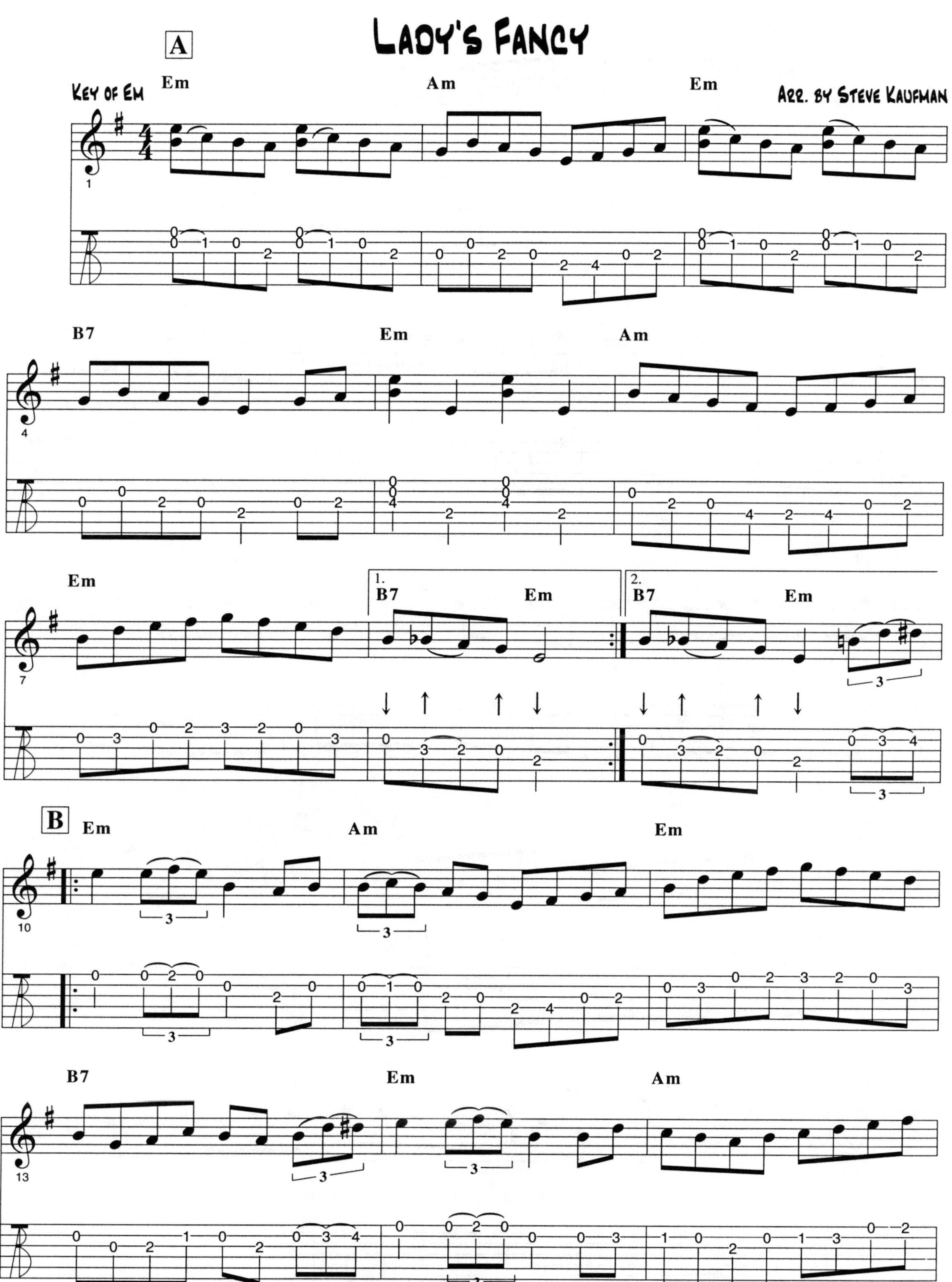

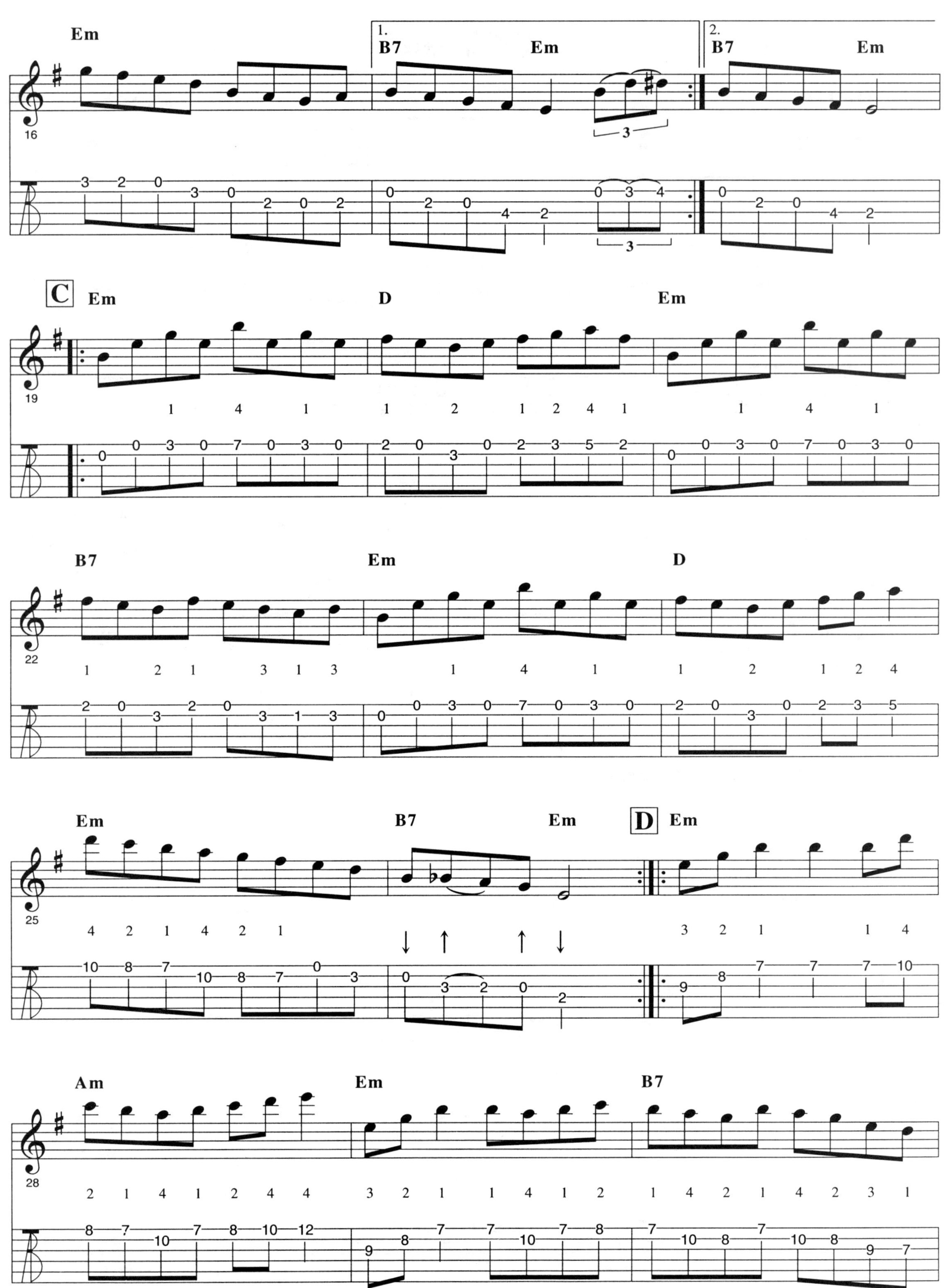

Em
1.
B7
Em
2.
B7
Em
16
C
Em
D
Em
19
B7
Em
D
22
Em
B7
Em
D
Em
25
Am
Em
B7
28

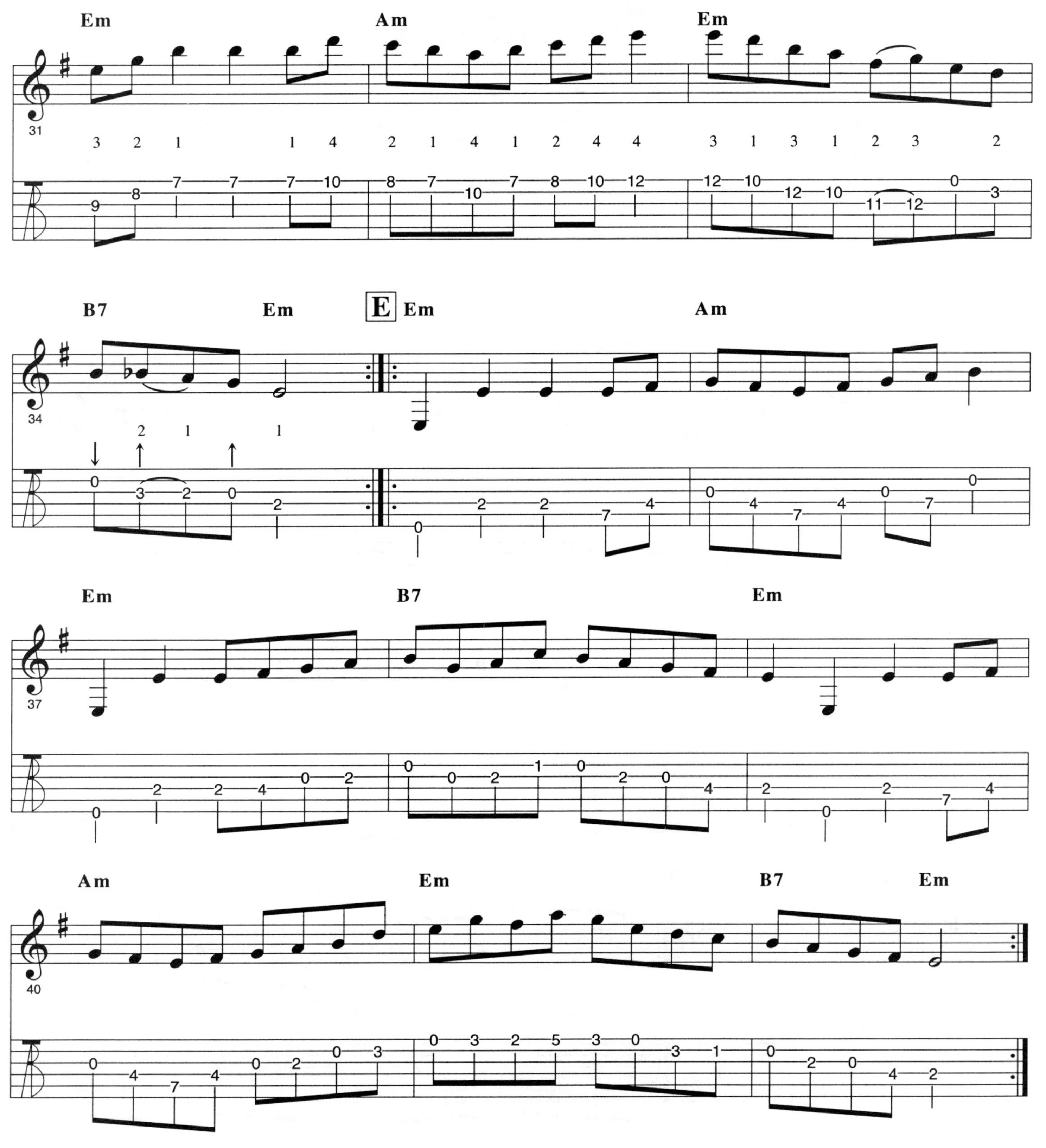

Em
Am
Em
31
B7
Em
E
Em
Am
34
Em
B7
Em
37
Am
Em
B7
Em
40

The Lime Rock

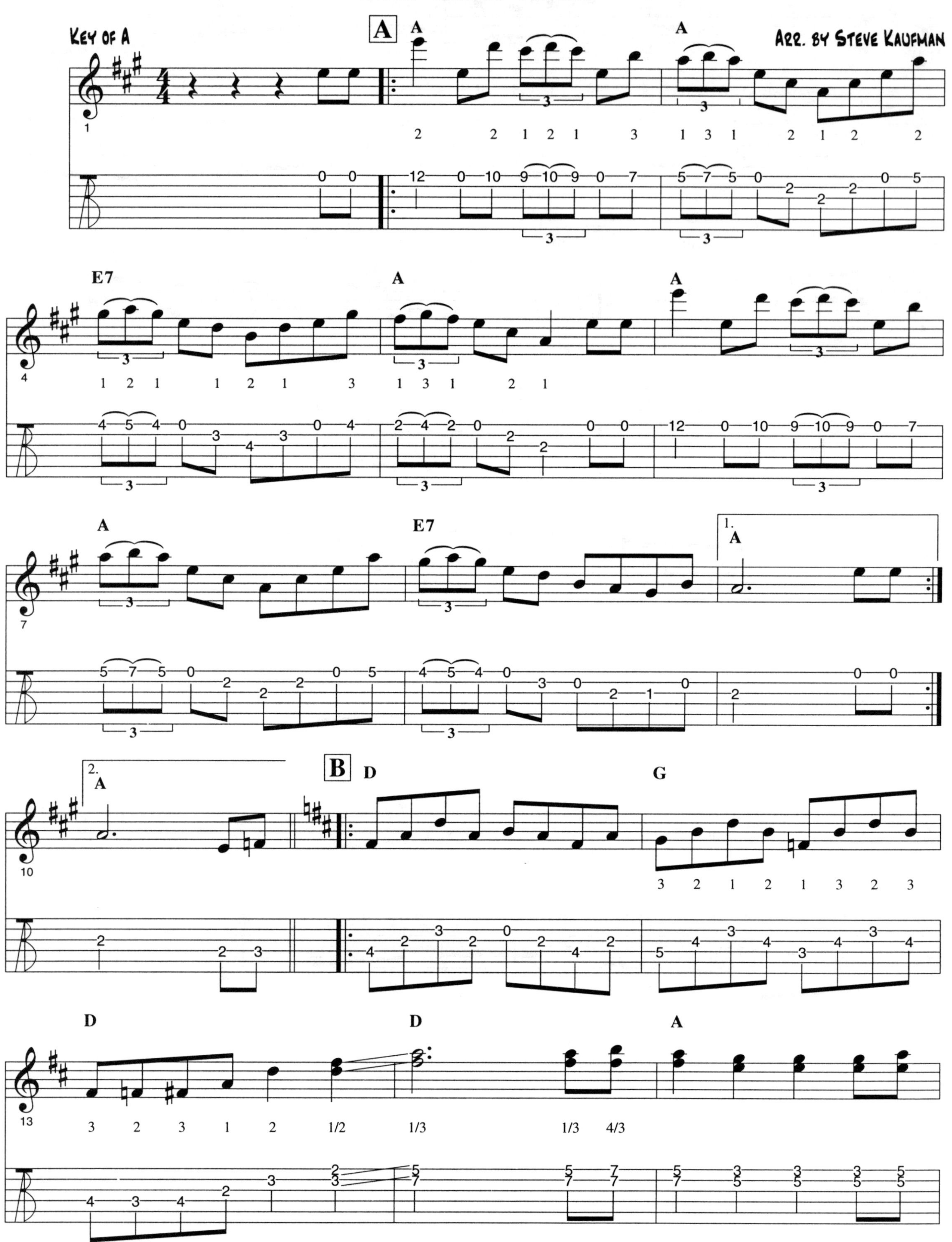

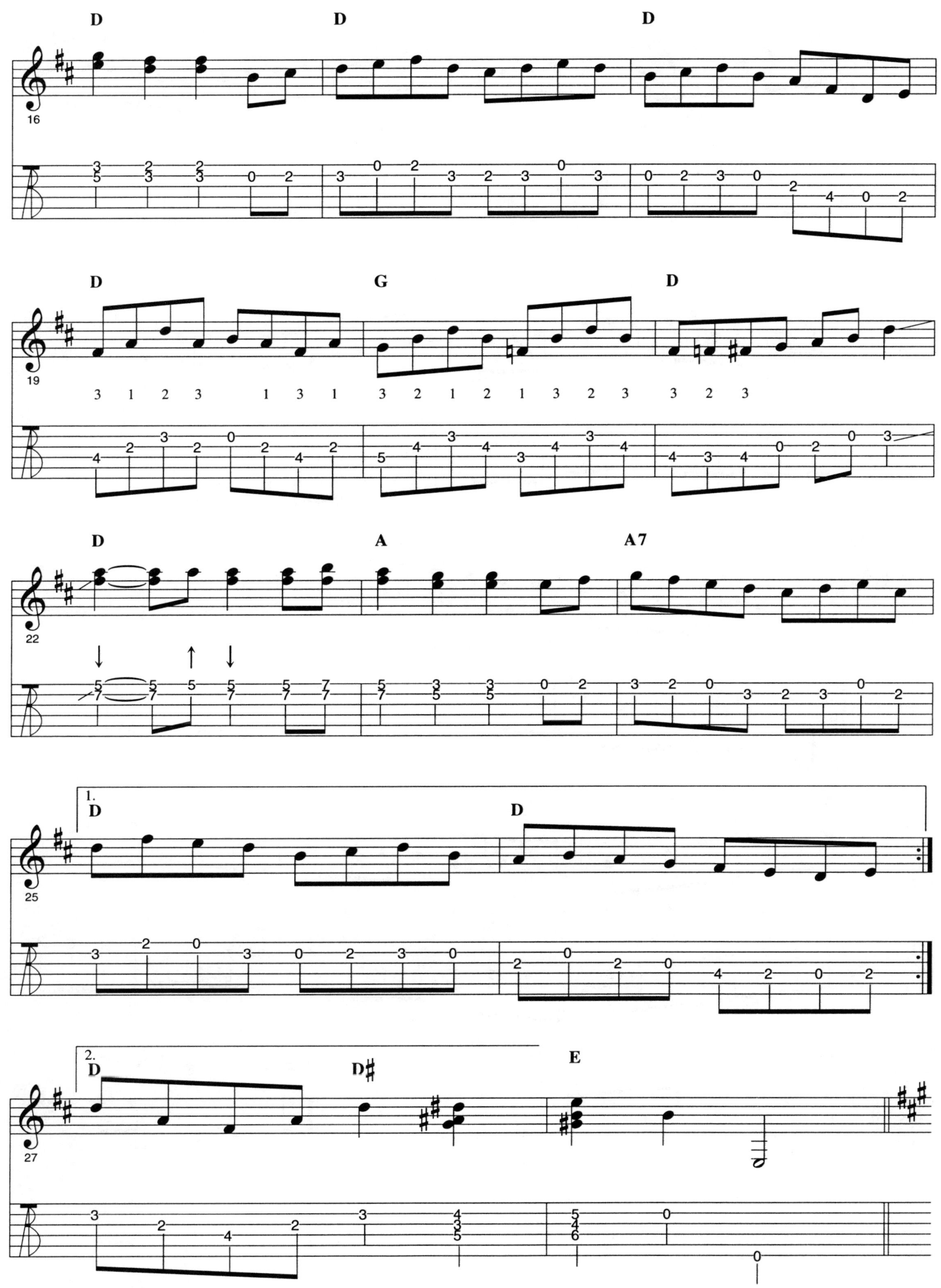
D
D
D
16
D
G
D
19
3 1 2 3 1 3 1
3 2 1 2 1 3 2 3
3 2 3
D
A
A7
22
1.
D
D
25
2.
D
D♯
E
27

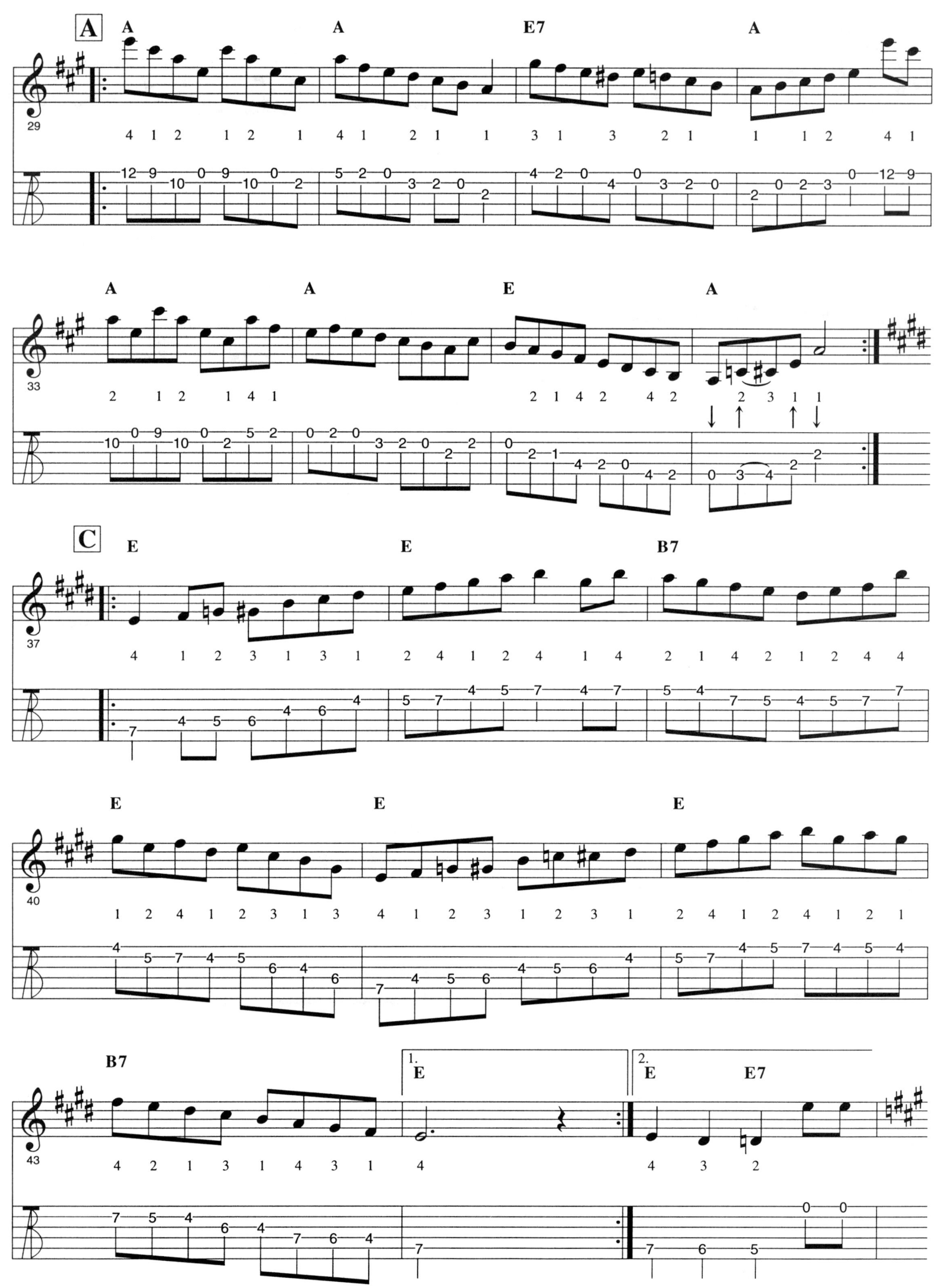
A
A
A
E7
A
29
4 1 2 1 2 1 4 1 2 1 1 3 1 3 2 1 1 1 2 4 1
A
A
E
A
33
2 1 2 1 4 1
2 1 4 2 4 2
2 3 1 1
C
E
E
B7
37
4 1 2 3 1 3 1 2 4 1 2 4 1 4 2 1 4 2 1 2 4 4
E
E
E
40
1 2 4 1 2 3 1 3 4 1 2 3 1 2 3 1 2 4 1 2 4 1 2 1
B7
1.
E
2.
E
E7
43
4 2 1 3 1 4 3 1 4 4 3 2

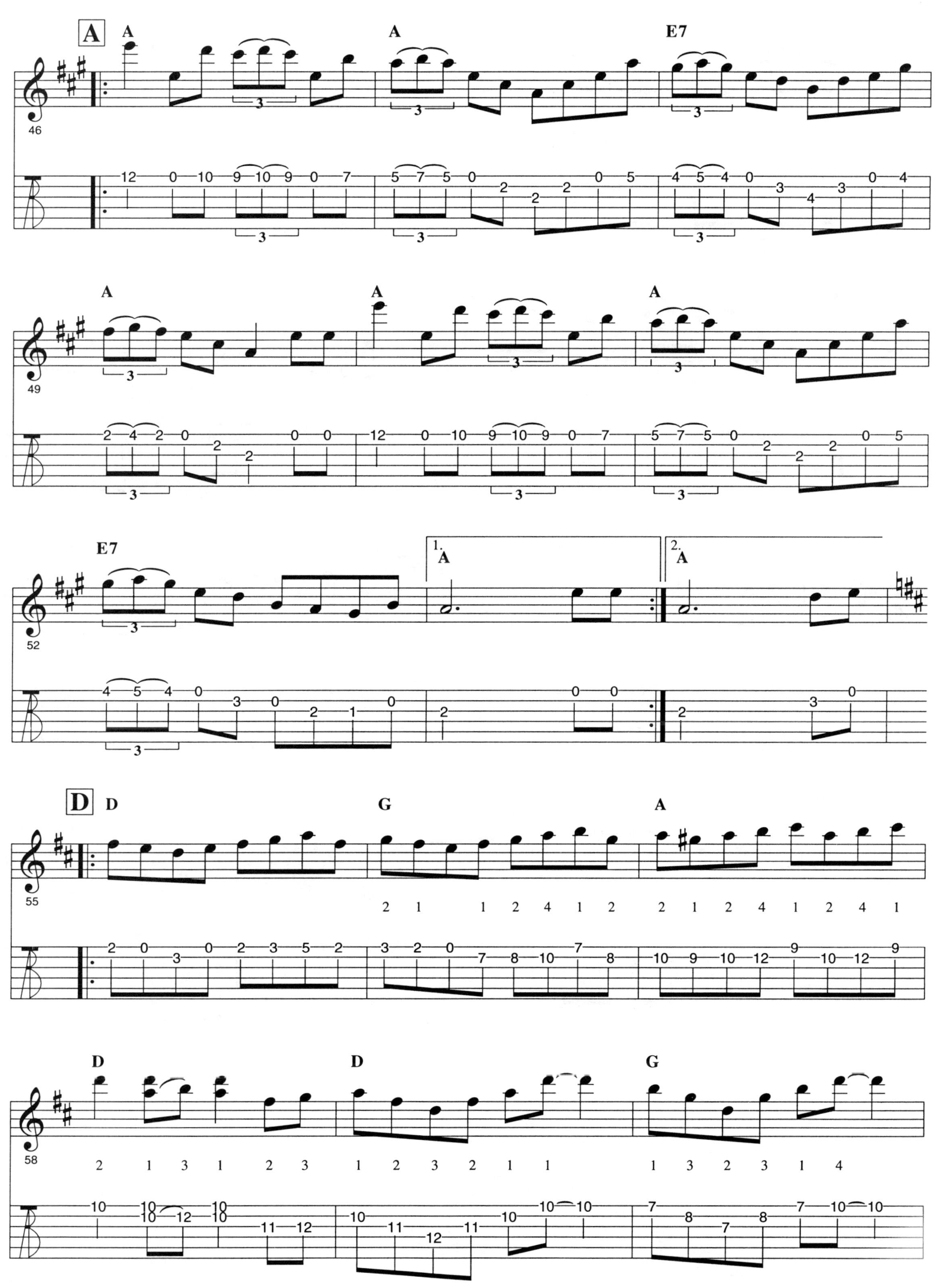
A
A A E7
46
A A A
49
E7 1. A 2. A
52
D
D G A
55
D D G
58

A
1. D
2. D
61
2 4 2 1 2 1 2 1 4 2
A
A
A
E7
64
A
A
A
67
E7
1. A
2. A
70

Maple Leaf Rag

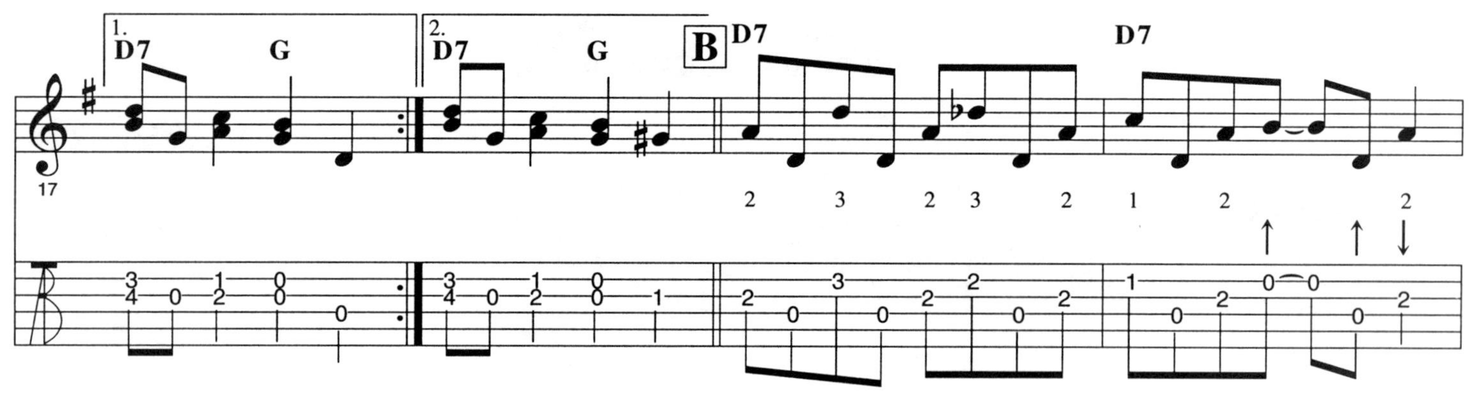
1.
D7
G
2.
D7
G
B
D7
D7
17

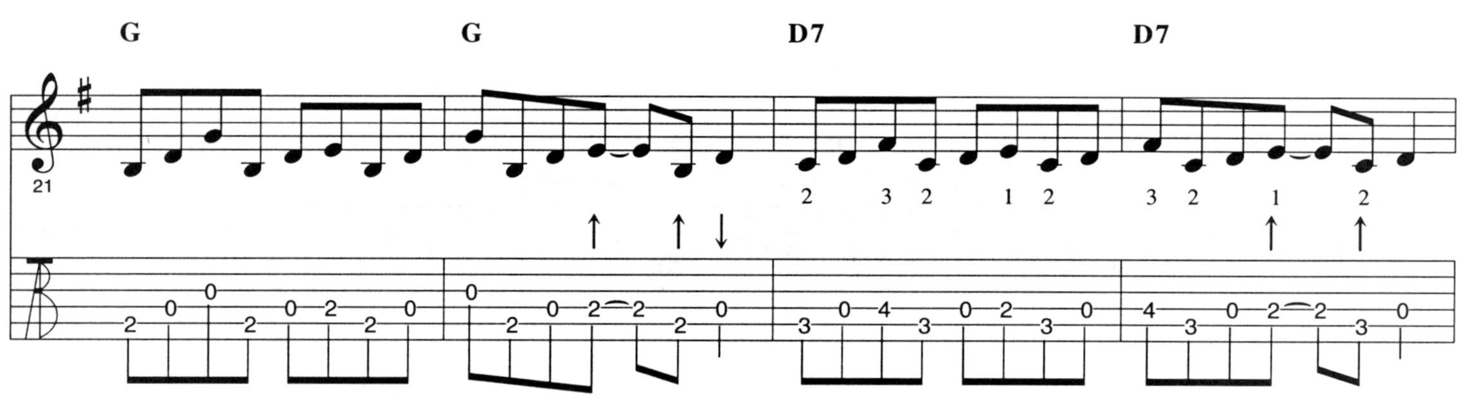
G
G
D7
D7
21

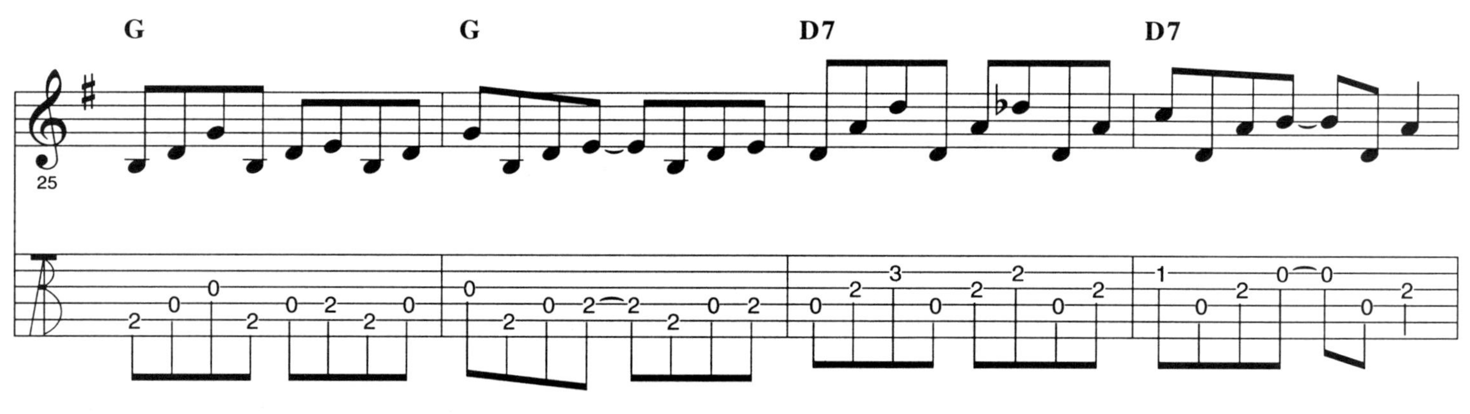
G
G
D7
D7
25

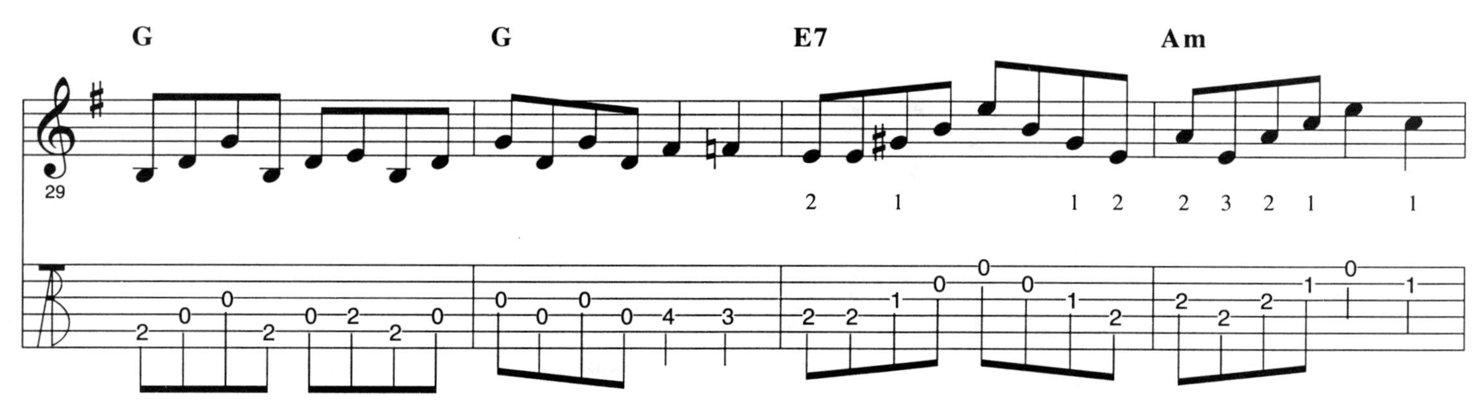
G
G
E7
Am
29

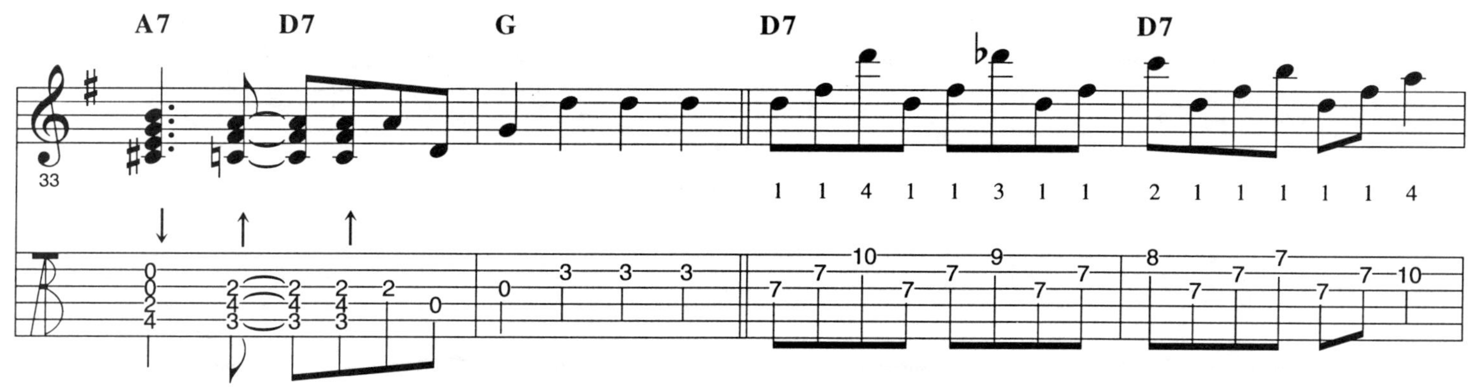
A7
D7
G
D7
D7
33
1 1 4 1 1 3 1 1
2 1 1 1 1 1 4

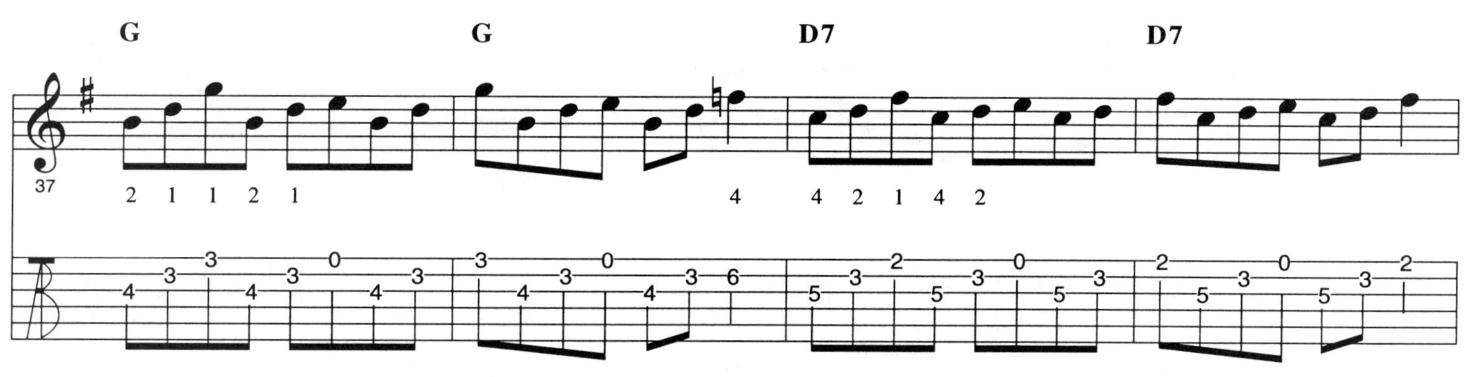
G
G
D7
D7
37
2 1 1 2 1
4
4 2 1 4 2

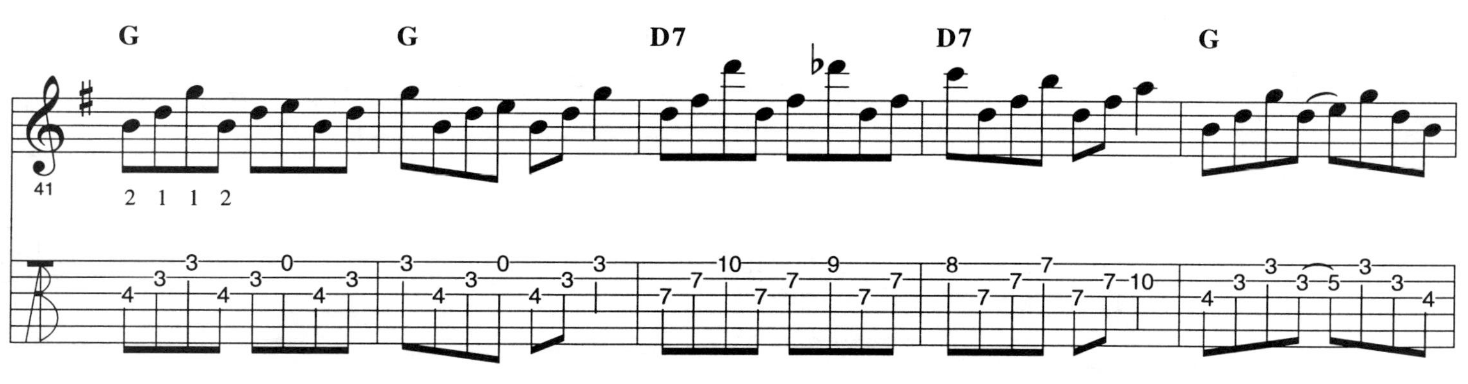
G
G
D7
D7
G
41
2 1 1 2

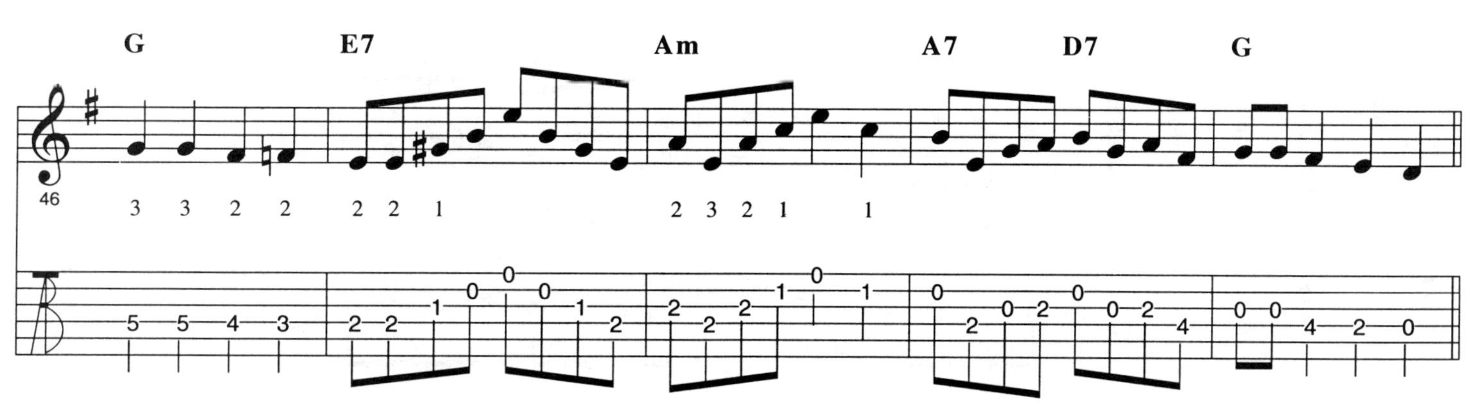
G
E7
Am
A7
D7
G
46
3 3 2 2
2 2 1
2 3 2 1
1

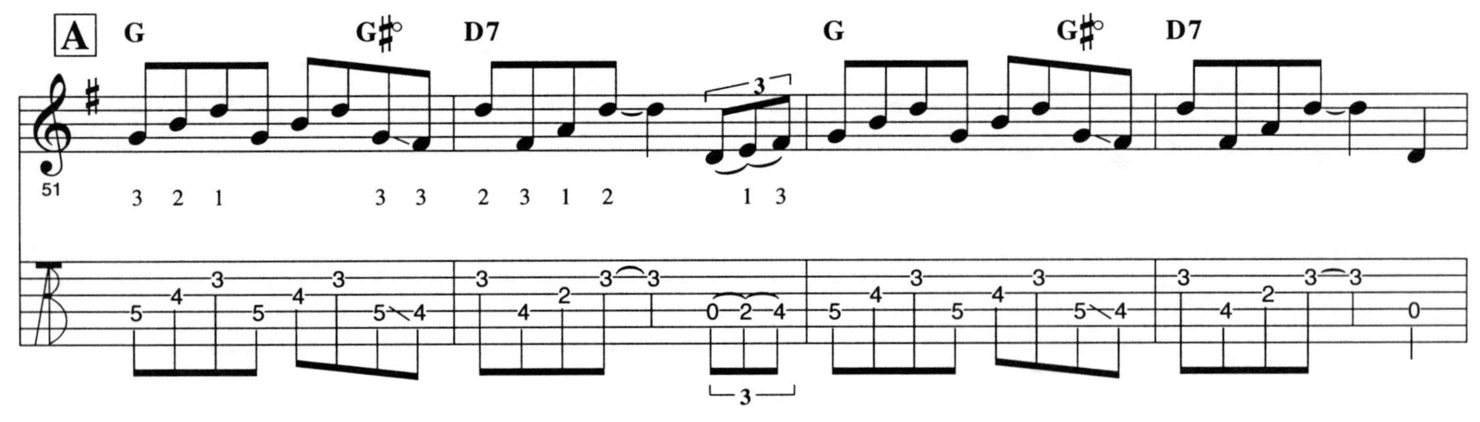
A
G
G#°
D7
G
G#°
D7
51

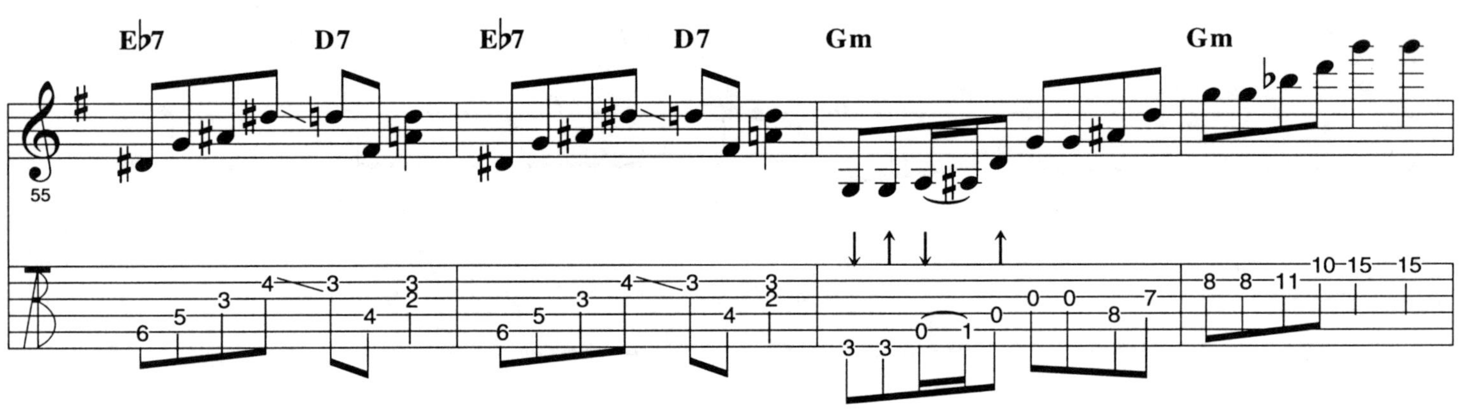
E♭7
D7
E♭7
D7
Gm
Gm
55

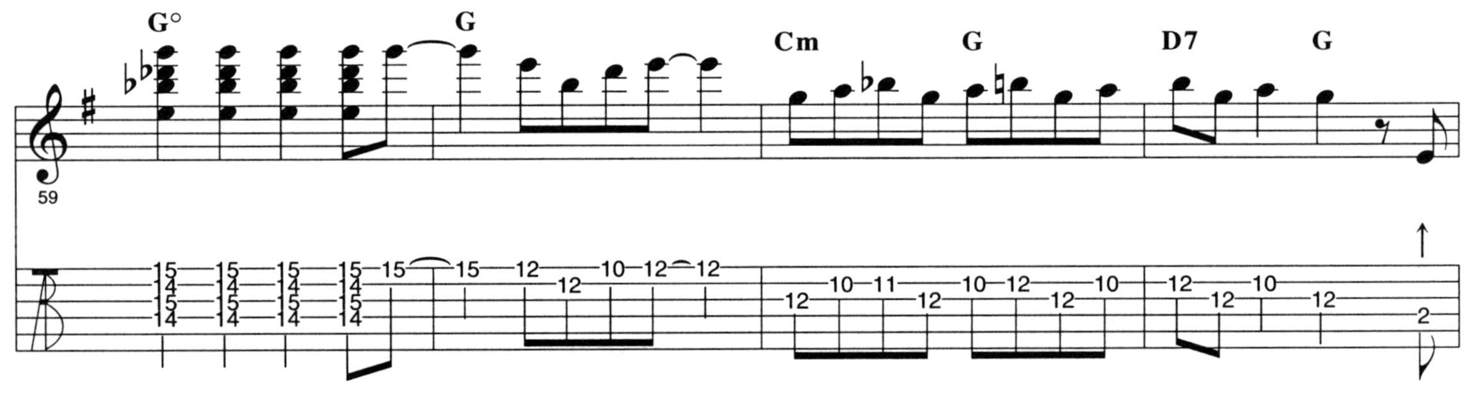
G°
G
Cm
G
D7
G
59

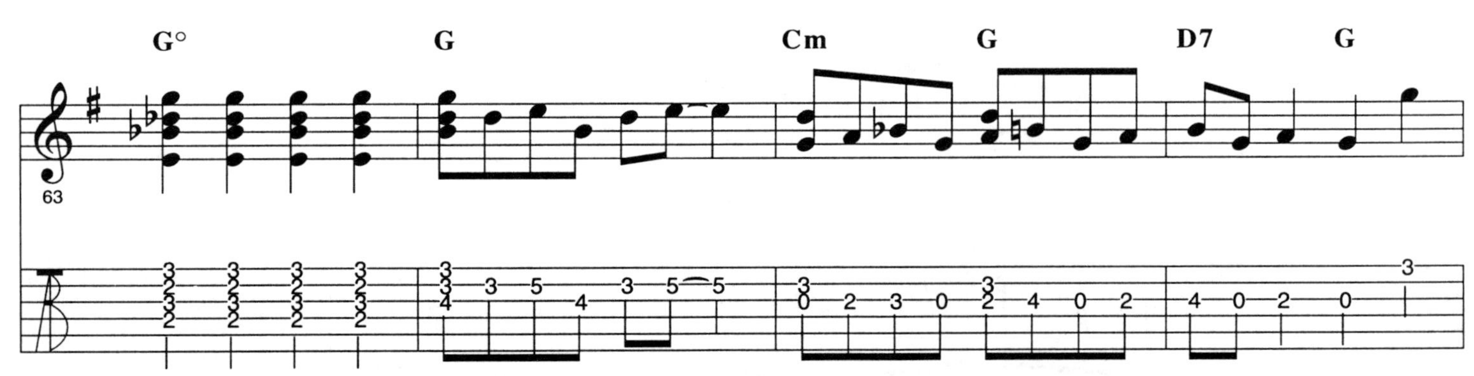
G°
G
Cm
G
D7
G
63

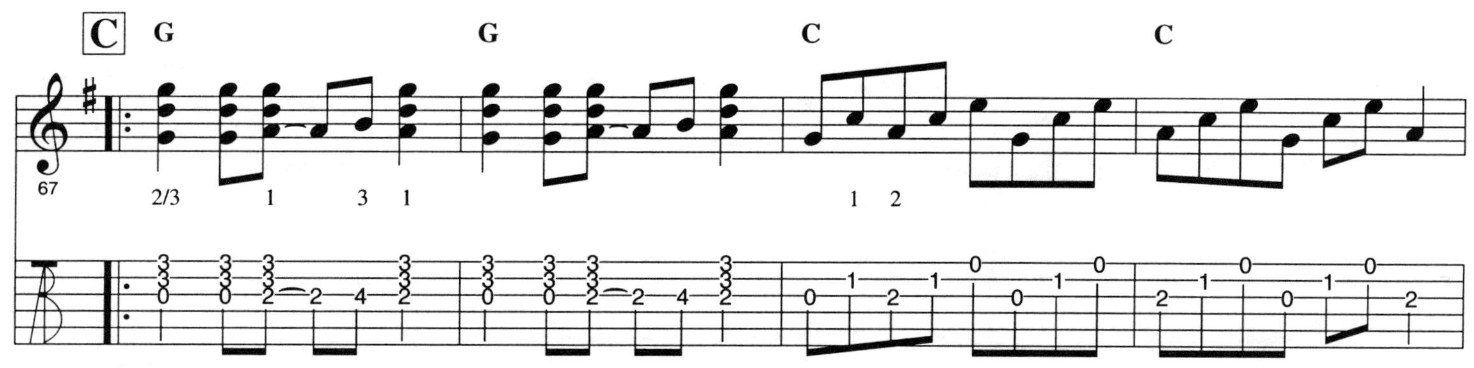
C
G
G
C
C
67
2/3 1 3 1
1 2

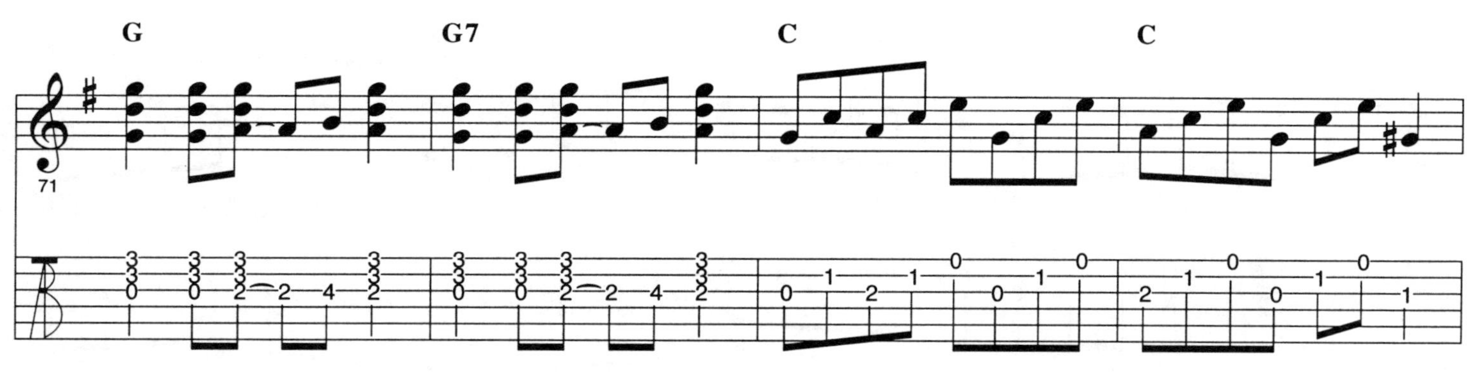
G
G7
C
C
71

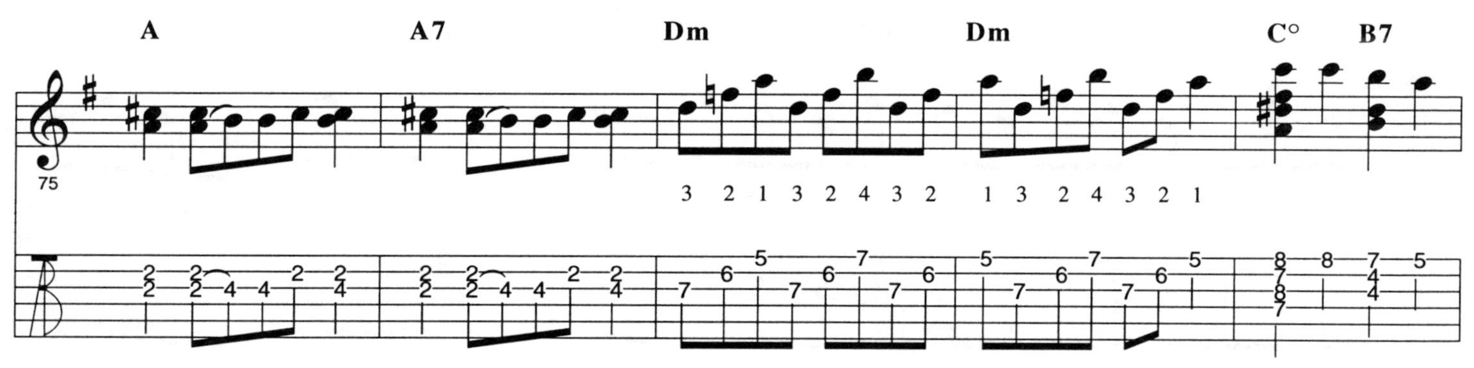
A
A7
Dm
Dm
C°
B7
75
3 2 1 3 2 4 3 2
1 3 2 4 3 2 1

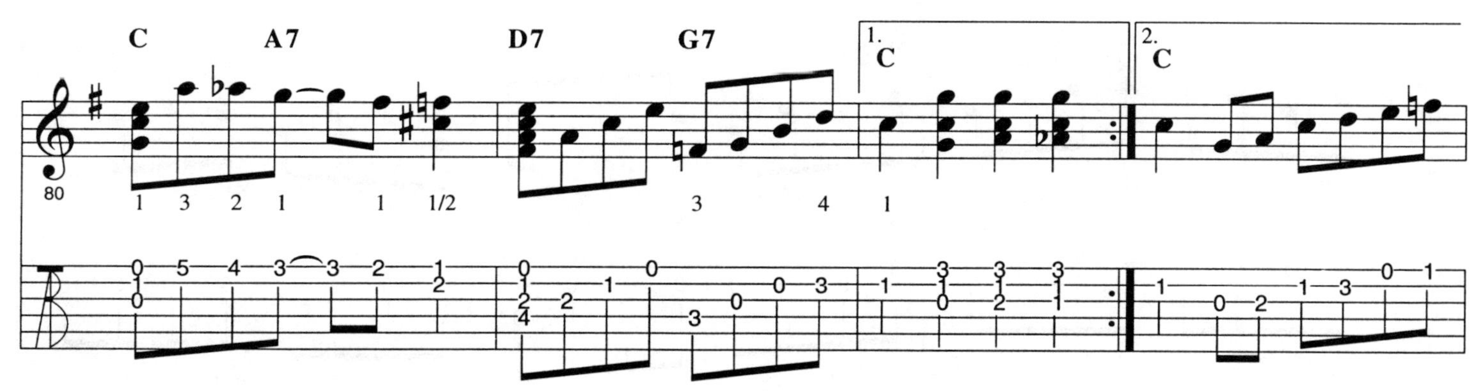
C
A7
D7
G7
1.
C
2.
C
80
1 3 2 1 1 1/2
3 4 1

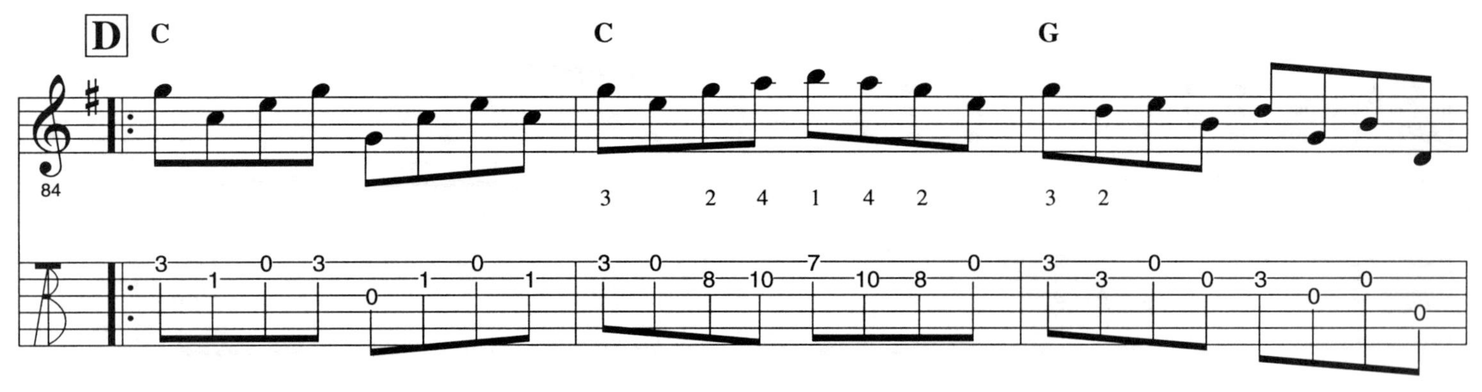
D
C
C
G
84
3 2 4 1 4 2
3 2

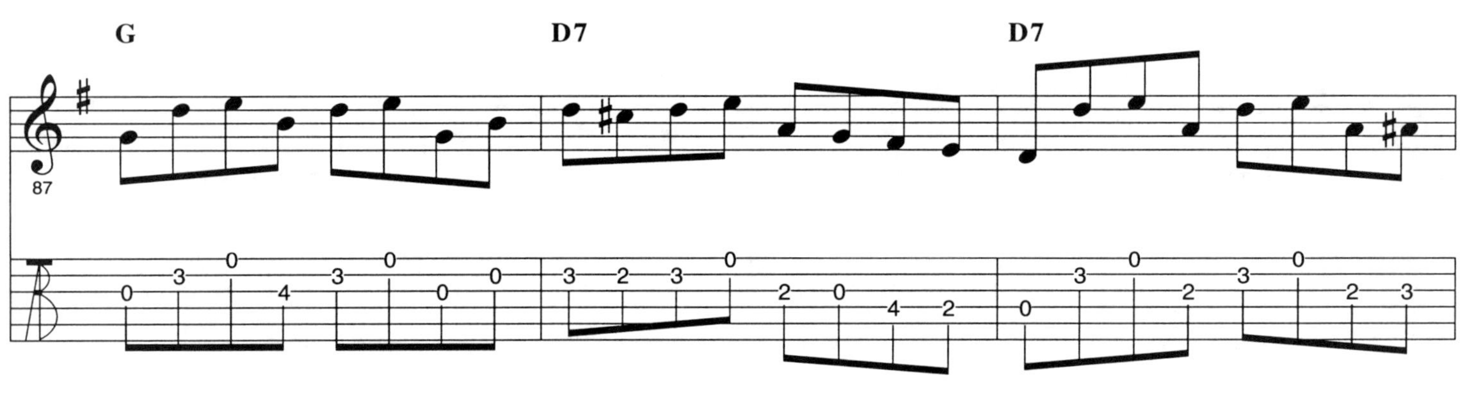
G
D7
D7
87

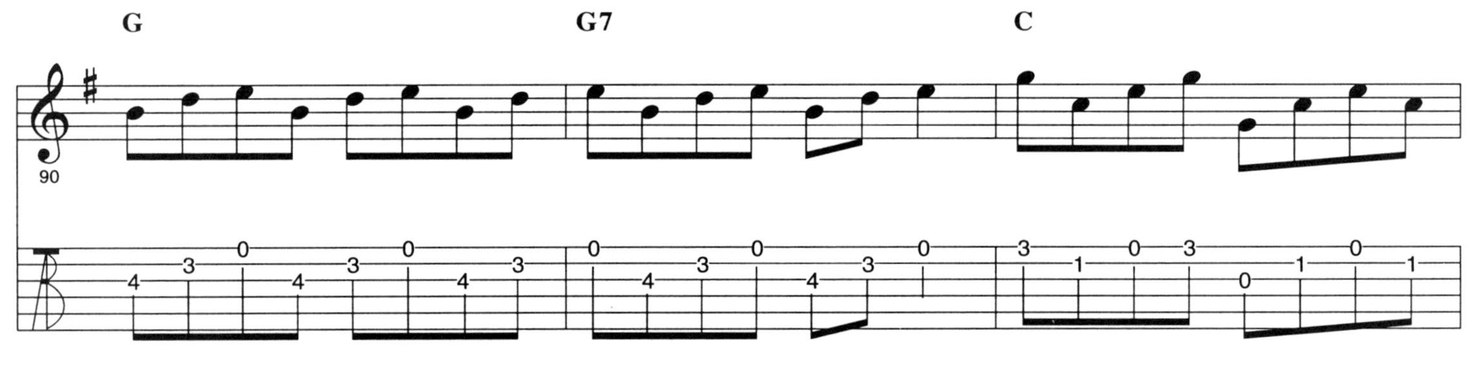
G
G7
C
90

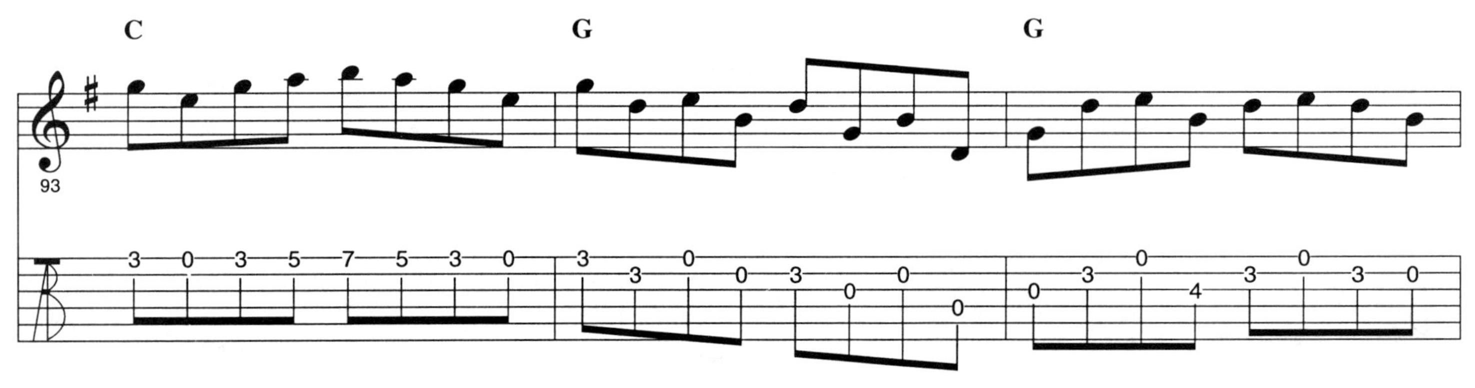
C
G
G
93

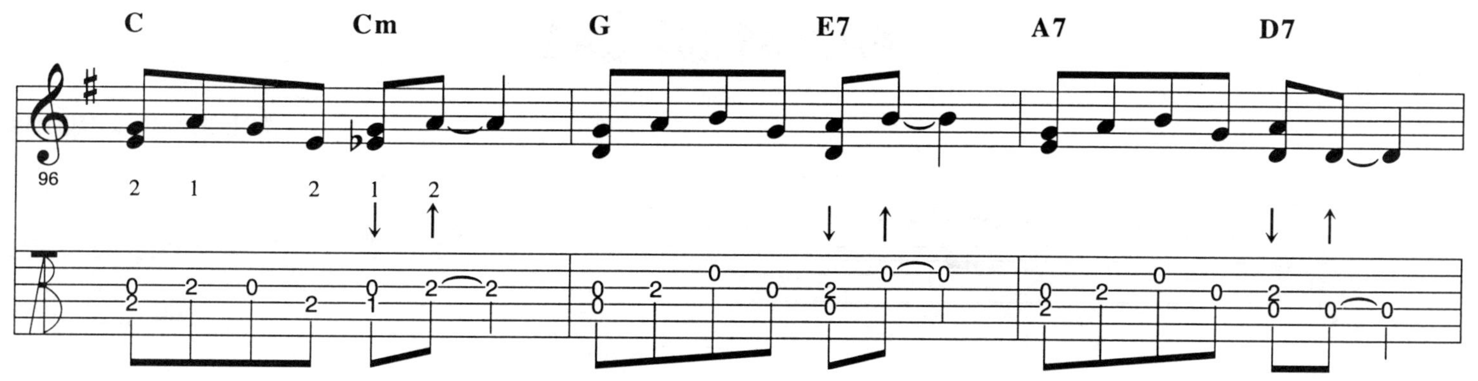
C
Cm
G
E7
A7
D7
96
2 1 2 1 2

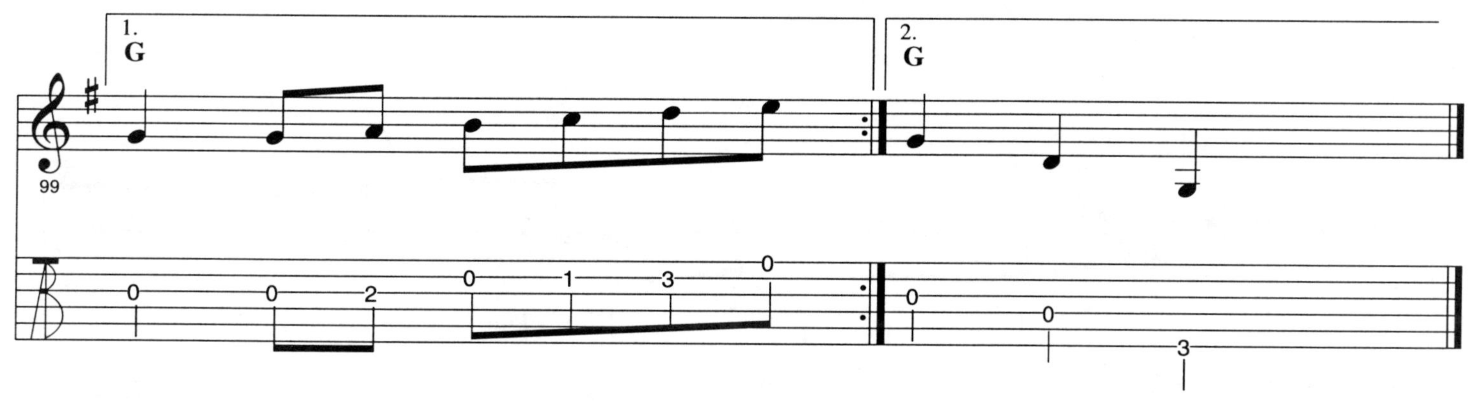
1.
G
2.
G
99

Temptation Rag

Arr. by Steve Kaufman

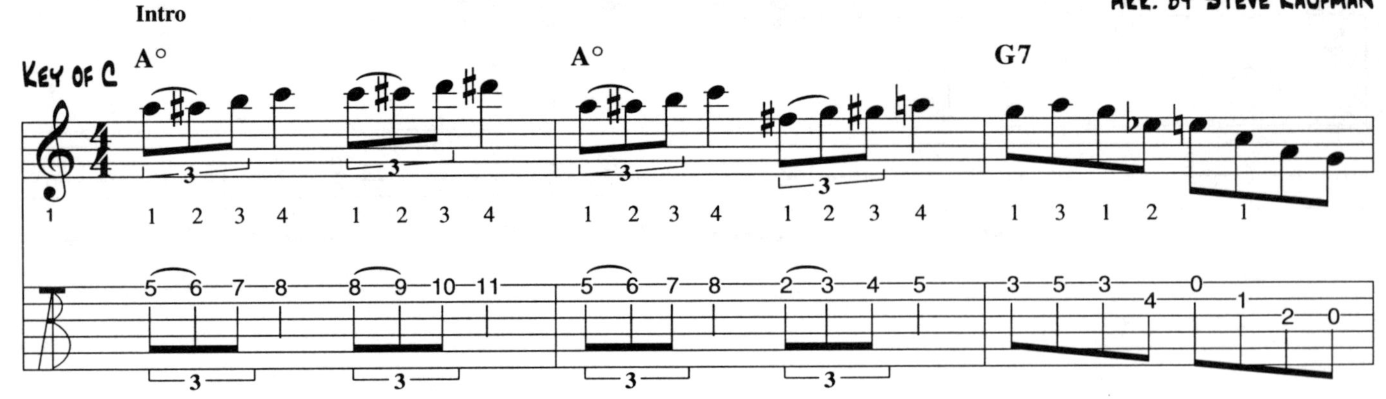

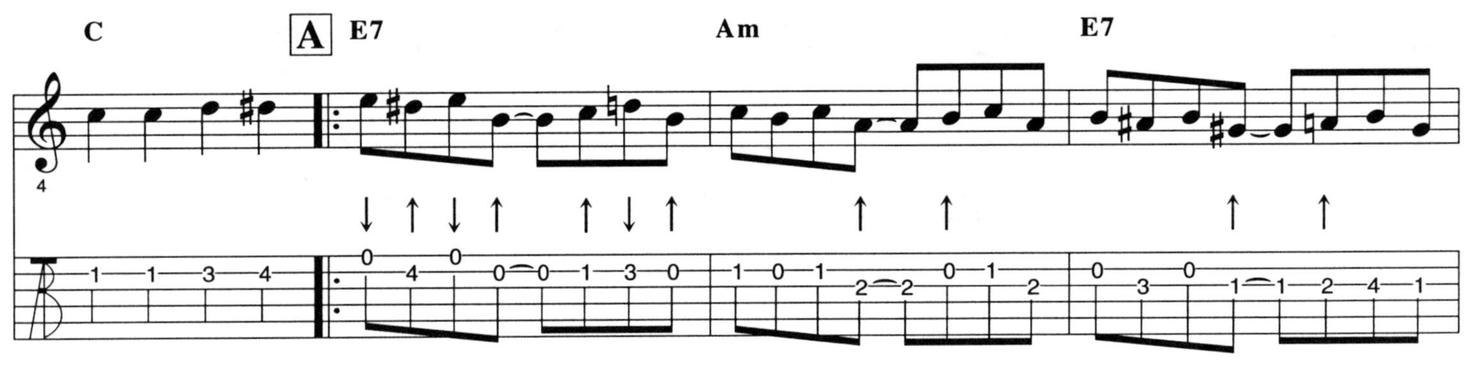

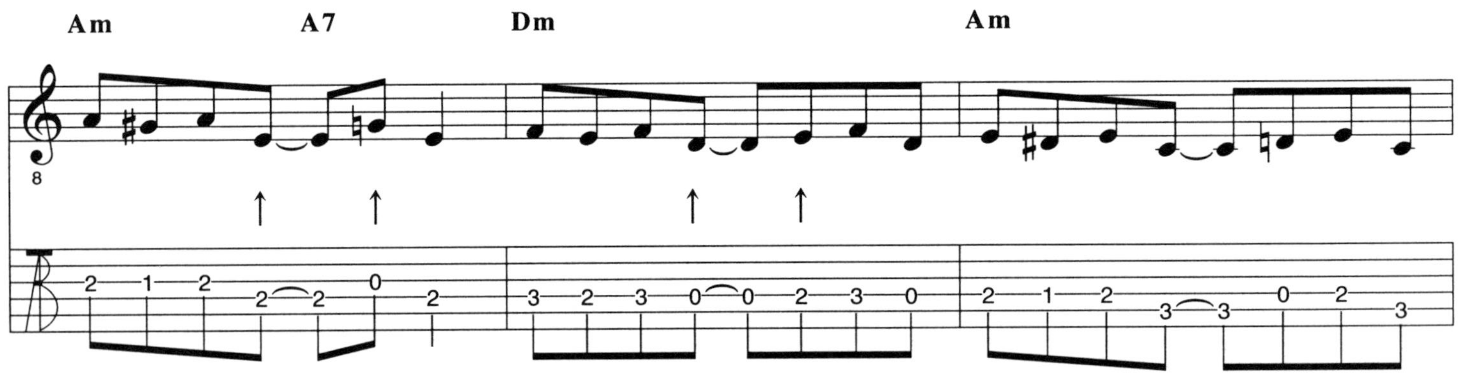

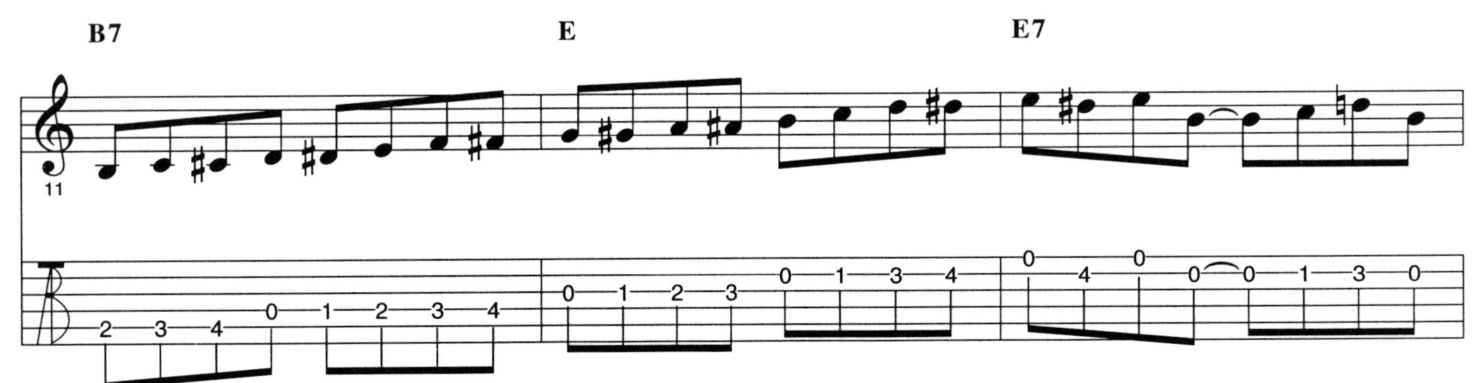

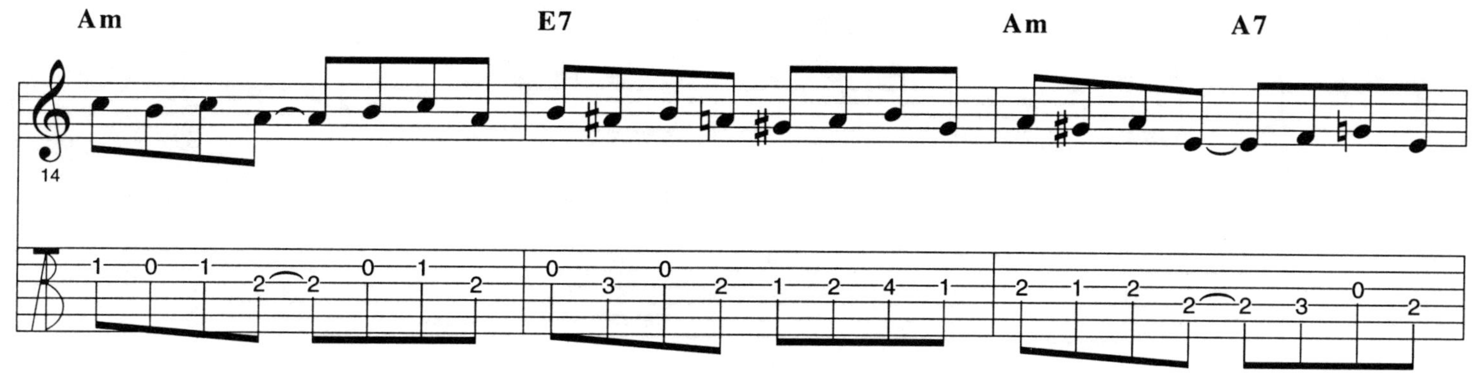
Am
E7
Am
A7
14

Dm
1.
Am
E7
Am
17
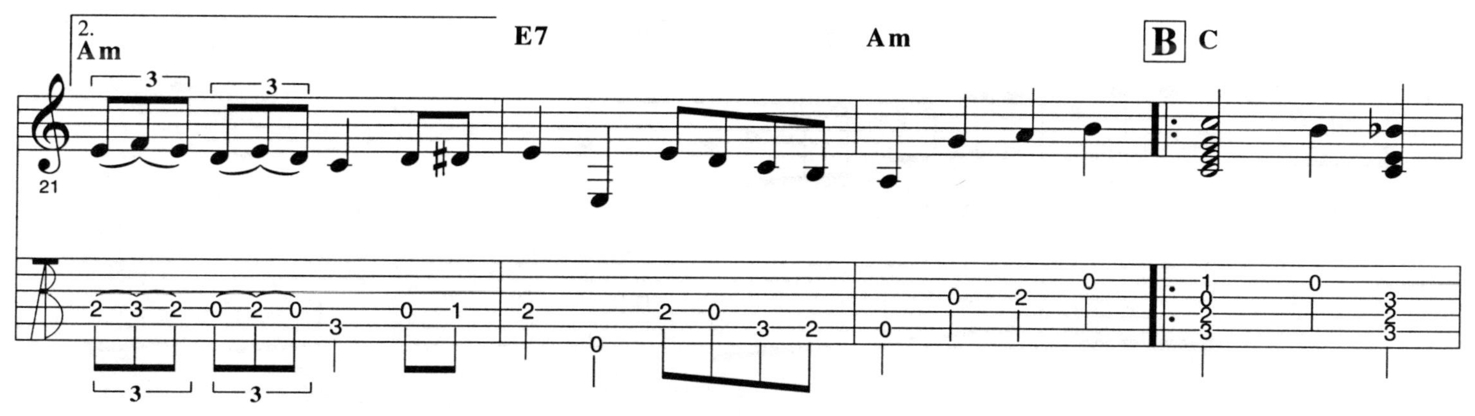
2.
Am
E7
Am
B
C
21
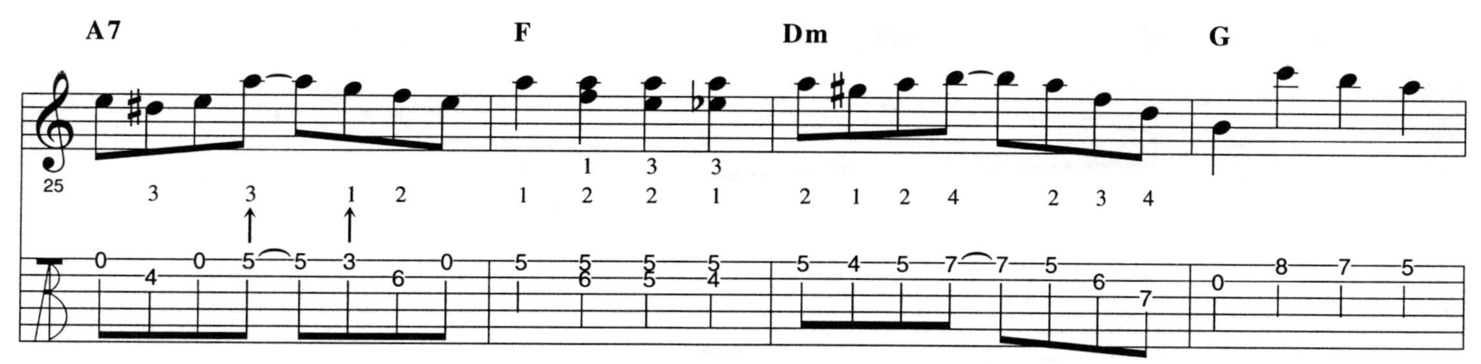
A7
F
Dm
G
25

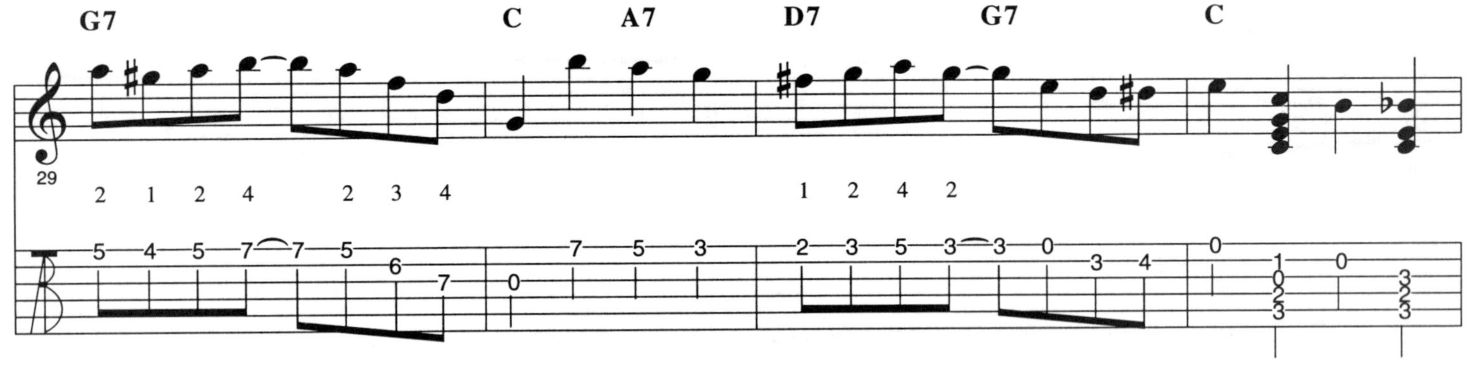
G7
C
A7
D7
G7
C
29

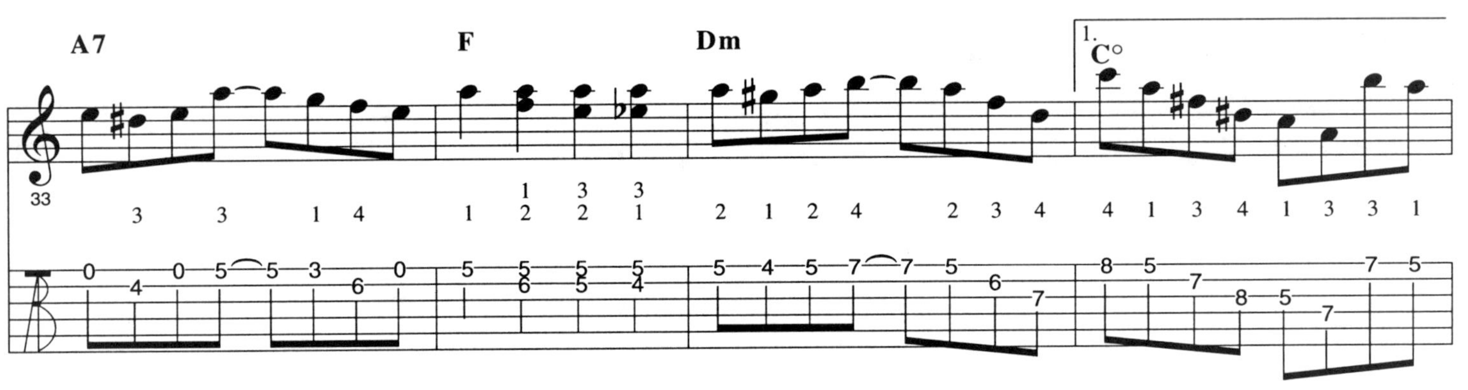
A7
F
Dm
1.
C°
33

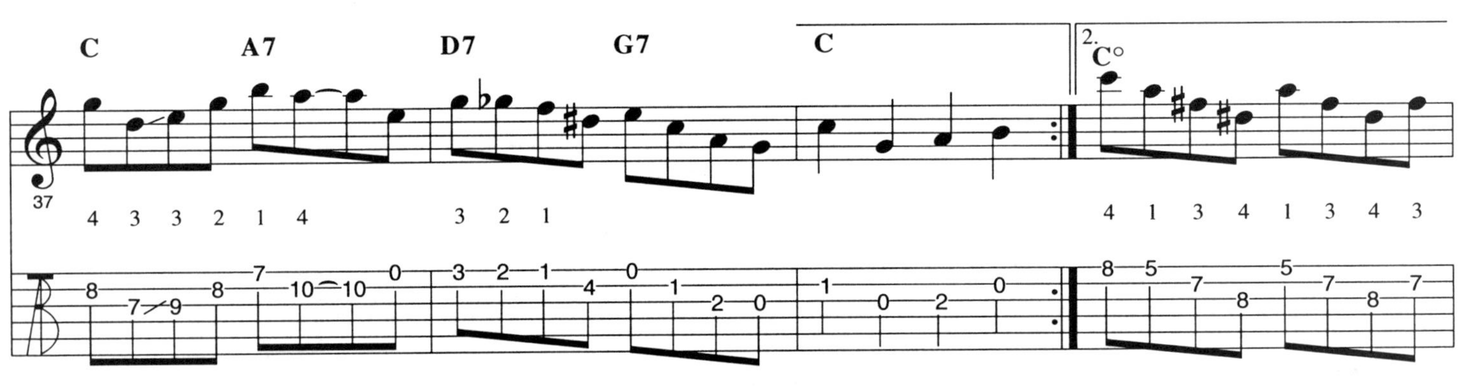
C
A7
D7
G7
C
2.
C°
37

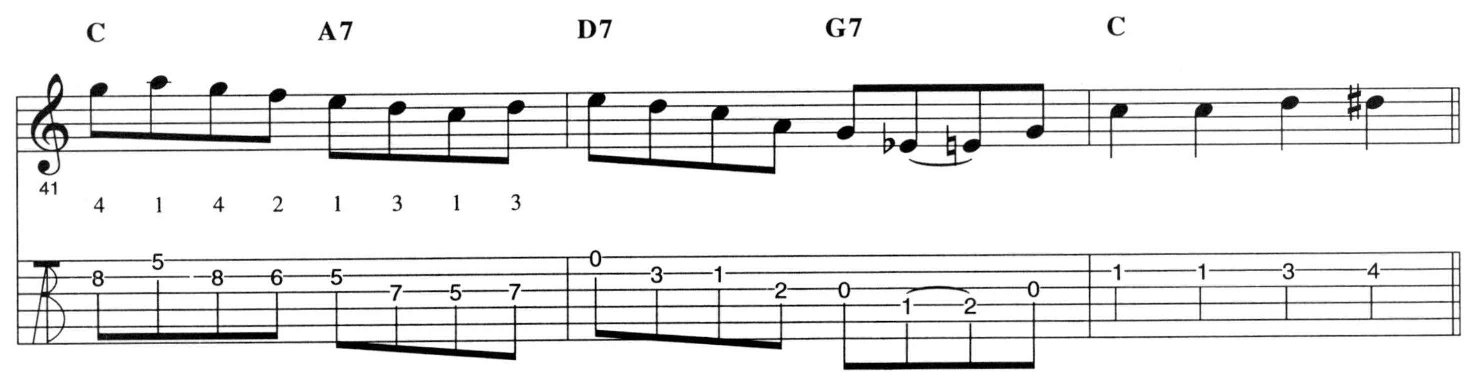
C
A7
D7
G7
C
41

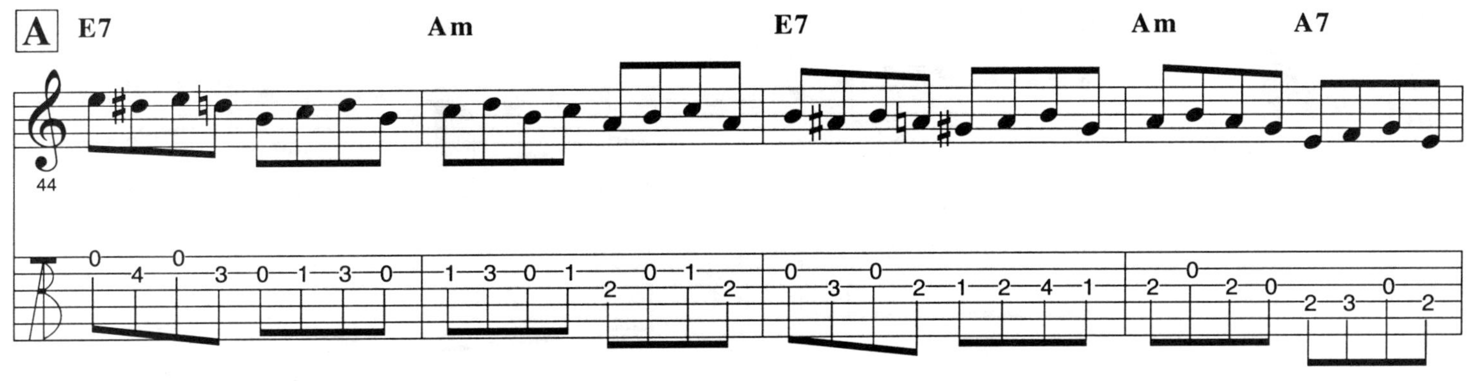
A
E7
Am
E7
Am
A7
44

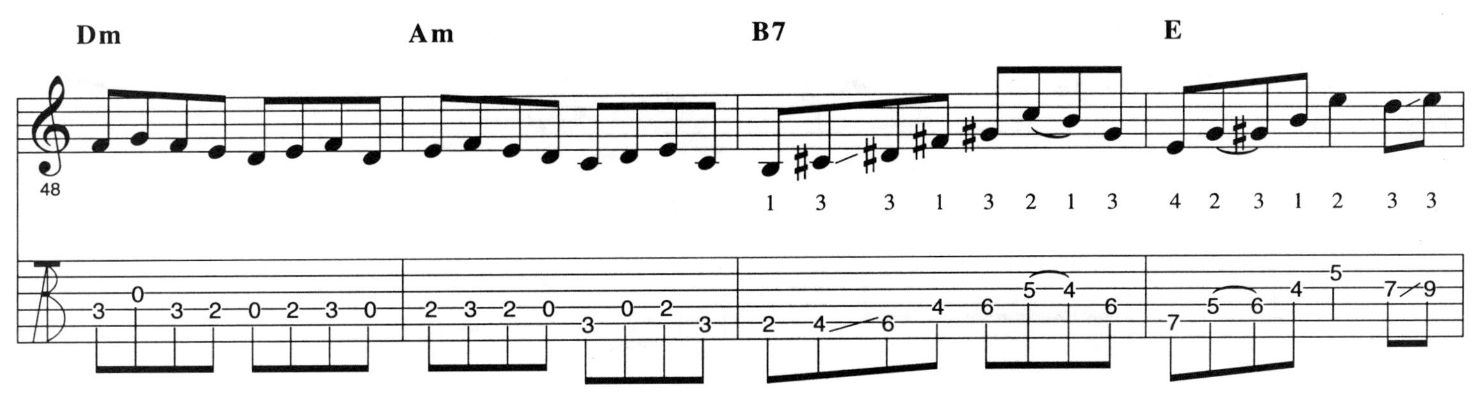
Dm
Am
B7
E
48

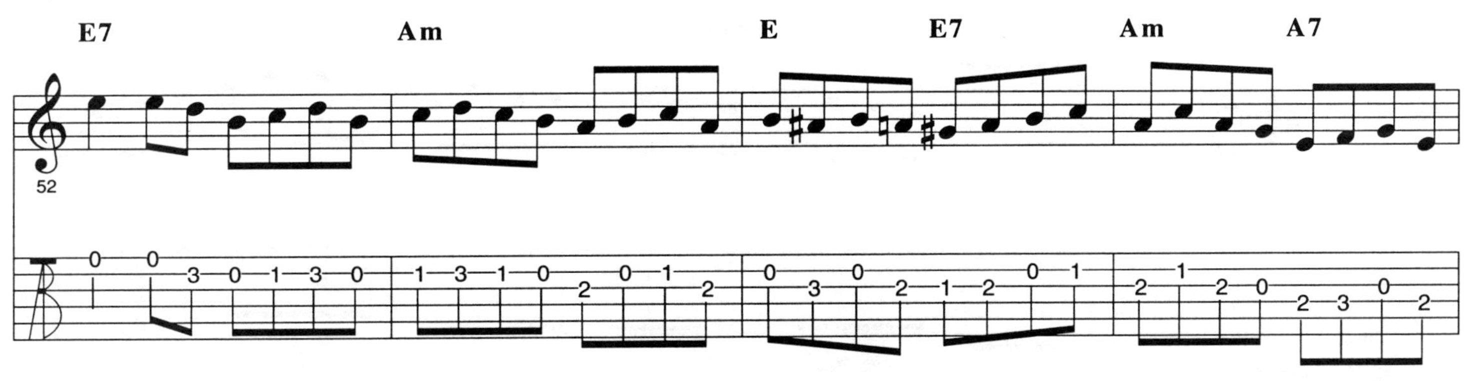
E7
Am
E
E7
Am
A7
52

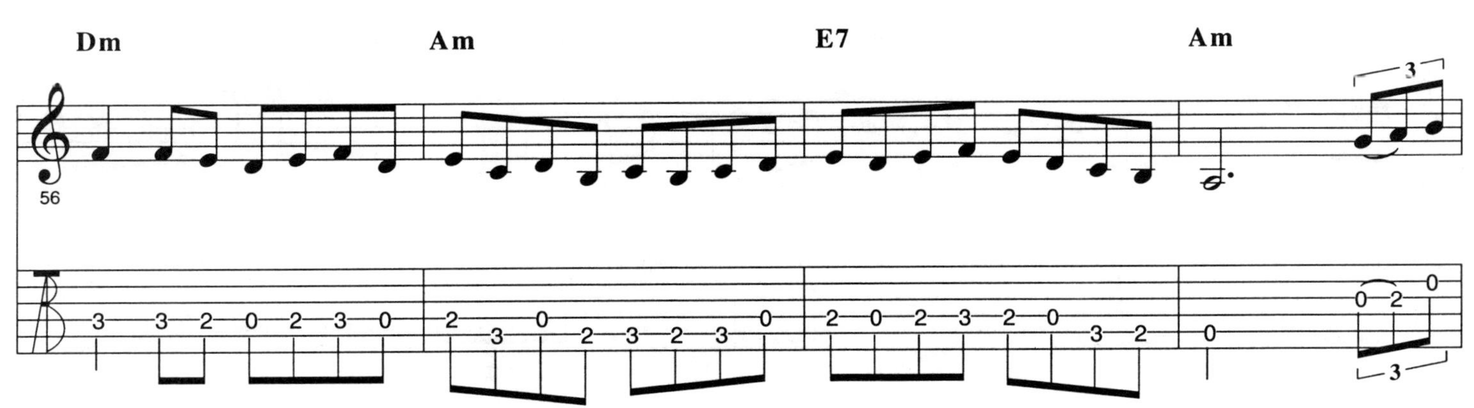
Dm
Am
E7
Am
56

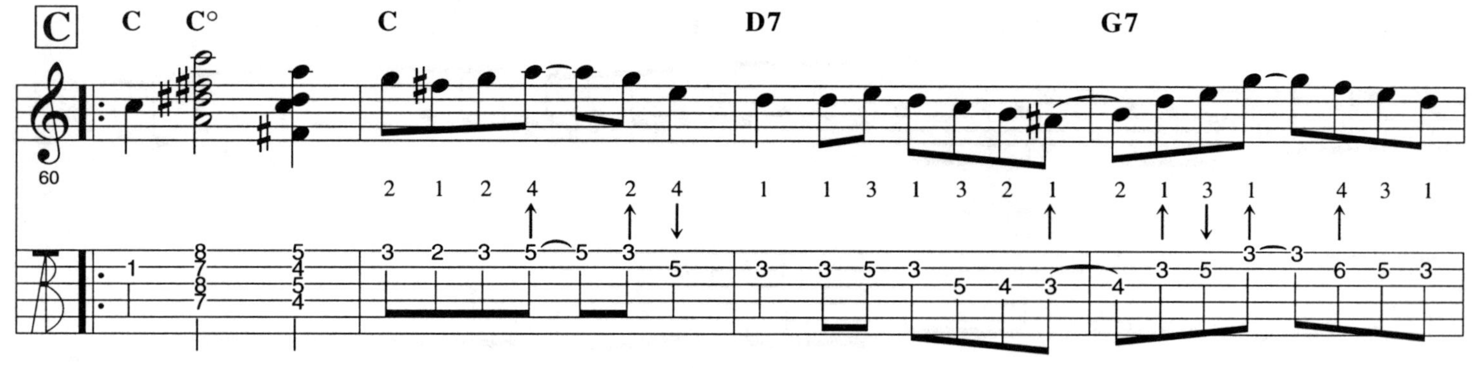
C
C
C°
C
D7
G7
60
2 1 2 4 2 4 1 1 3 1 3 2 1 2 1 3 1 4 3 1

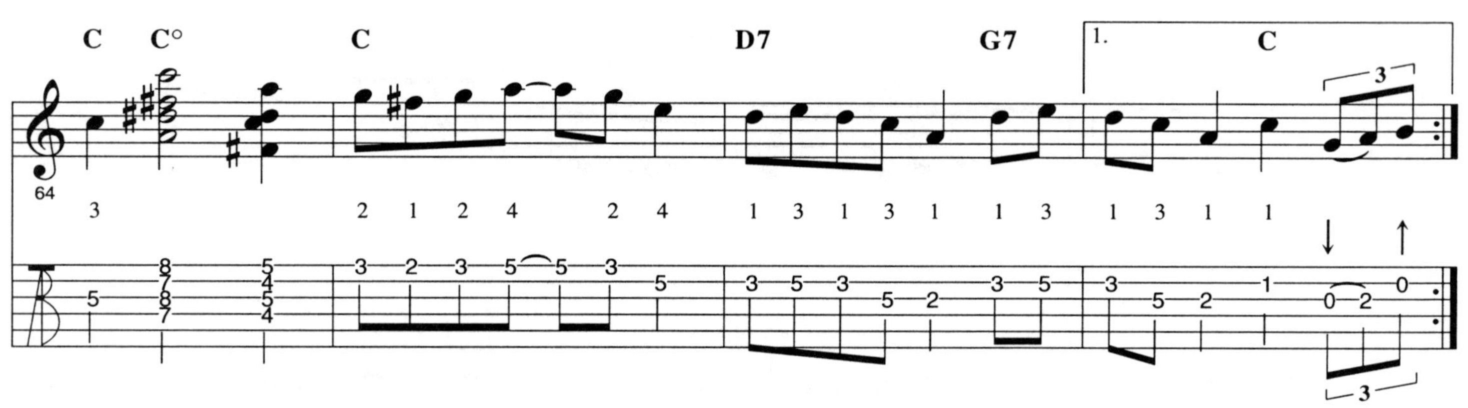
C
C°
C
D7
G7
1.
C
64
3
2 1 2 4 2 4 1 3 1 3 1 1 3 1 3 1 1

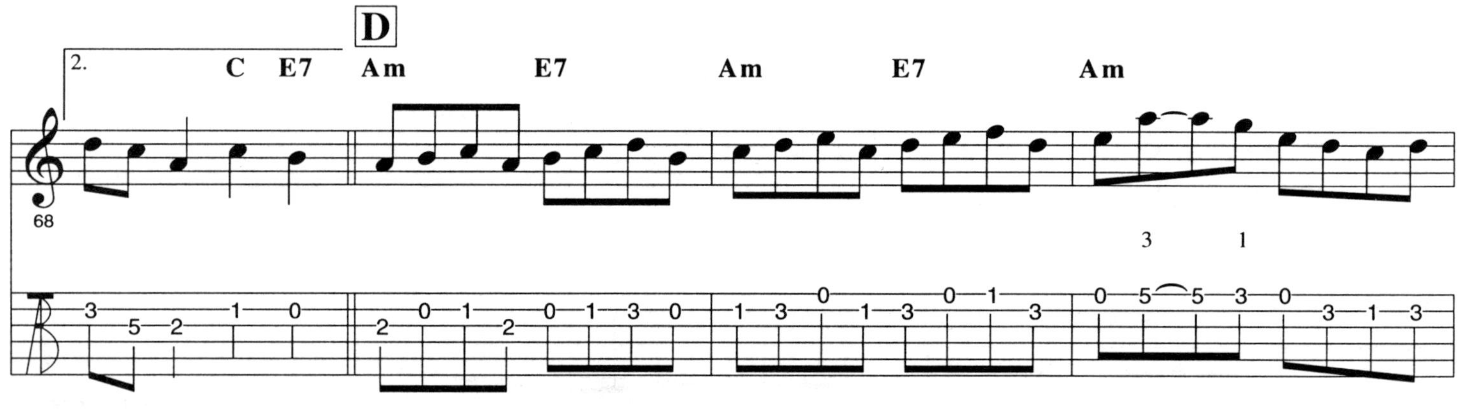
2.
C
E7
D
Am
E7
Am
E7
Am
68
3 1

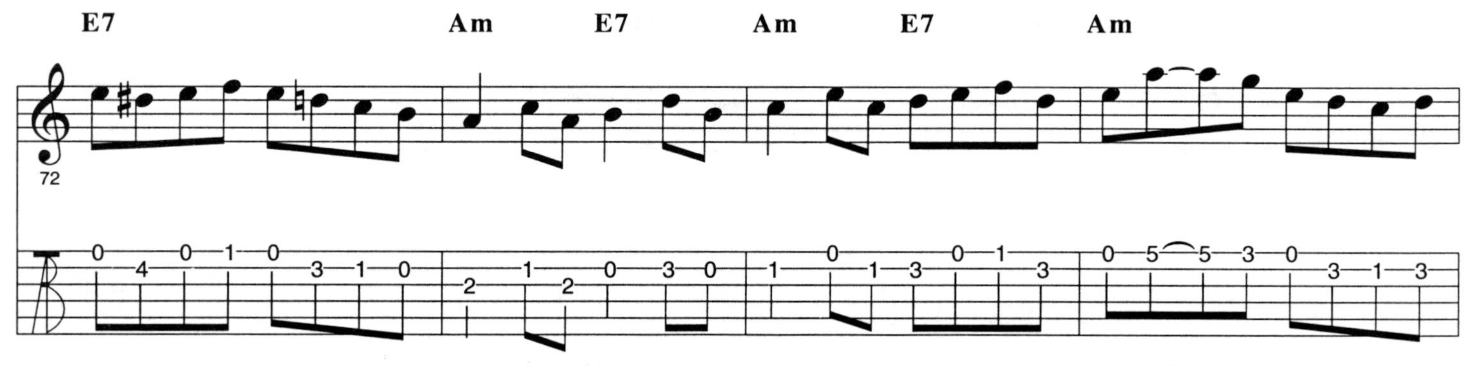
E7
Am
E7
Am
E7
Am
72

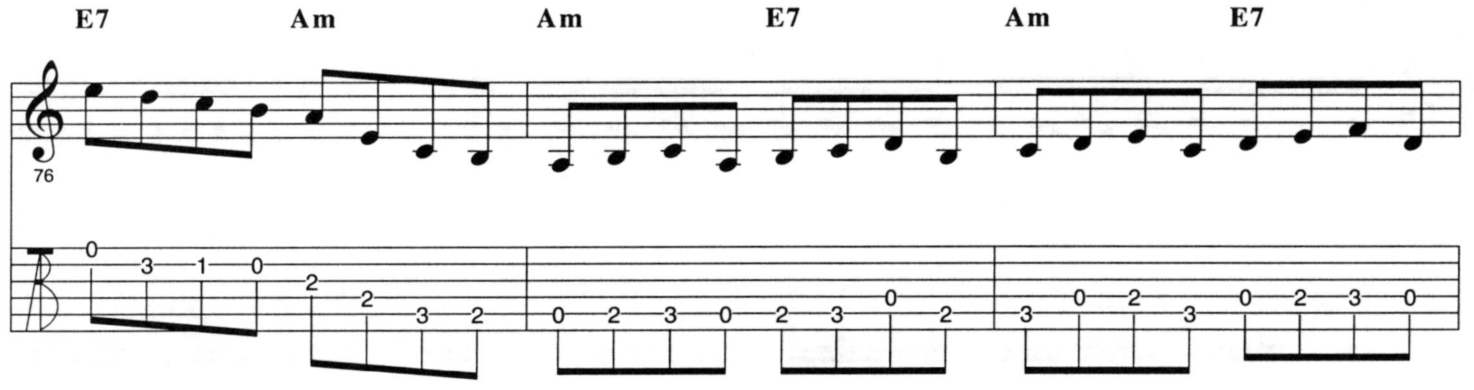
E7
Am
Am
E7
Am
E7
76

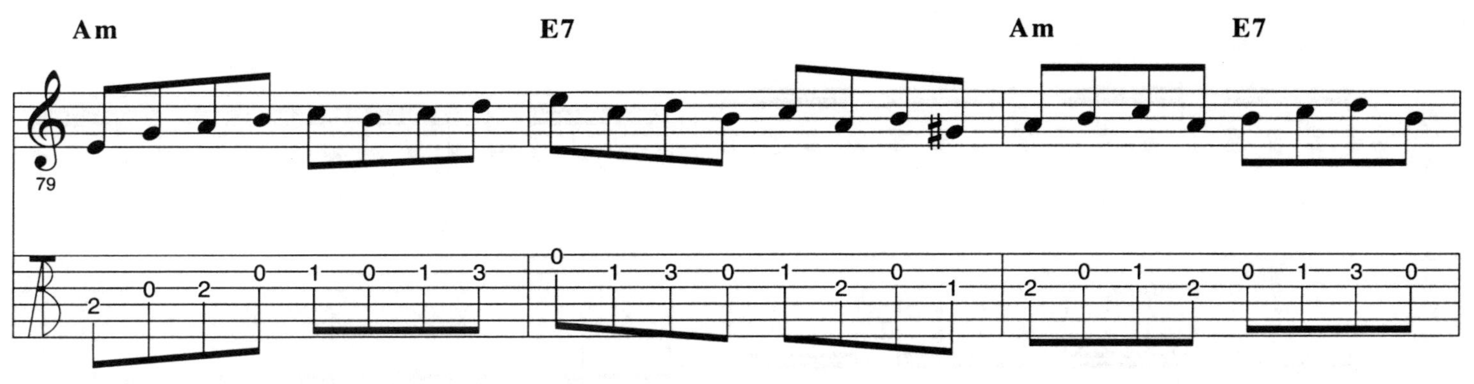
Am
E7
Am
E7
79

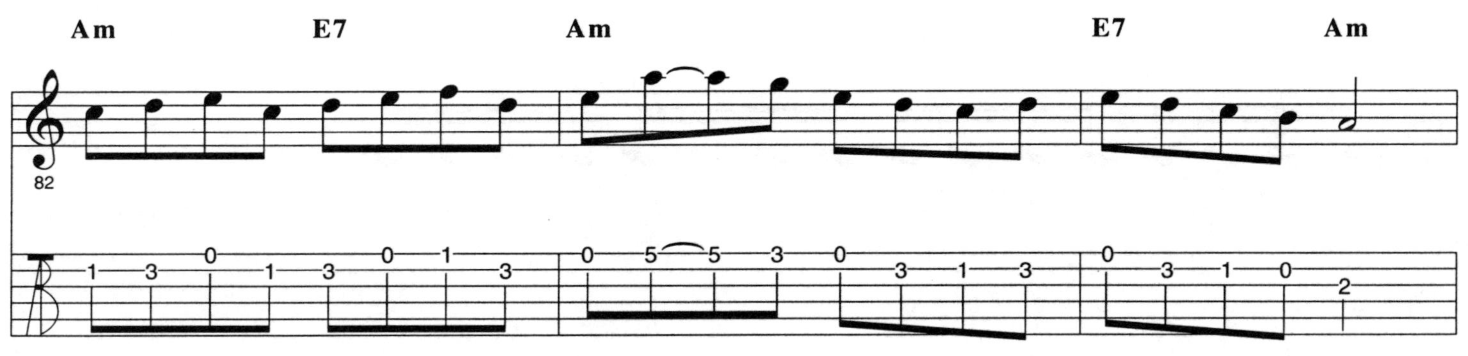
Am
E7
Am
E7
Am
82

G Stop Chord
85

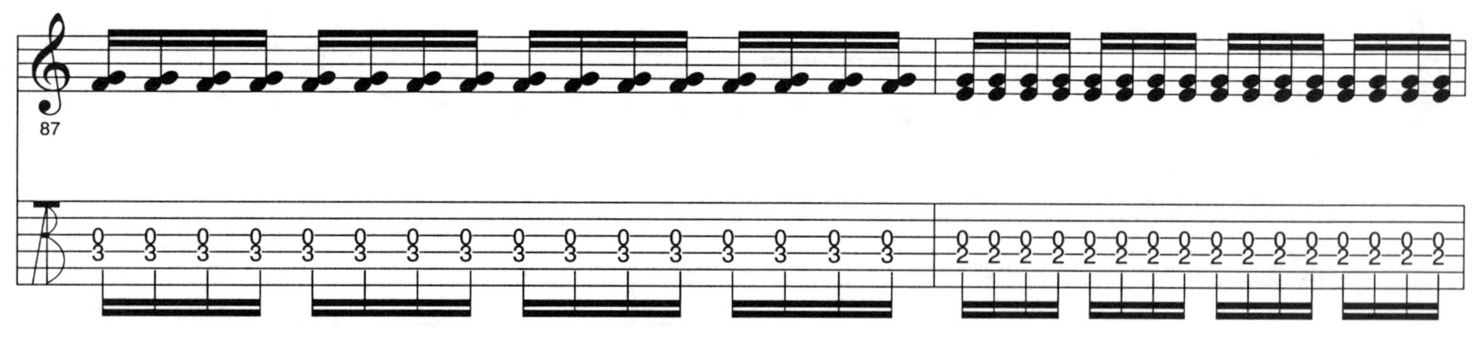
87

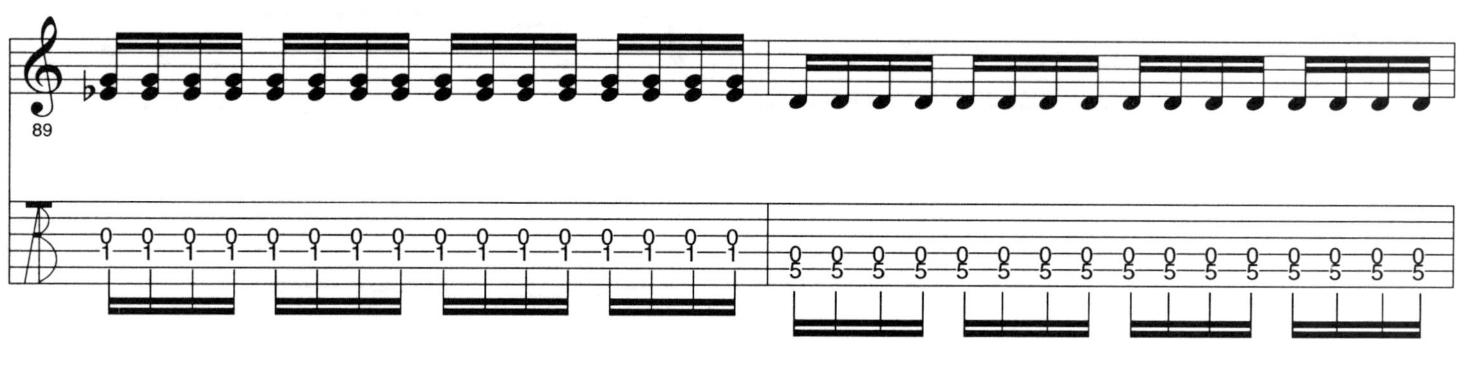
89

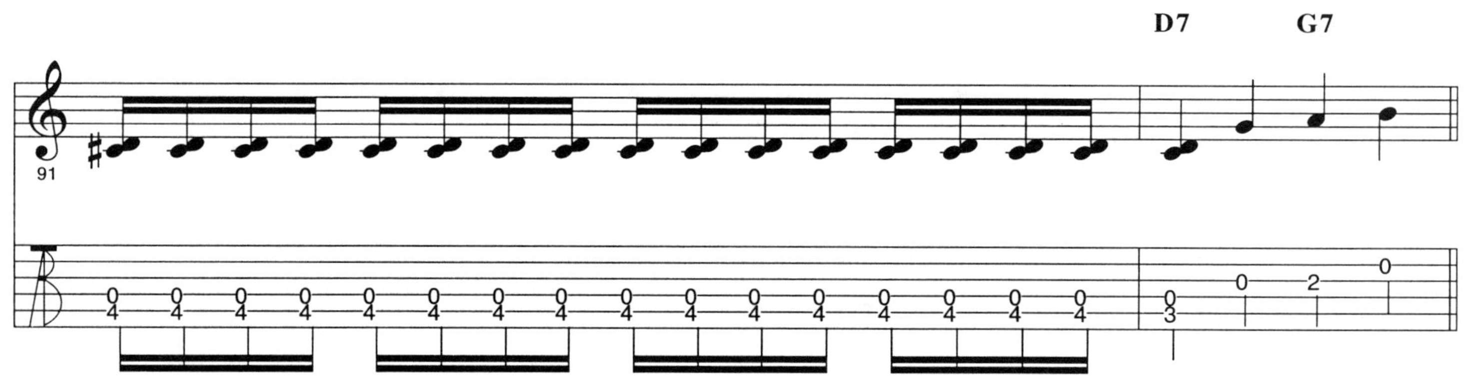
D7
G7
91

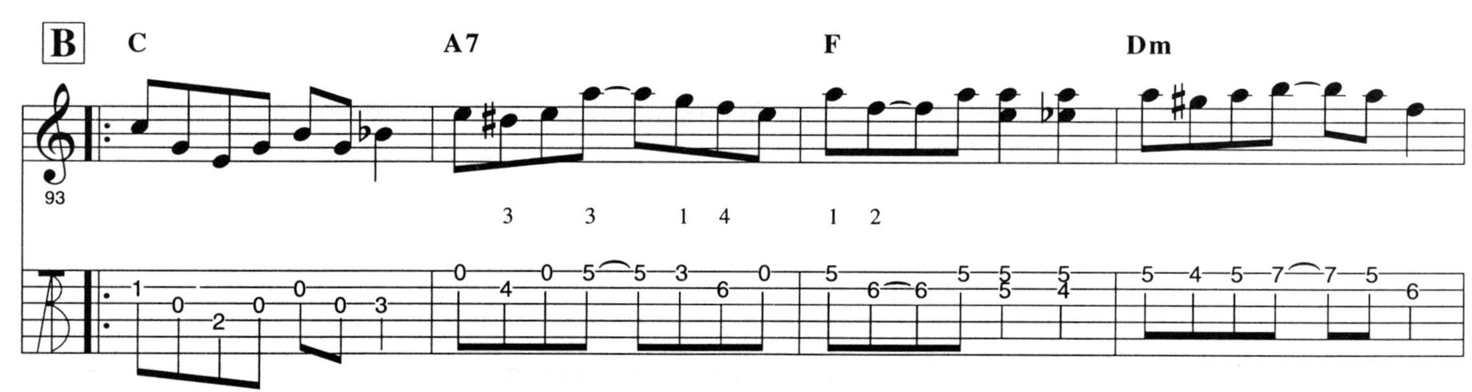
B
C
A7
F
Dm
93

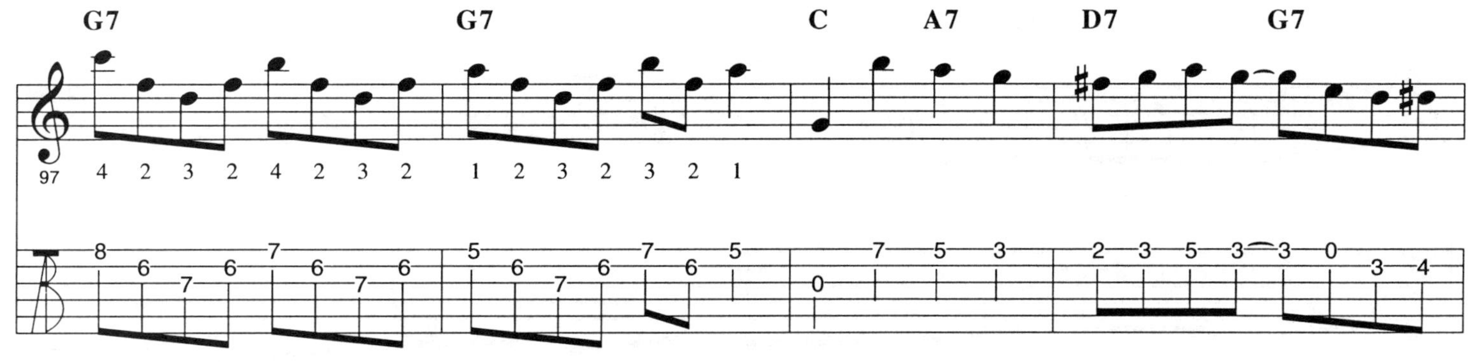
G7
G7
C
A7
D7
G7
97

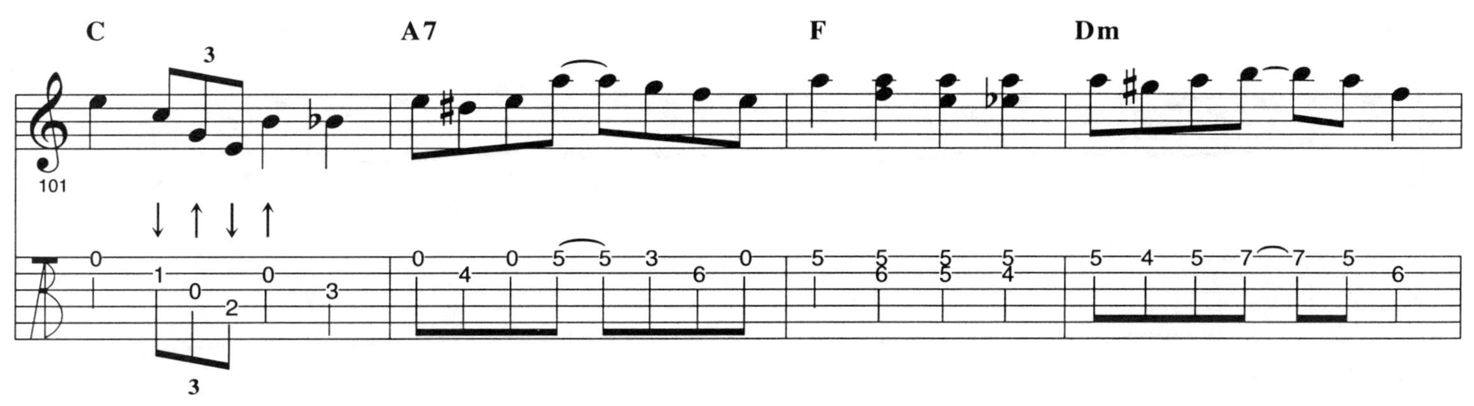
C
A7
F
Dm
101

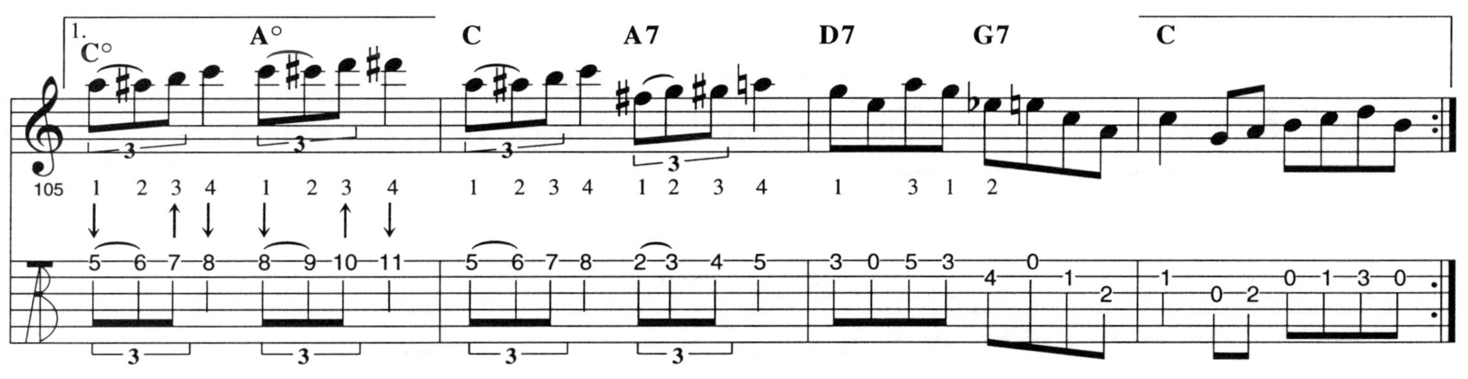
1.
C○
A○
C
A7
D7
G7
C
105

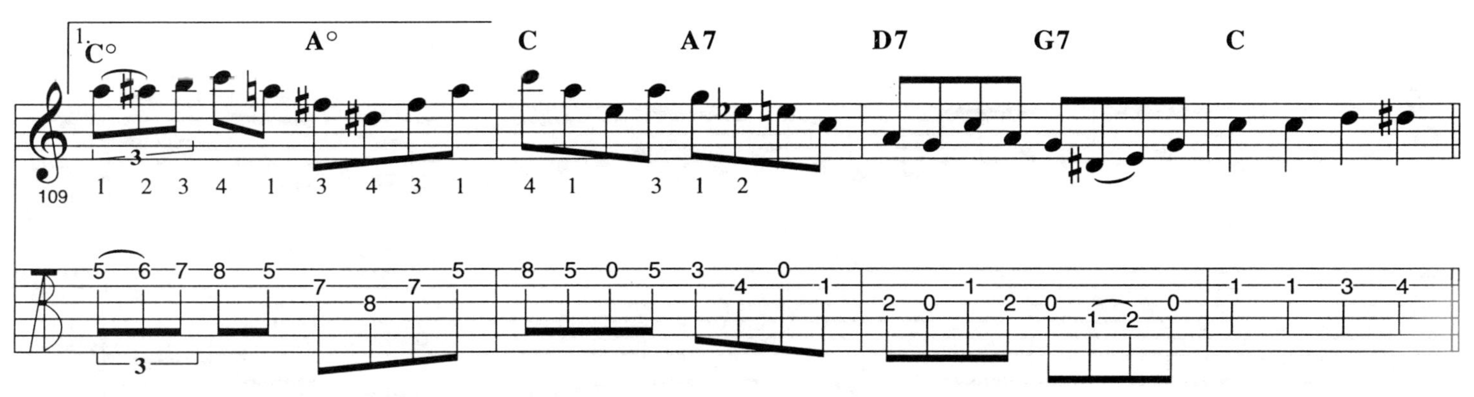
1.
C○
A○
C
A7
D7
G7
C
109

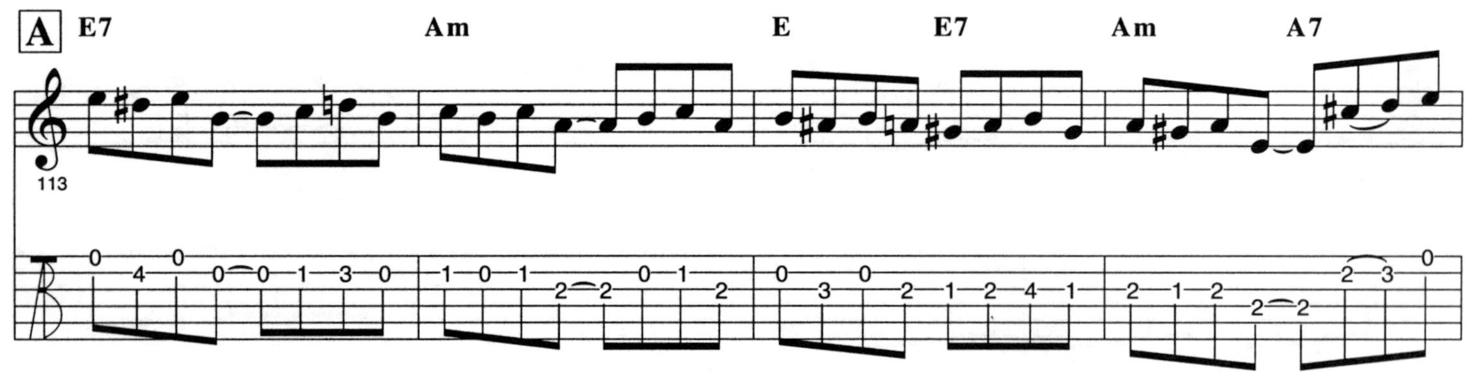
A
E7
Am
E
E7
Am
A7
113

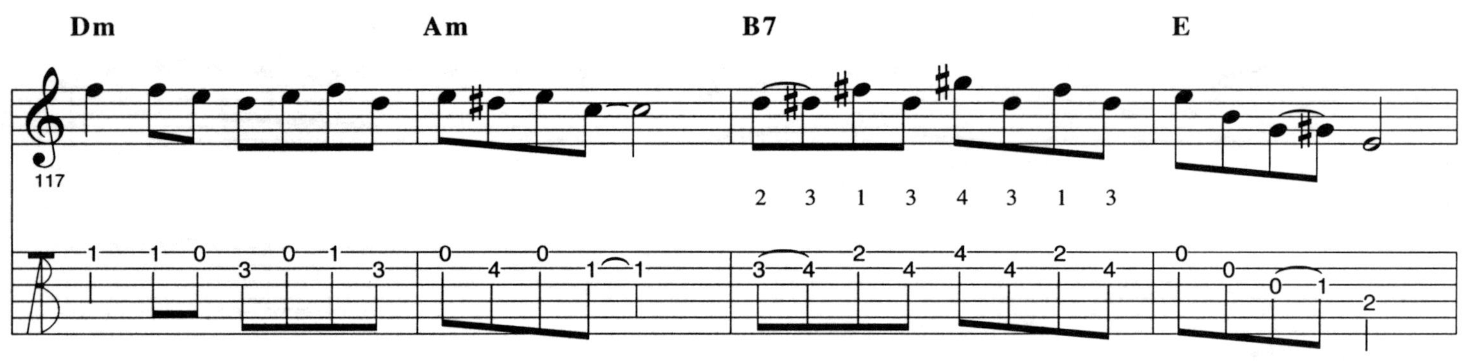
Dm
Am
B7
E
117
2 3 1 3 4 3 1 3

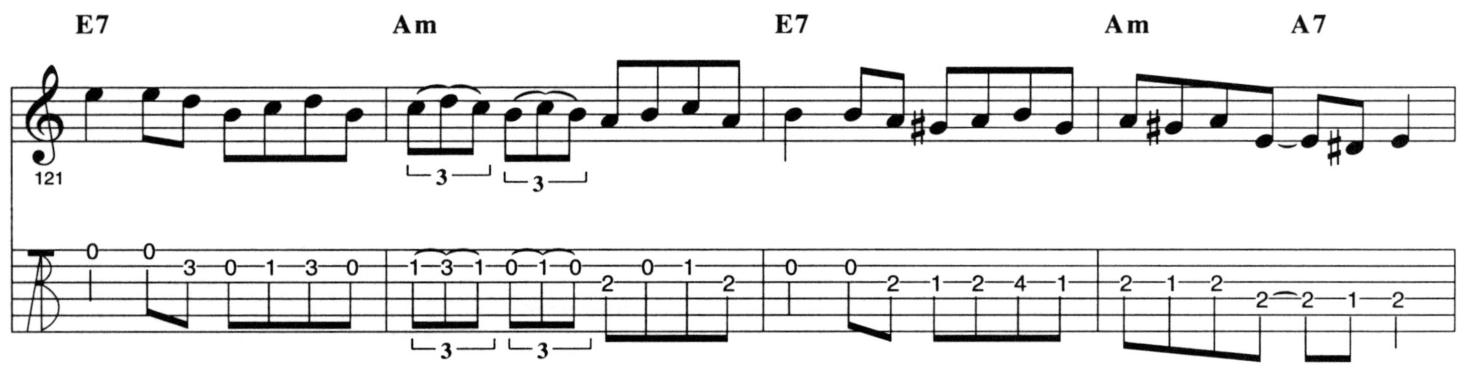
E7
Am
E7
Am
A7
121

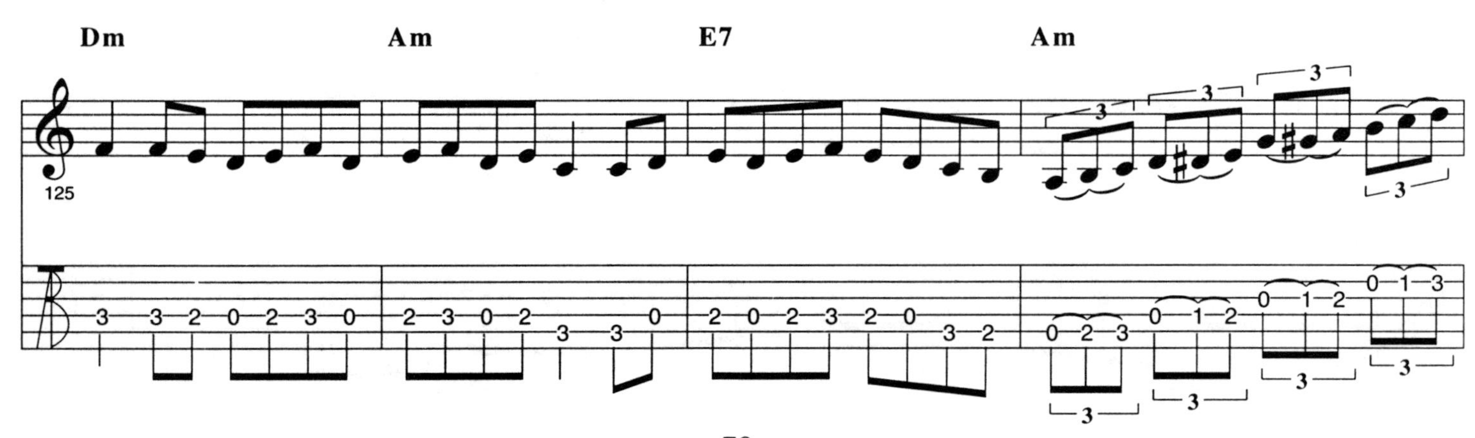
Dm
Am
E7
Am
125

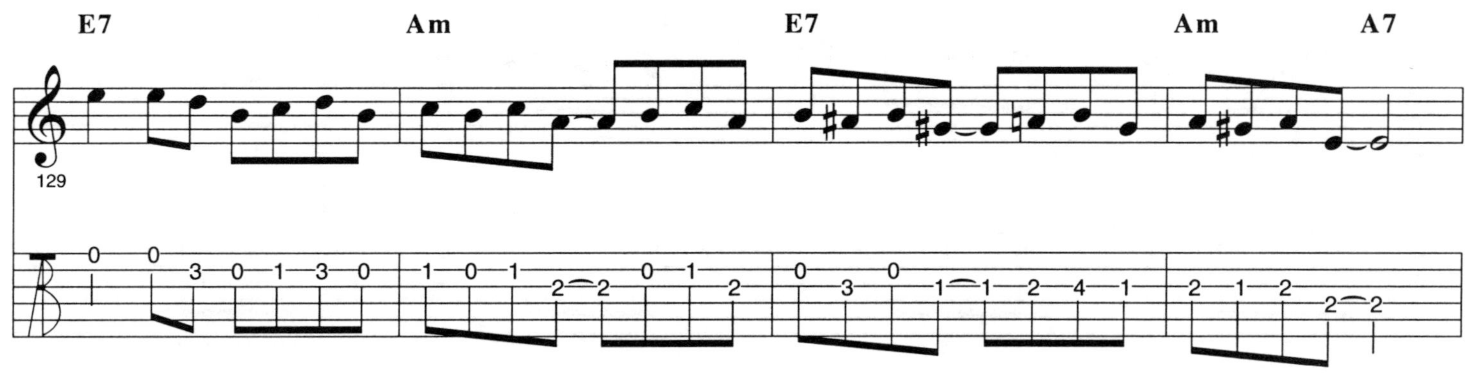
E7 Am E7 Am A7
129

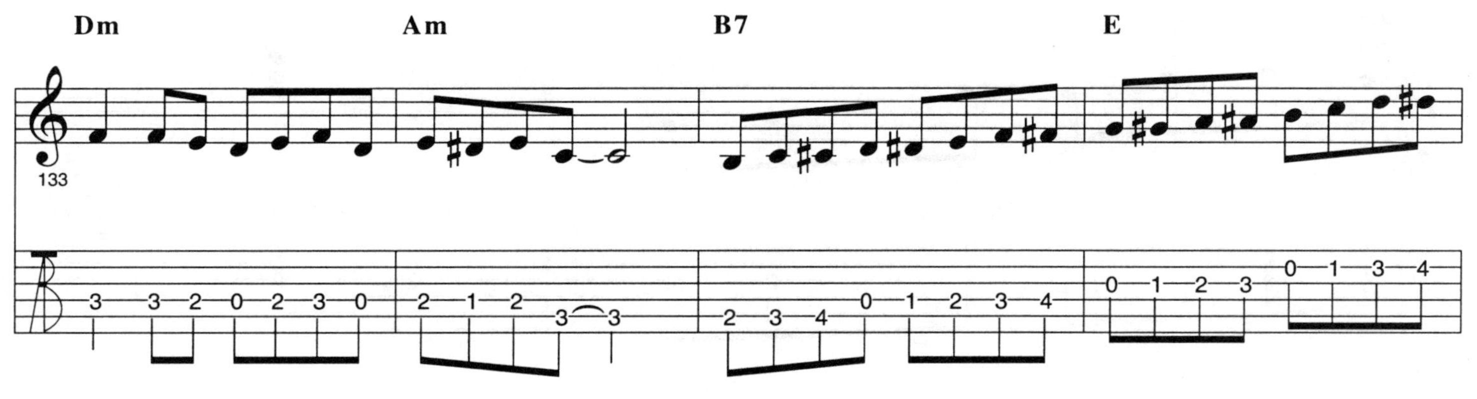
Dm Am B7 E
133

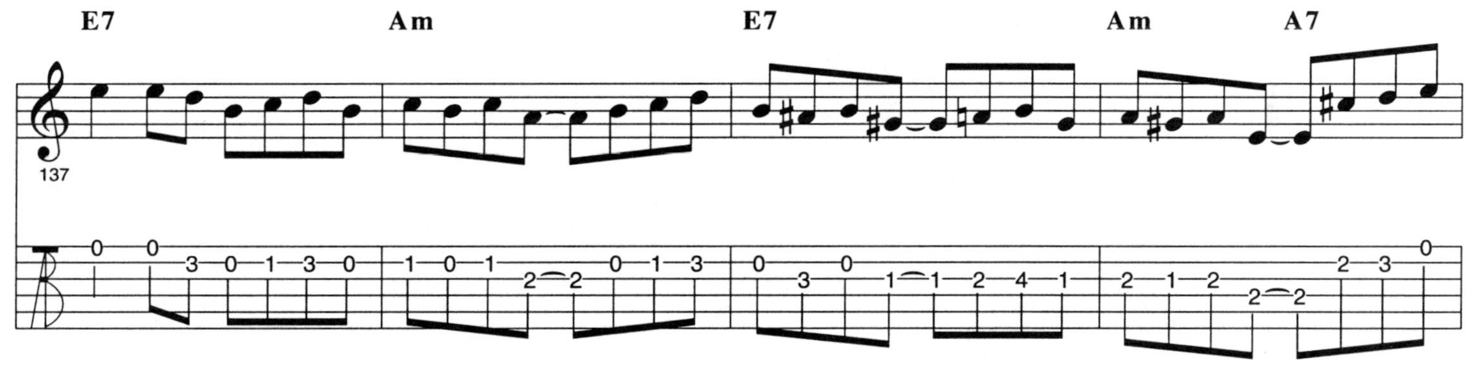
E7 Am E7 Am A7
137

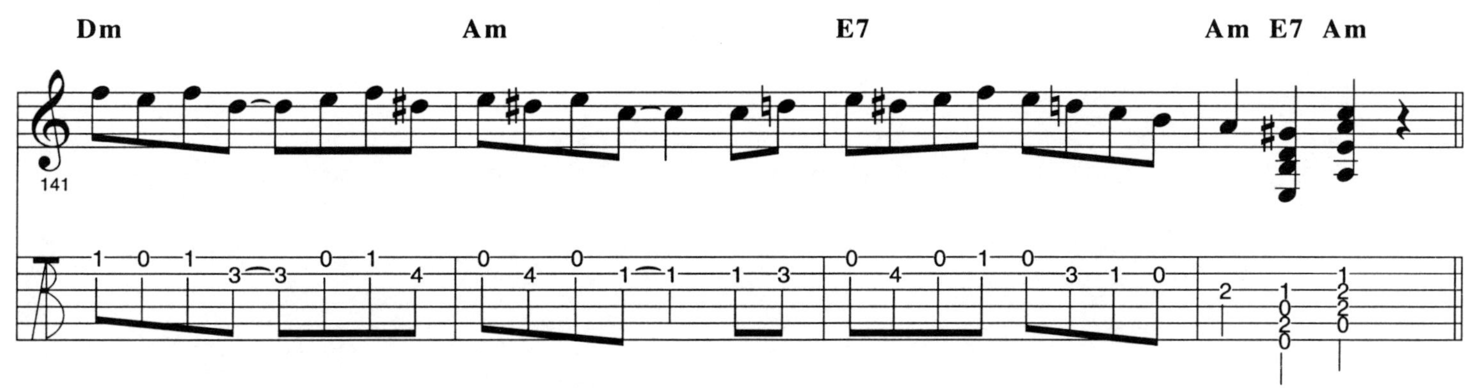
Dm Am E7 Am E7 Am
141

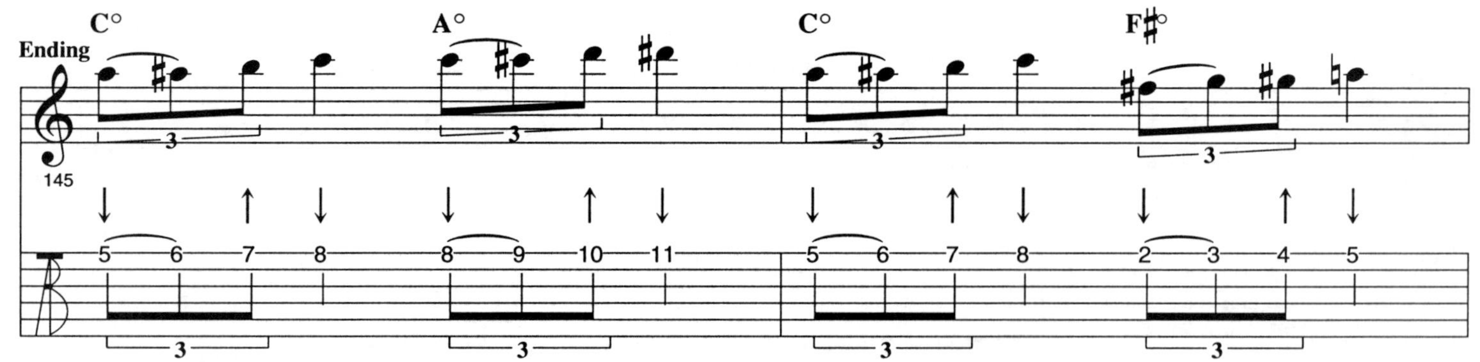
Ending
C°
A°
C°
F♯°
145
3
3
3
3
5 6 7 8
8 9 10 11
5 6 7 8
2 3 4 5

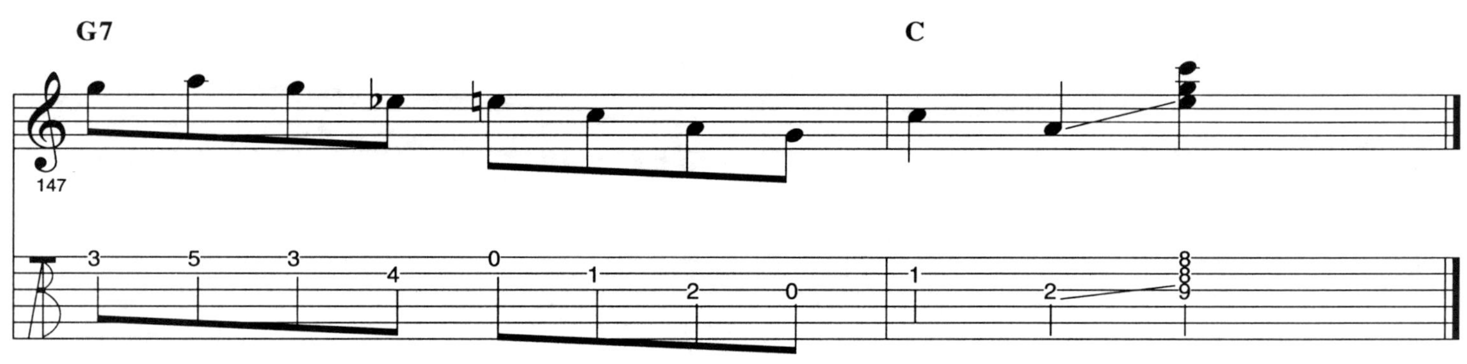
G7
C
147
3 5 3 4
0 1 2 0
1 2 8 8 9

Tico Taco No Fuba

Abreu

Arr. by Steve Kaufman

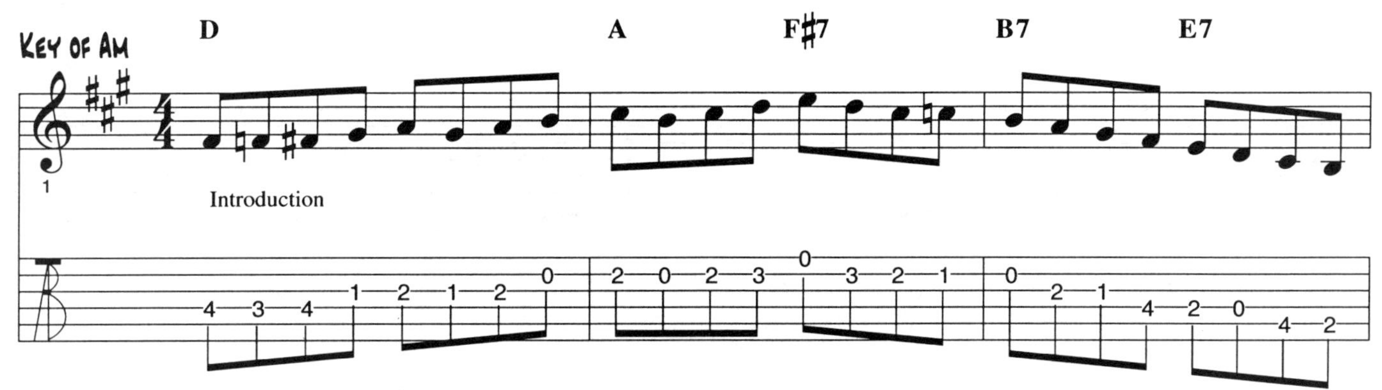

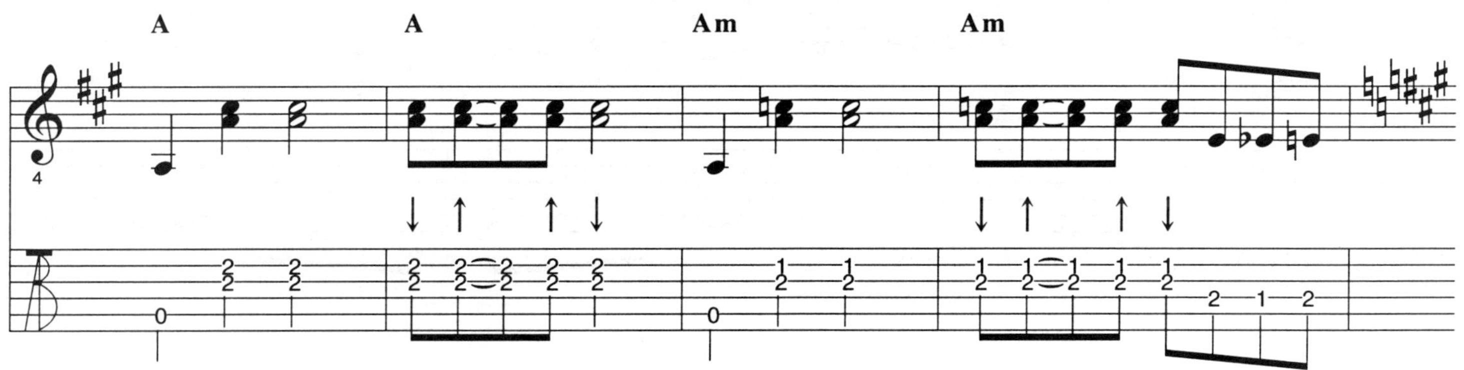

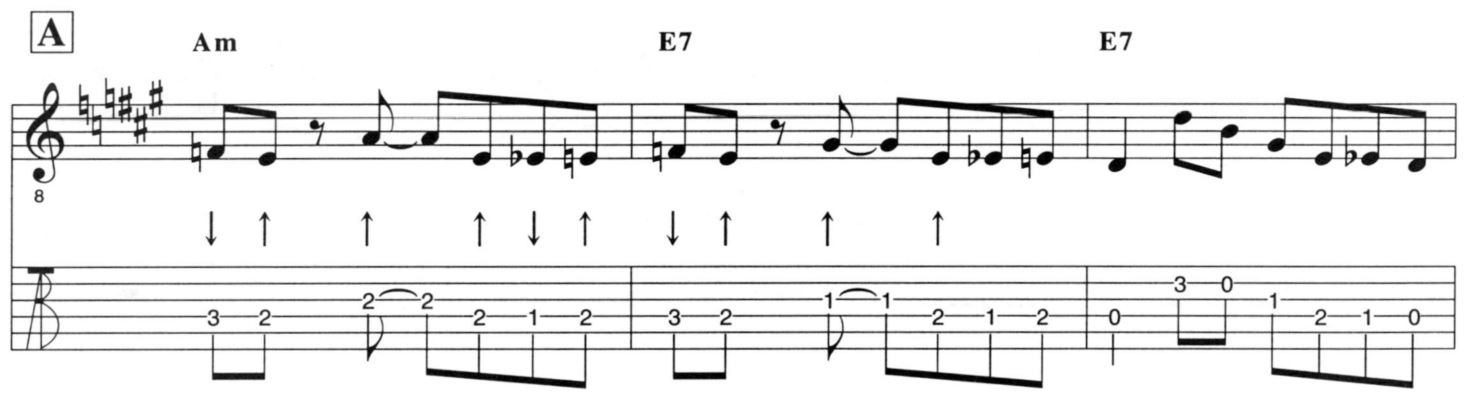

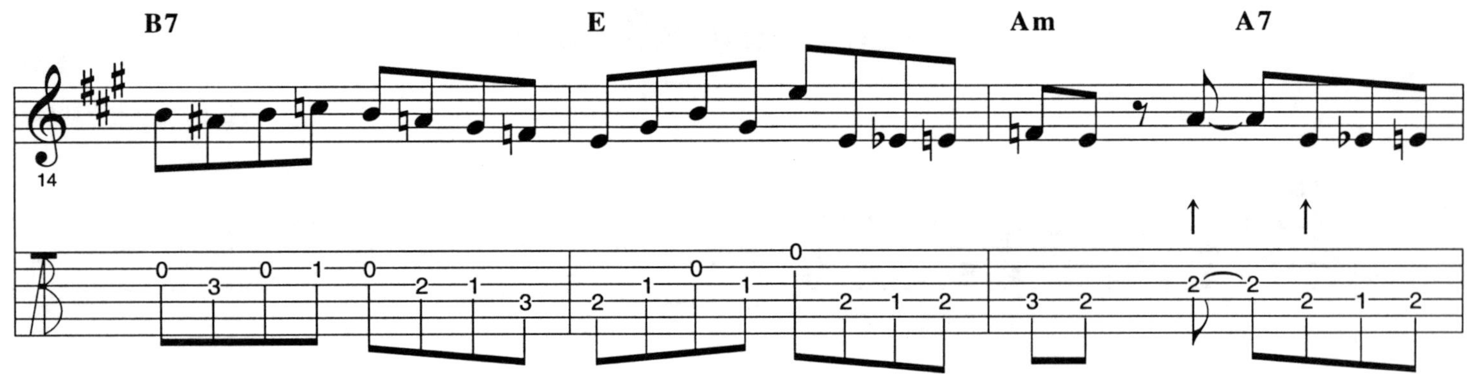
B7
E
Am
A7
14
0 3 0 1 0 2 1 3
2 1 0 1 0 2 1 2
3 2 2 2 2 1 2

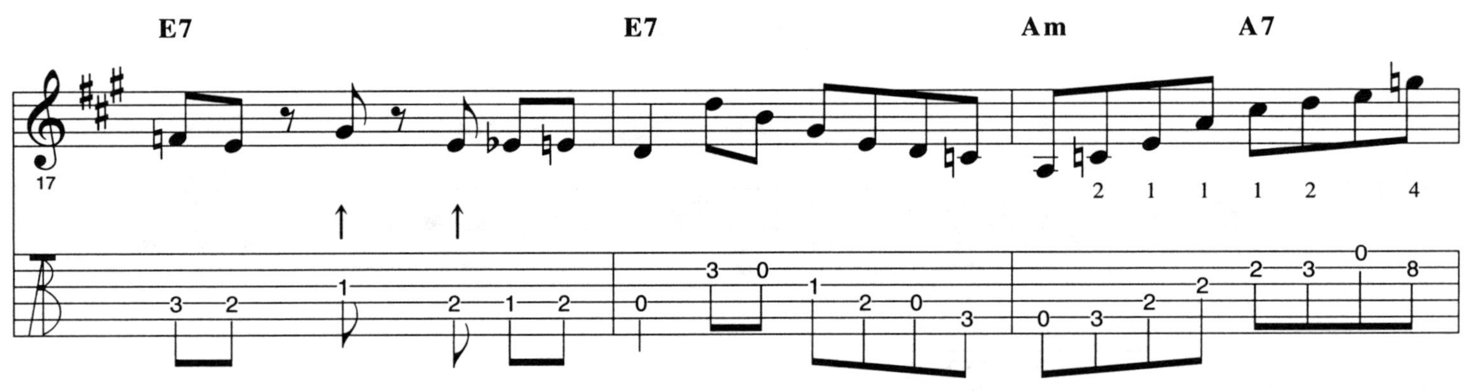
E7
E7
Am
A7
17
2 1 1 1 2 4
3 2 1 2 1 2
0 3 0 1 2 0 3
0 3 2 2 2 3 0 8

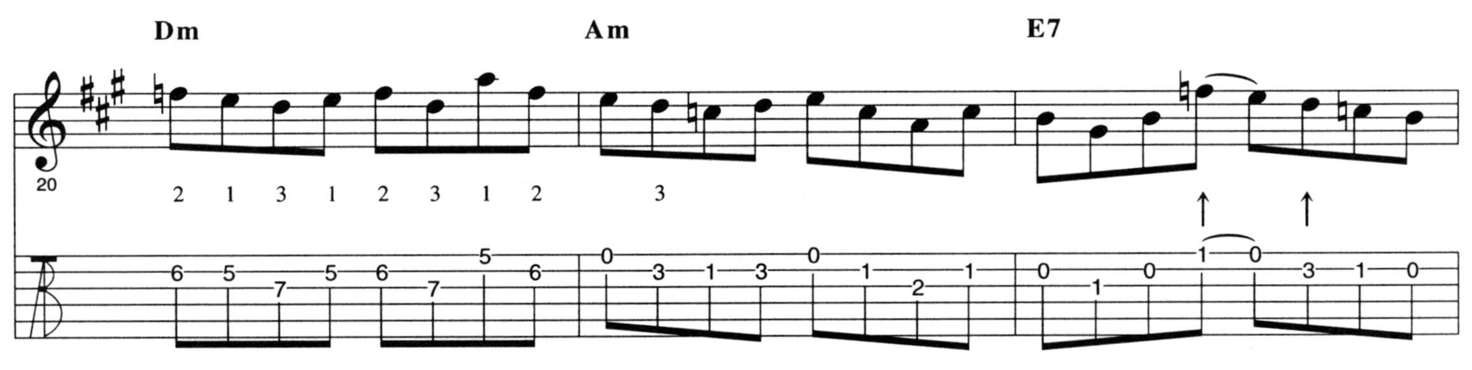
Dm
Am
E7
20
2 1 3 1 2 3 1 2
3
6 5 7 5 6 7 5 6
0 3 1 3 0 1 2 1
0 1 0 1 0 3 1 0

Am
Am
E7
23
2 2 3 2 0 2 1 2
3 2 2 2 1 2
3 2 1 2 1 2

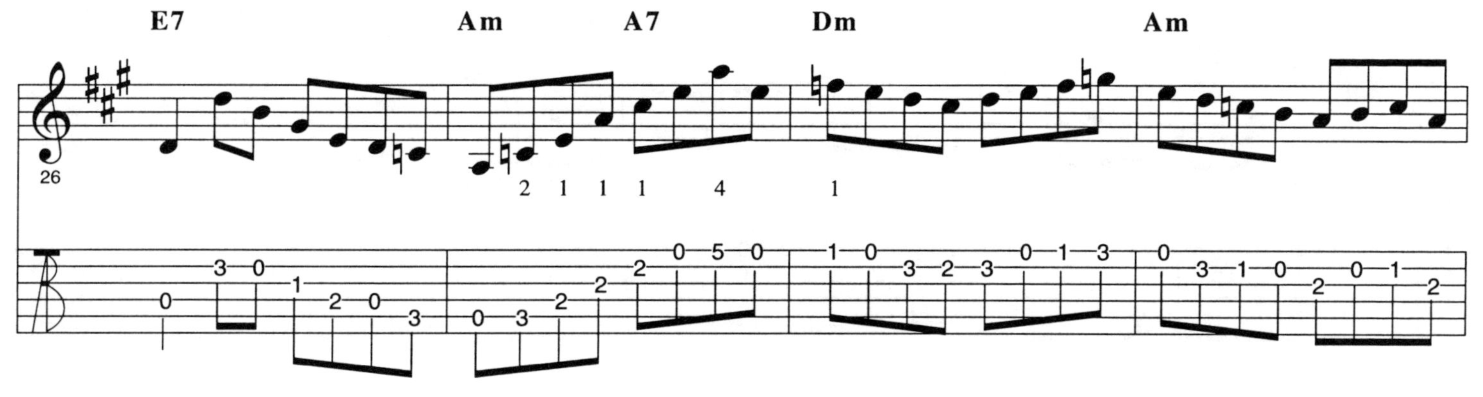
E7 Am A7 Dm Am
26

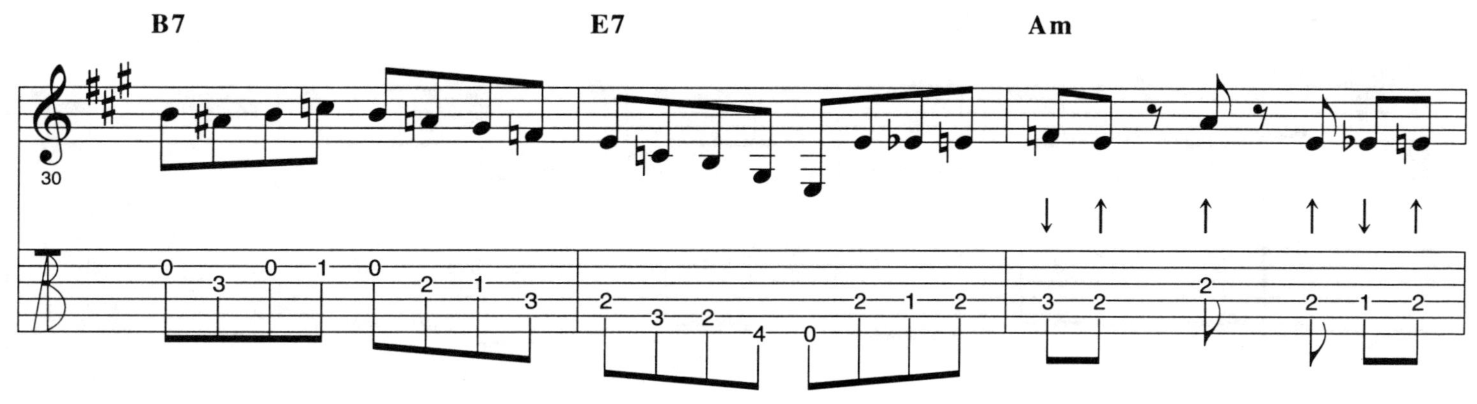
B7 E7 Am
30

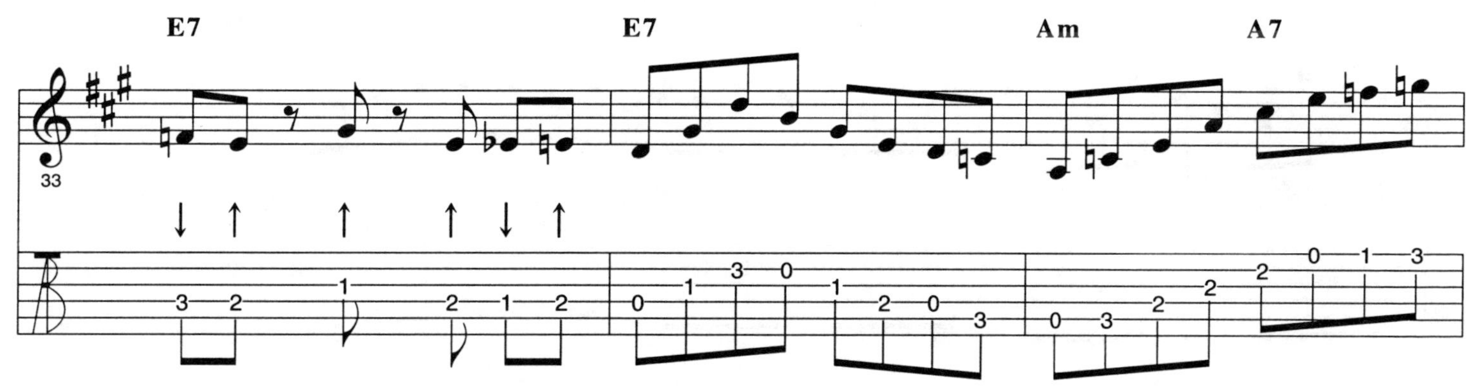
E7 E7 Am A7
33

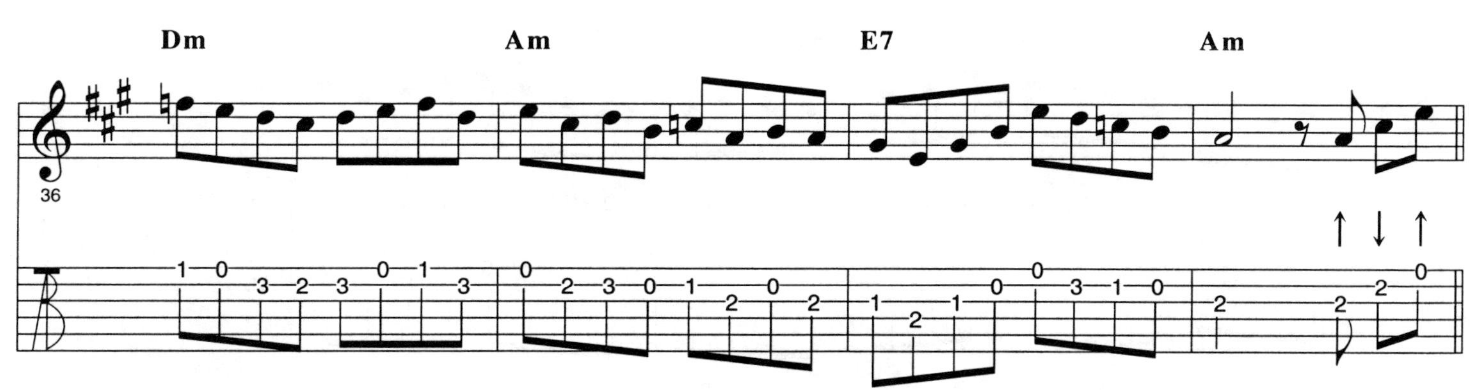
Dm Am E7 Am
36

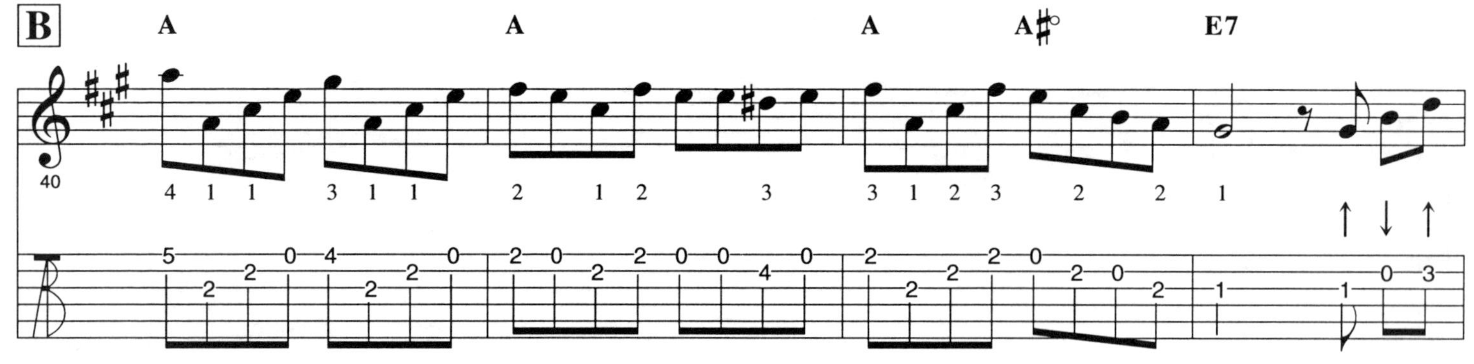
B
A
A
A
A♯°
E7
40

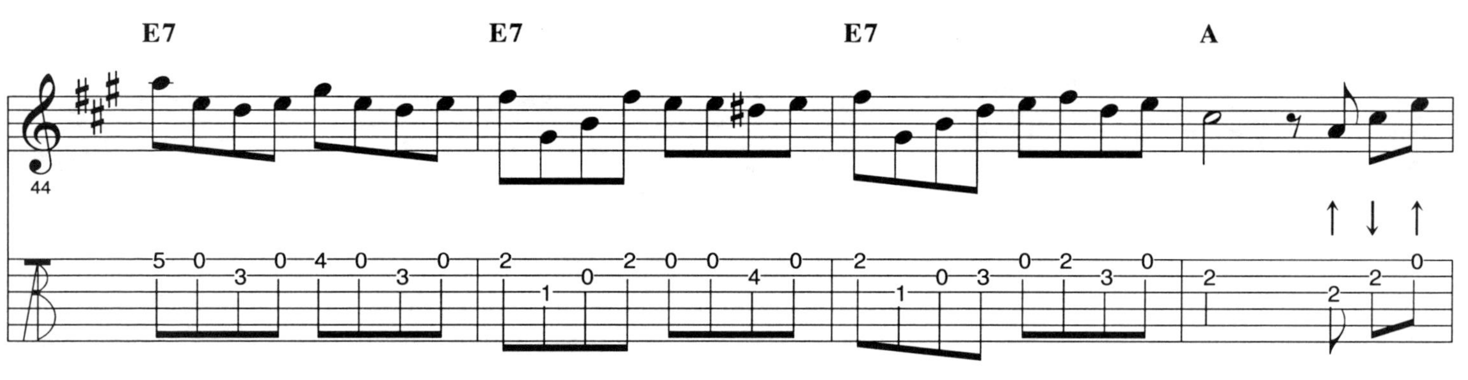
E7
E7
E7
A
44

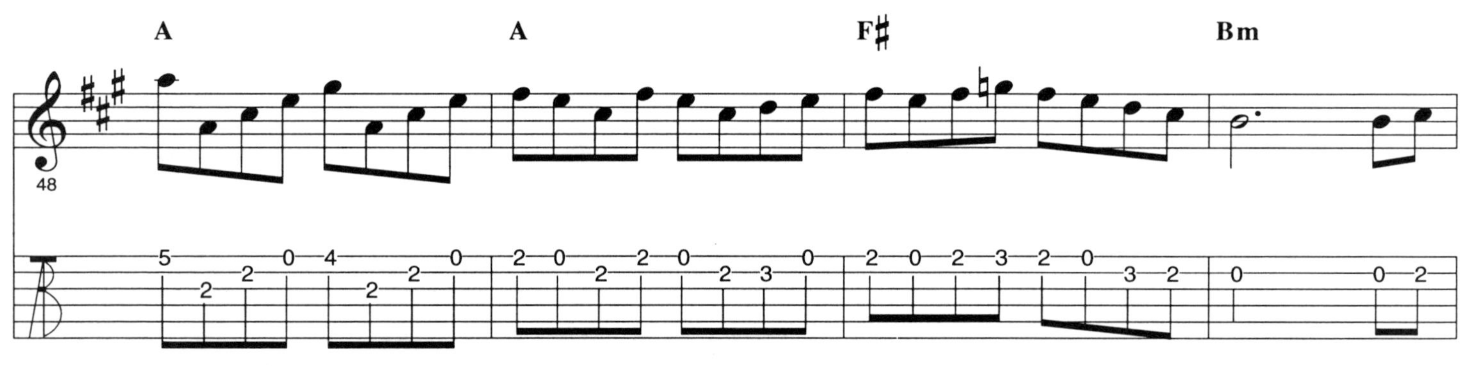
A
A
F♯
Bm
48

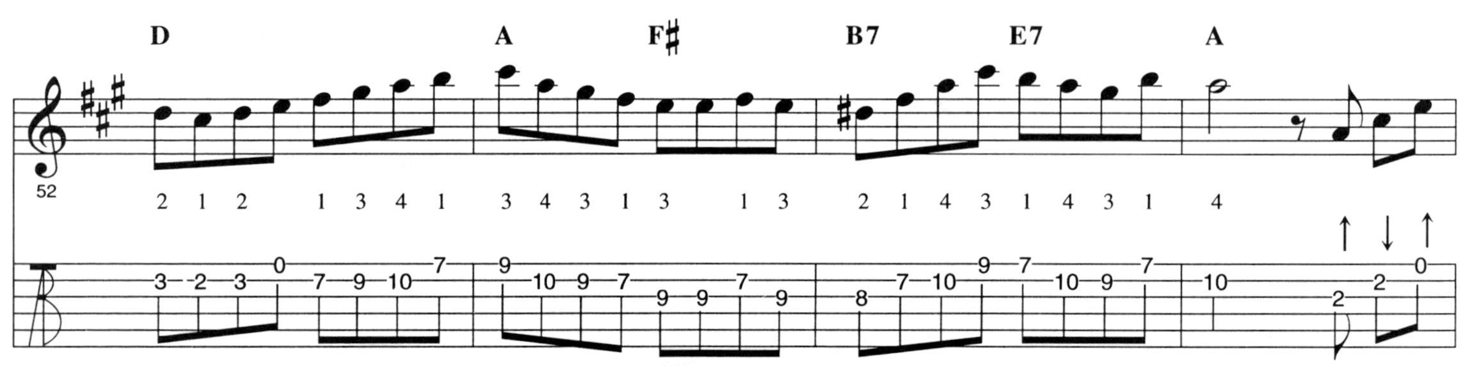
D
A
F♯
B7
E7
A
52

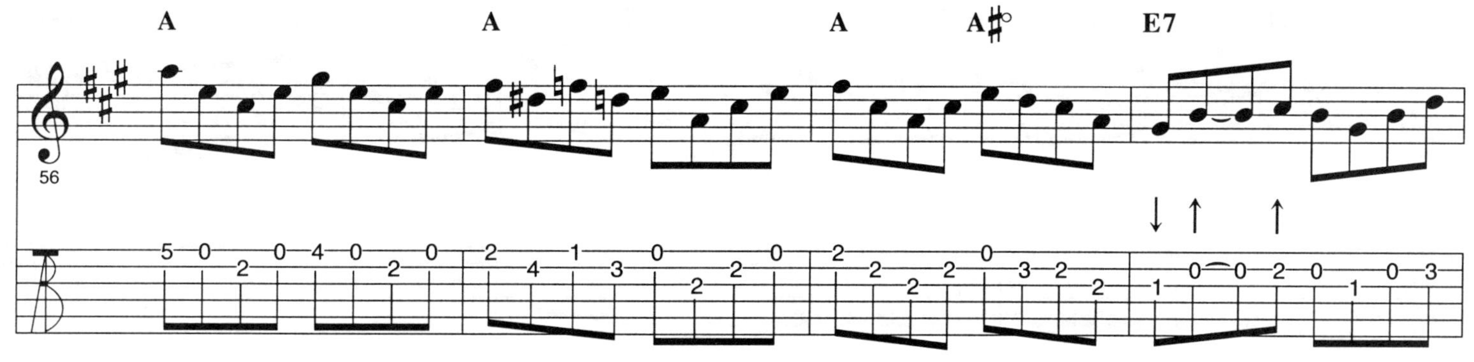
A
A
A
A#°
E7
56

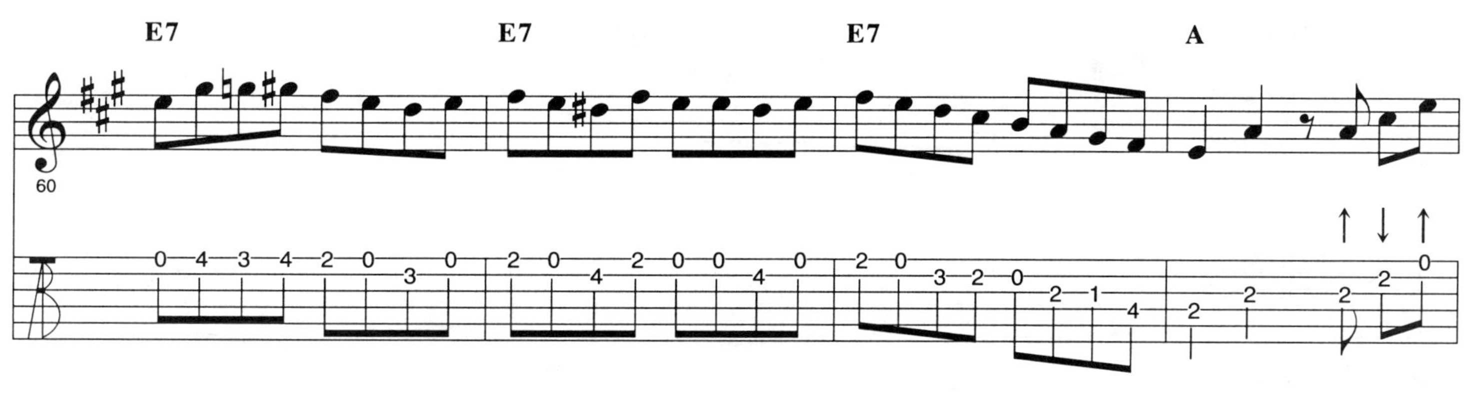
E7
E7
E7
A
60

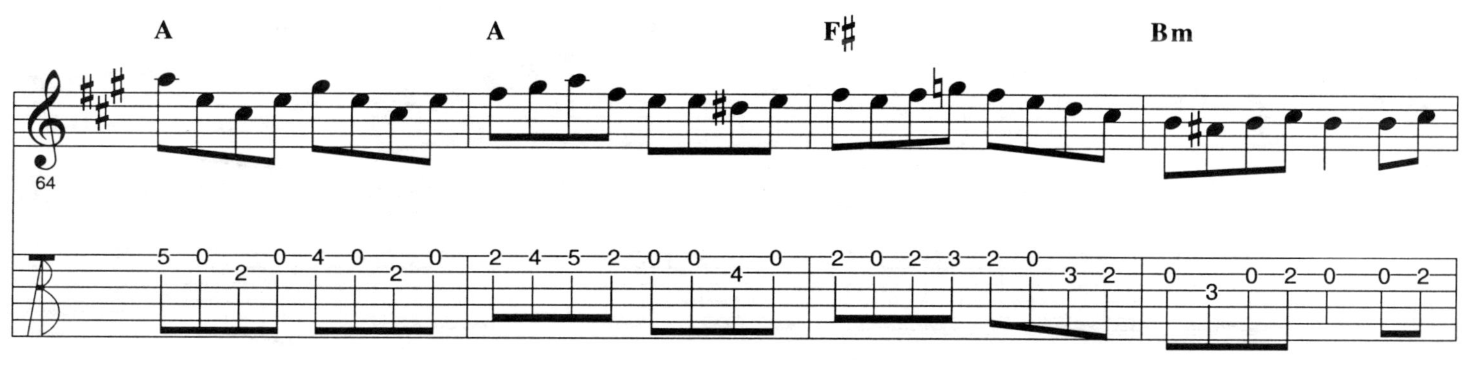
A
A
F#
Bm
64

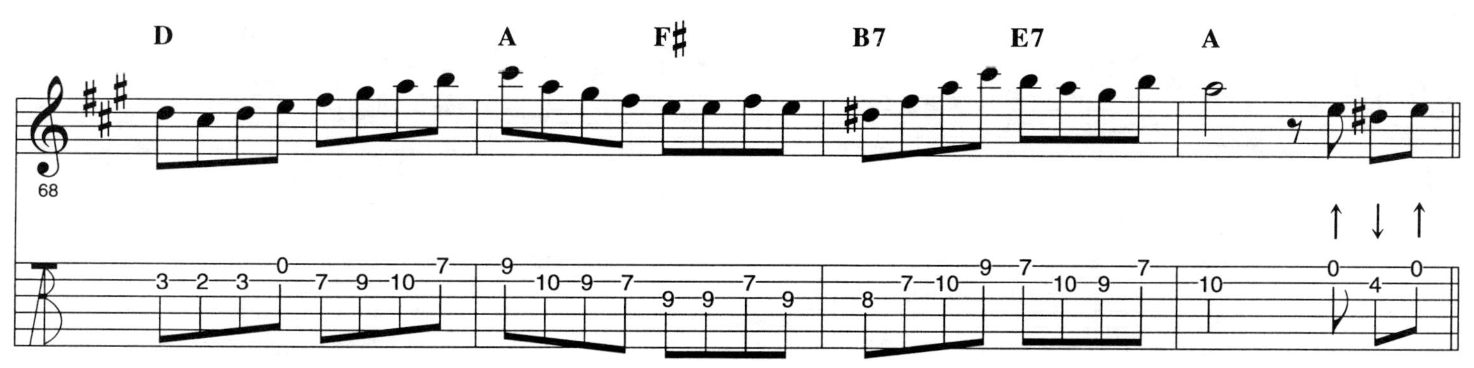
D
A
F#
B7
E7
A
68

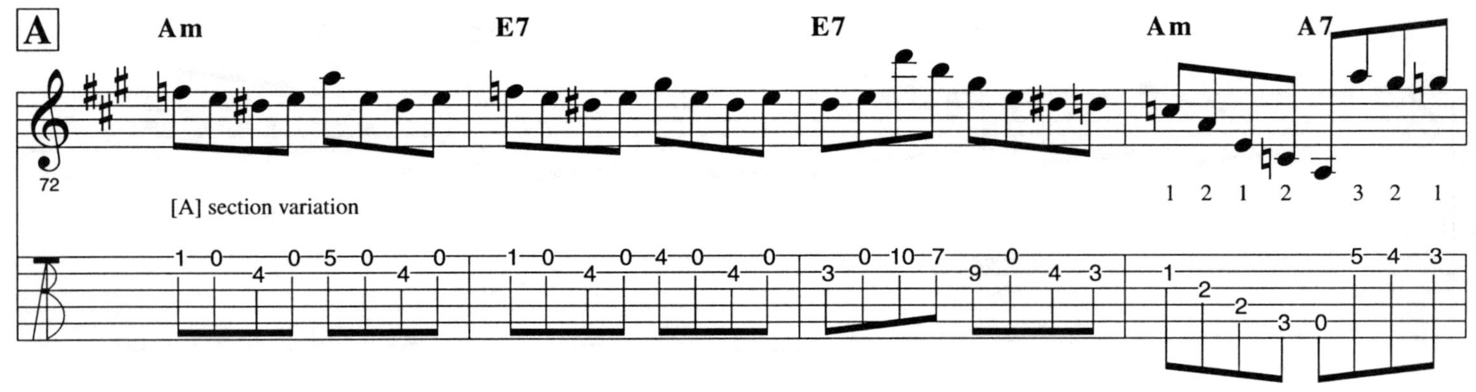
A
Am
E7
E7
Am
A7
72
[A] section variation

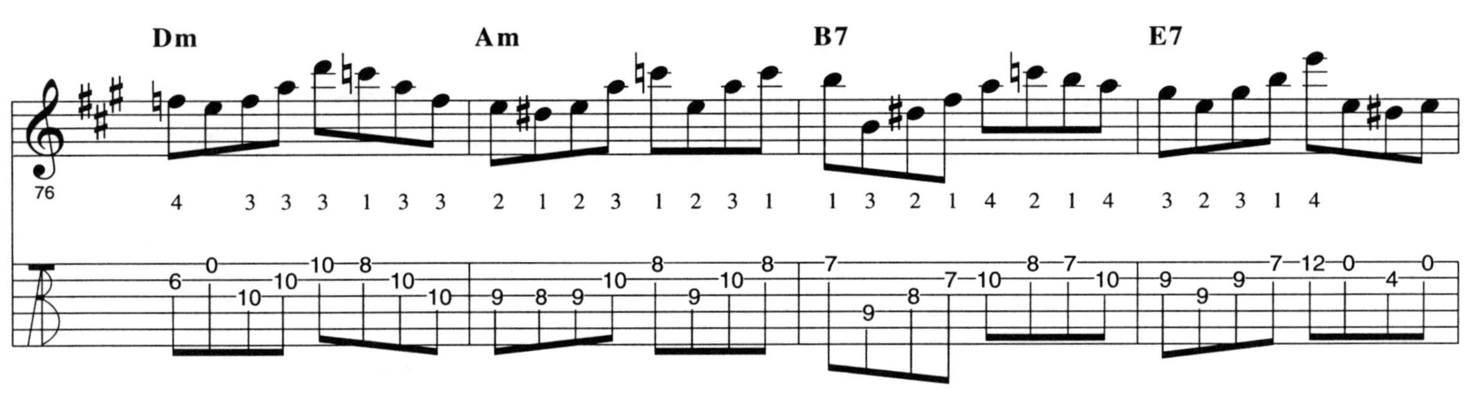
Dm
Am
B7
E7
76

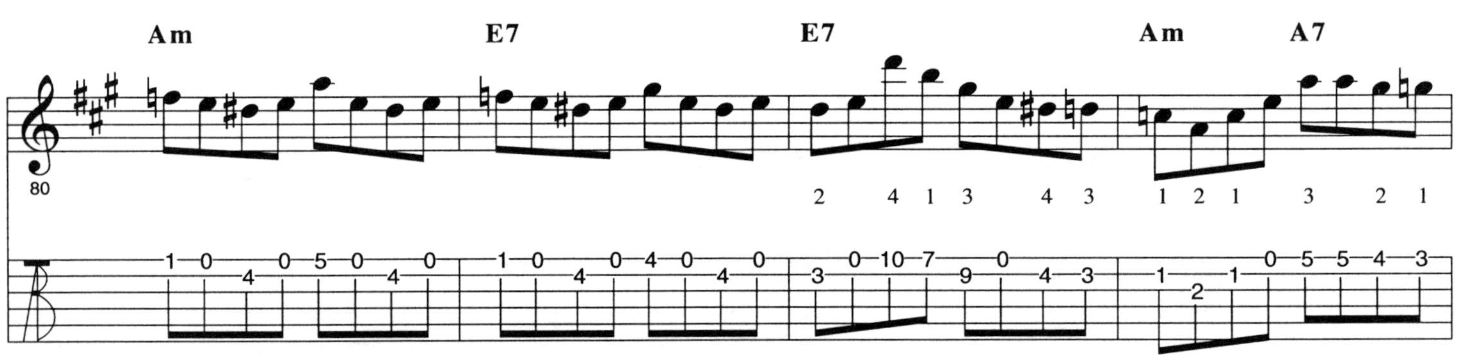
Am
E7
E7
Am
A7
80

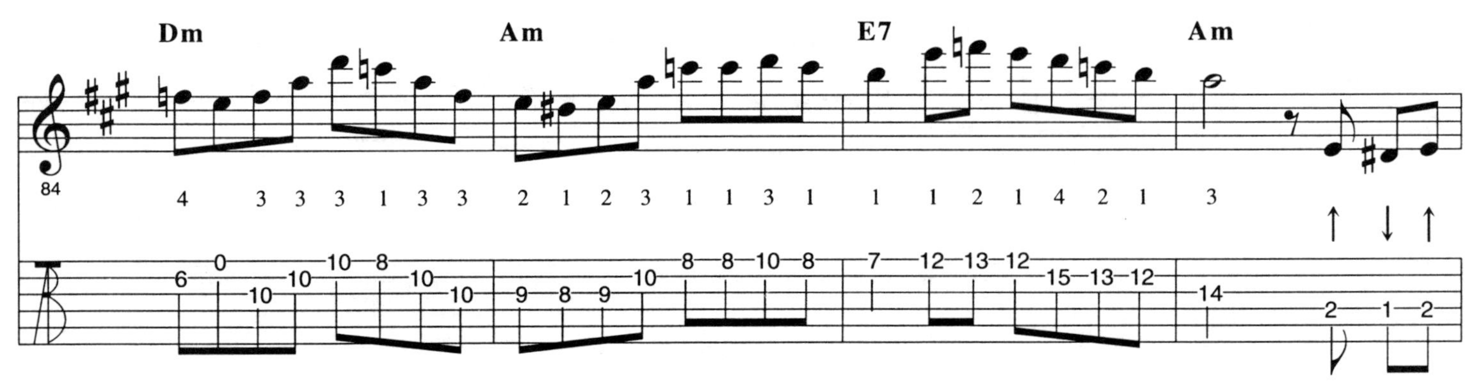
Dm
Am
E7
Am
84

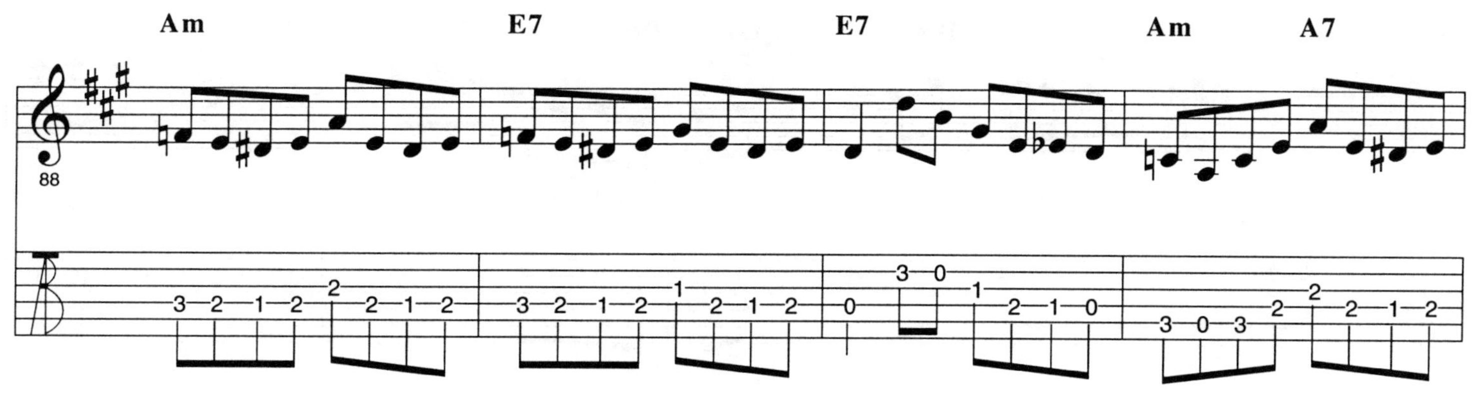
Am
E7
E7
Am
A7
88

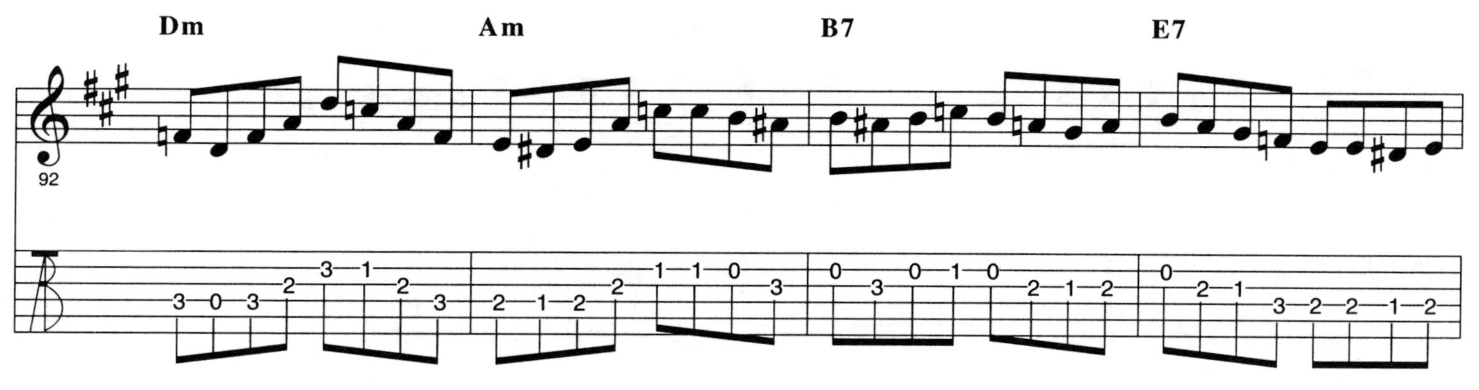
Dm
Am
B7
E7
92

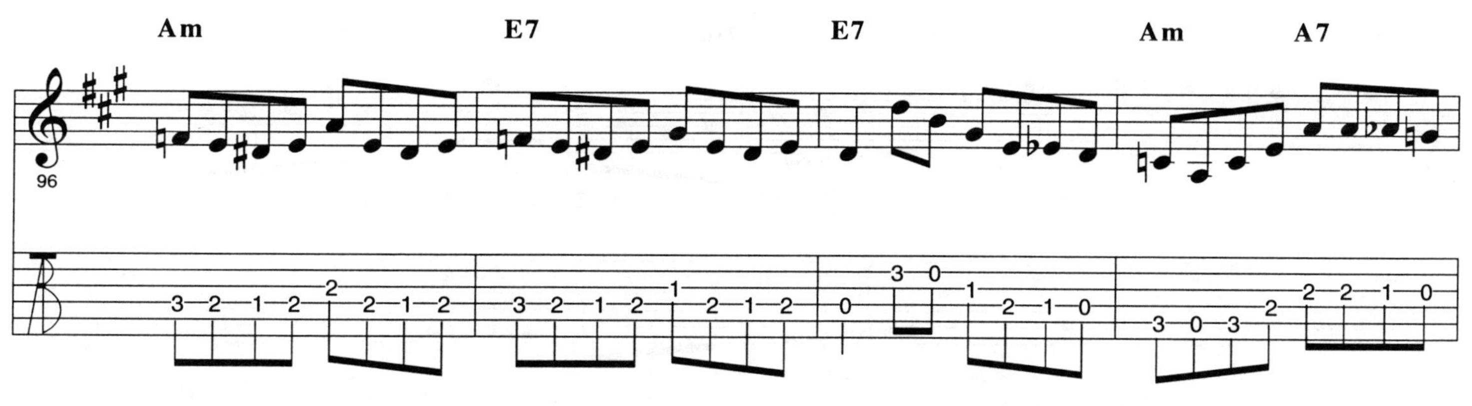
Am
E7
E7
Am
A7
96

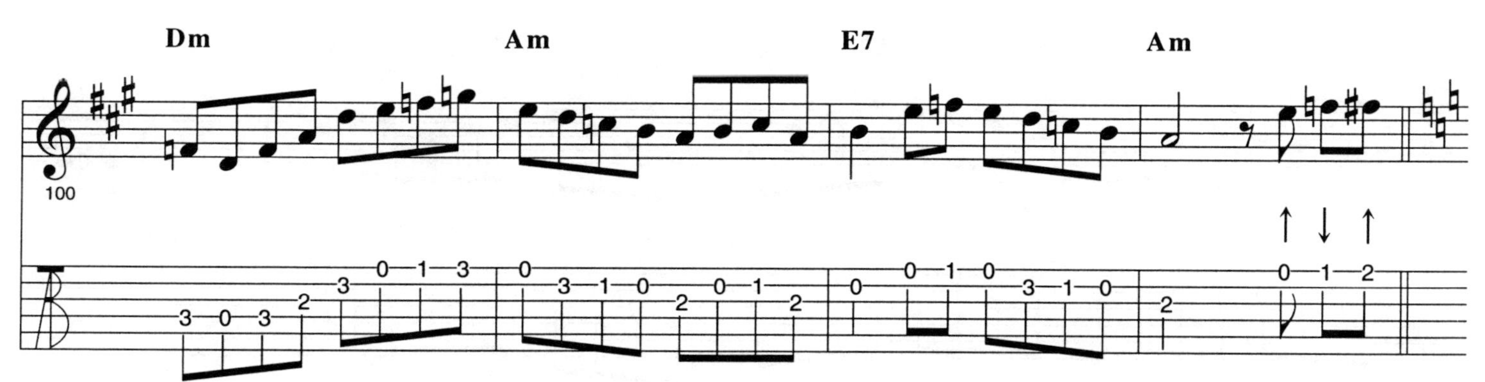
Dm
Am
E7
Am
100

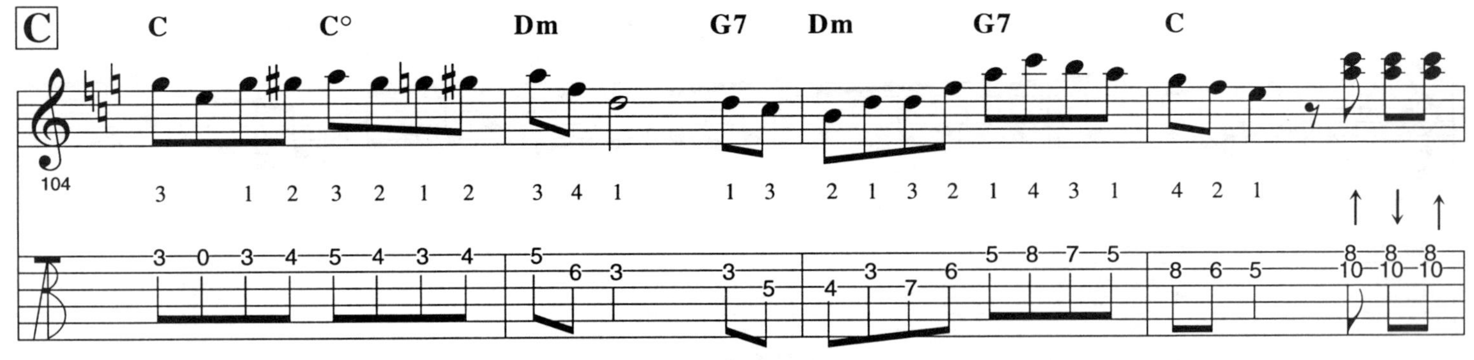
C
C
C°
Dm
G7
Dm
G7
C
104
3 1 2 3 2 1 2 3 4 1 1 3 2 1 3 2 1 4 3 1 4 2 1

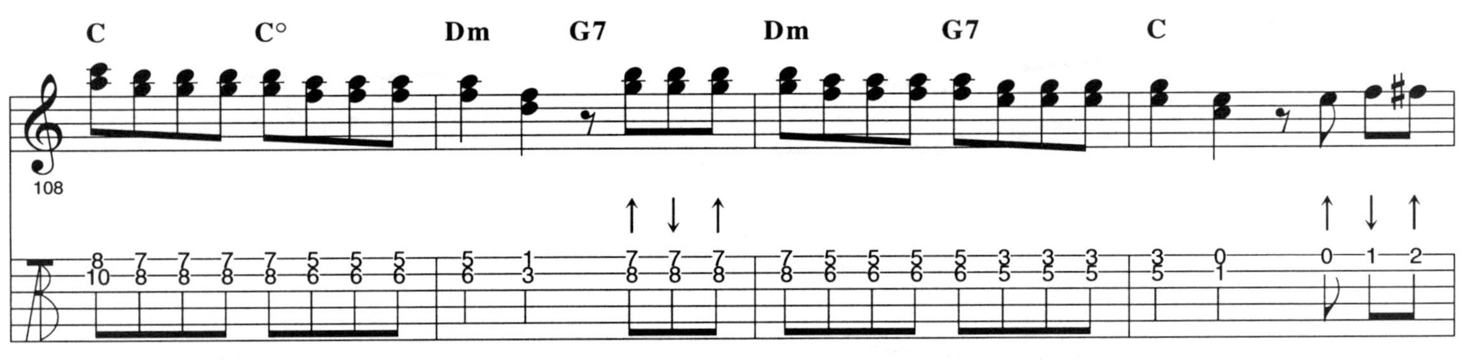
C
C°
Dm
G7
Dm
G7
C
108

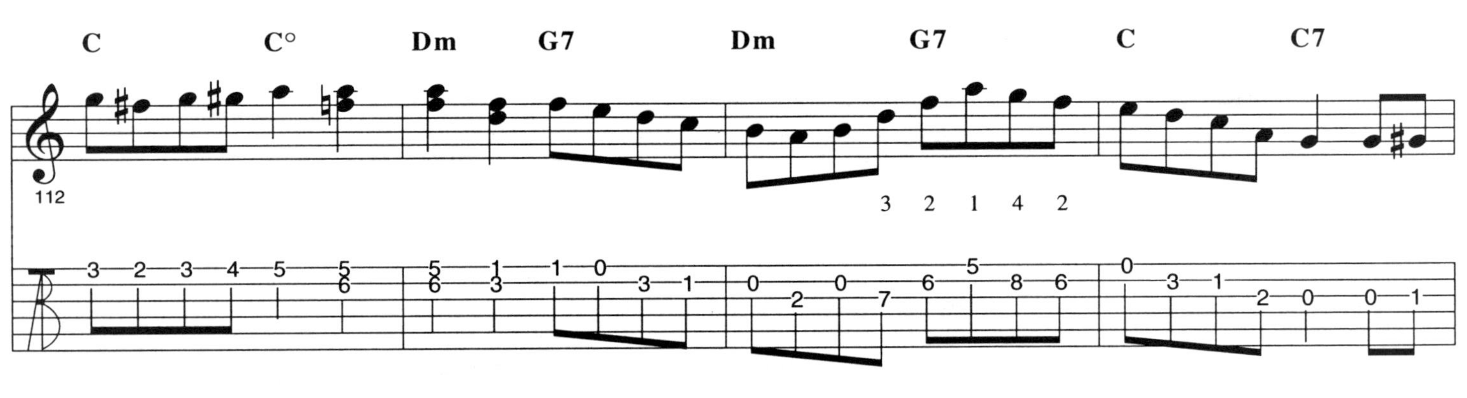
C
C°
Dm
G7
Dm
G7
C
C7
112
3 2 1 4 2

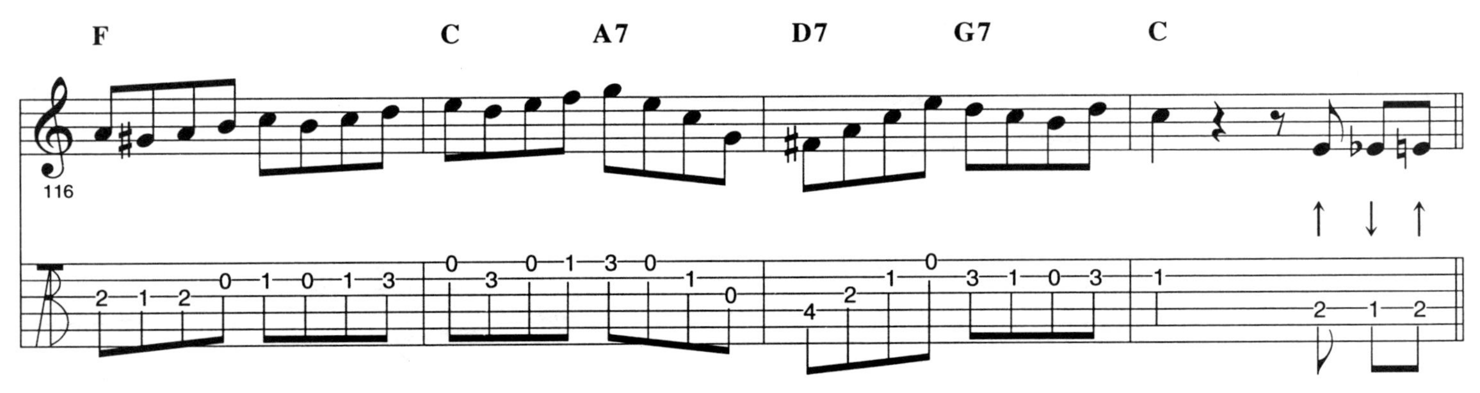
F
C
A7
D7
G7
C
116

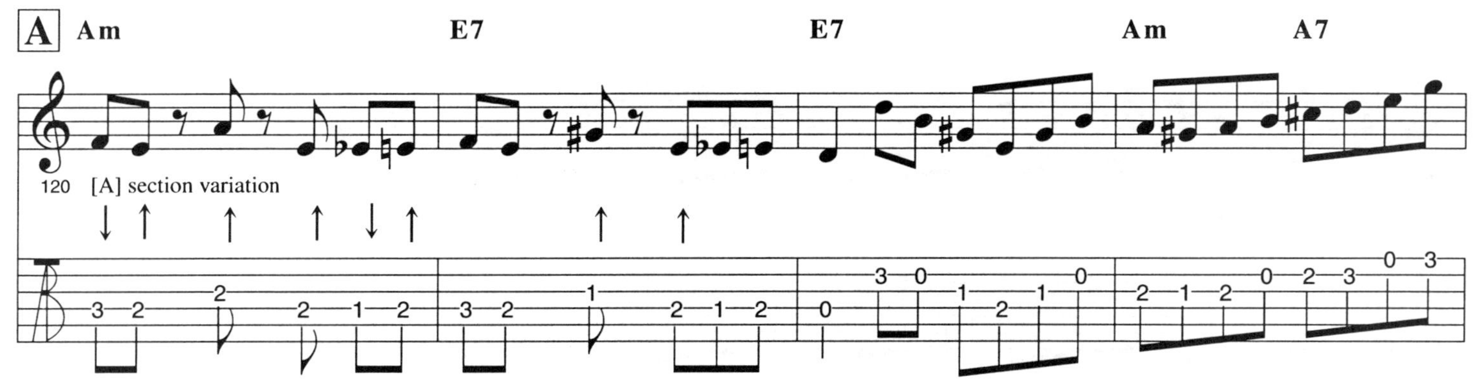
A
Am
E7
E7
Am
A7
120
[A] section variation

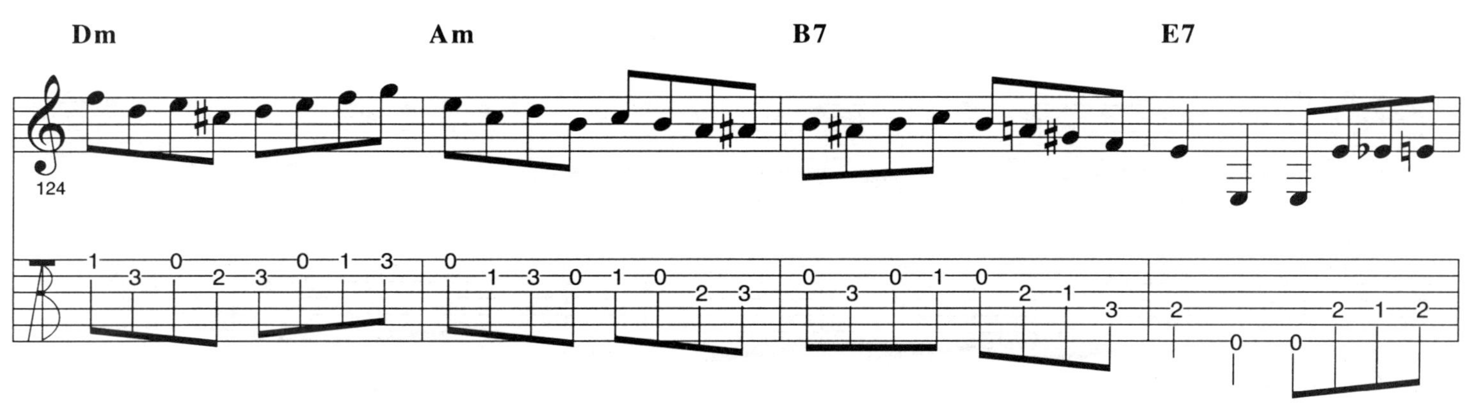
Dm
Am
B7
E7
124

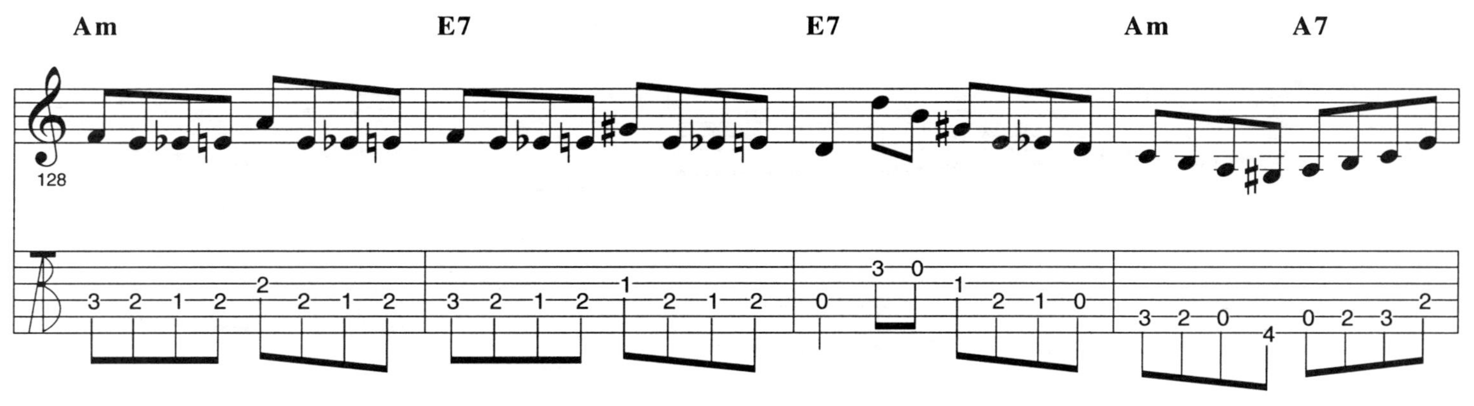
Am
E7
E7
Am
A7
128

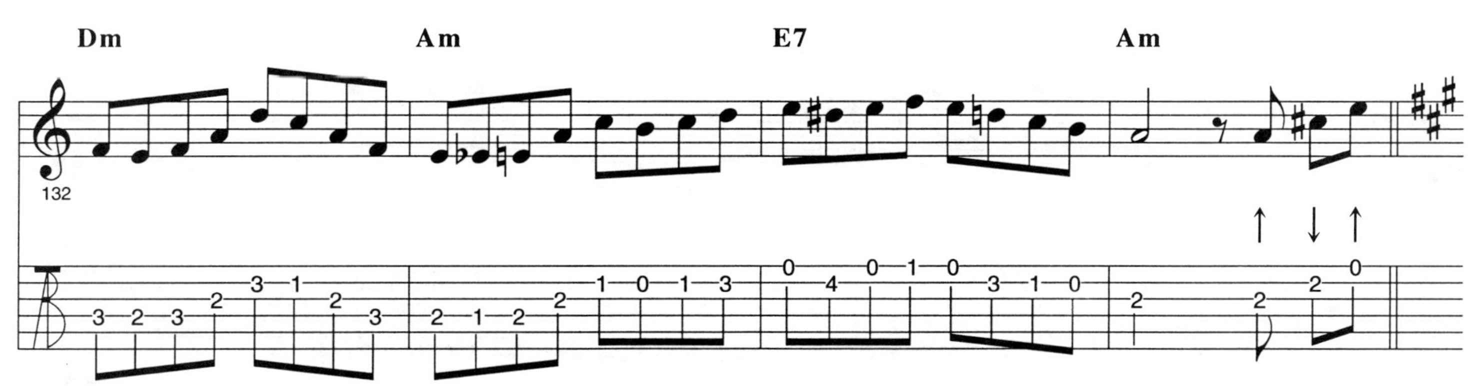
Dm
Am
E7
Am
132

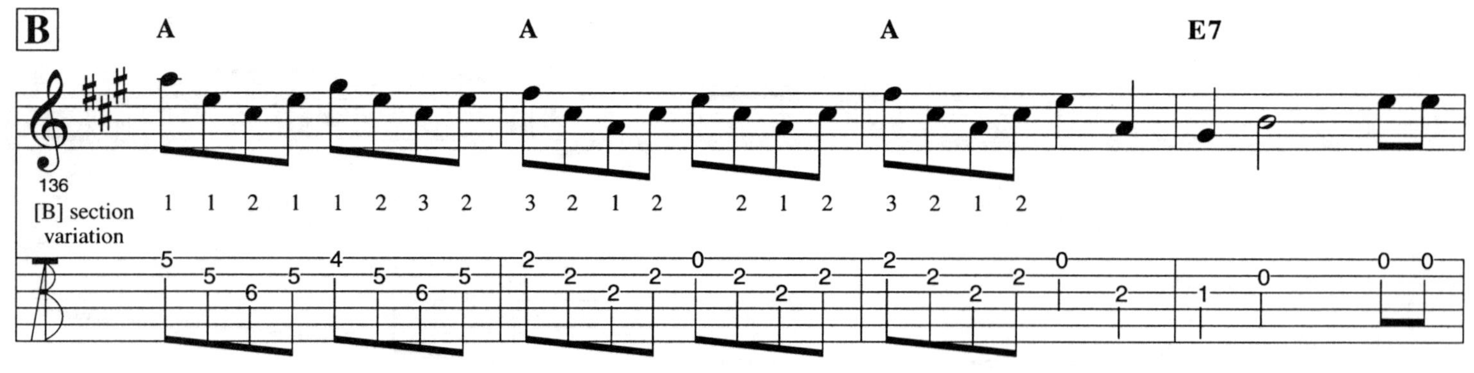
B
A
A
A
E7
136
[B] section
variation

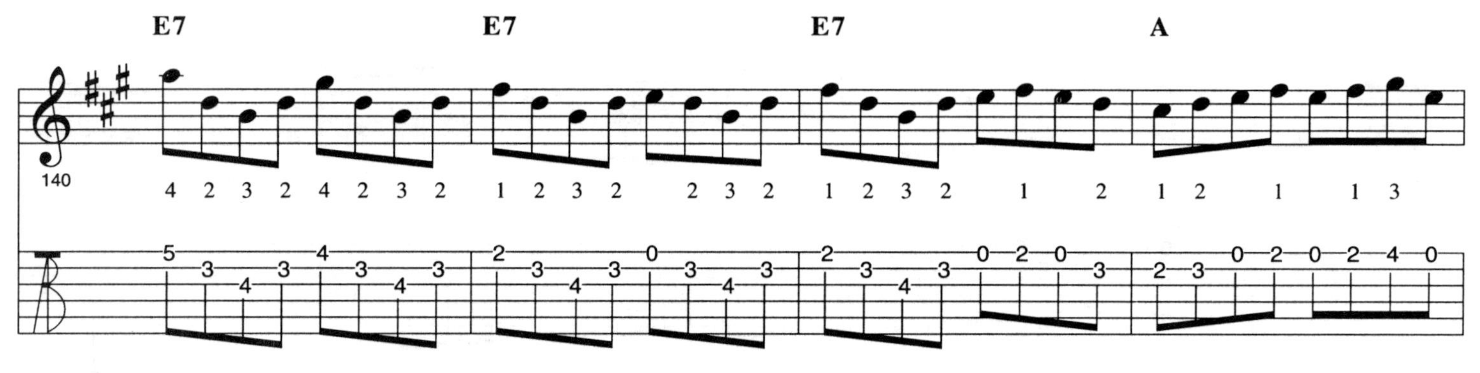
E7
E7
E7
A
140

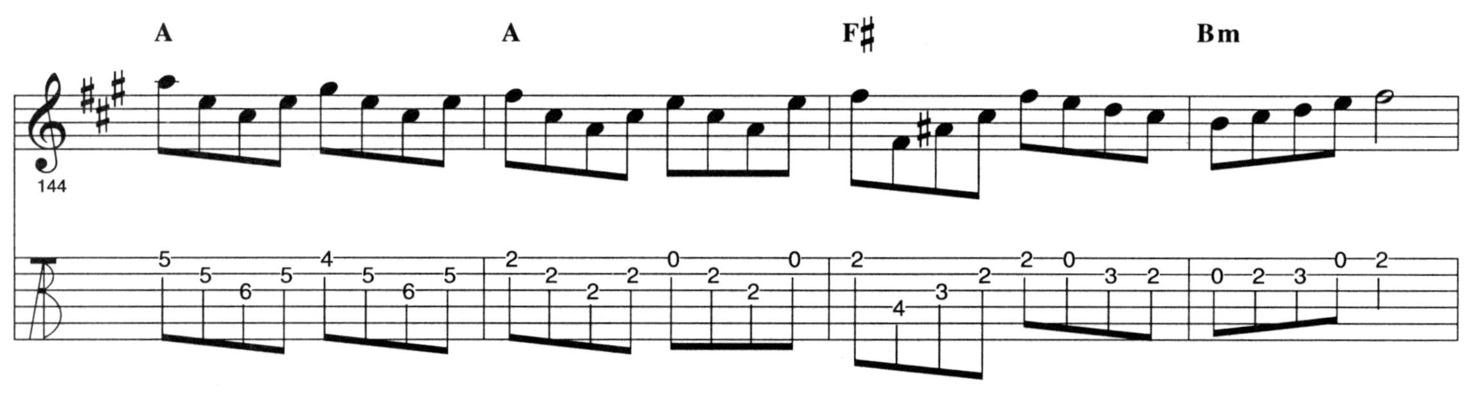
A
A
F♯
Bm
144

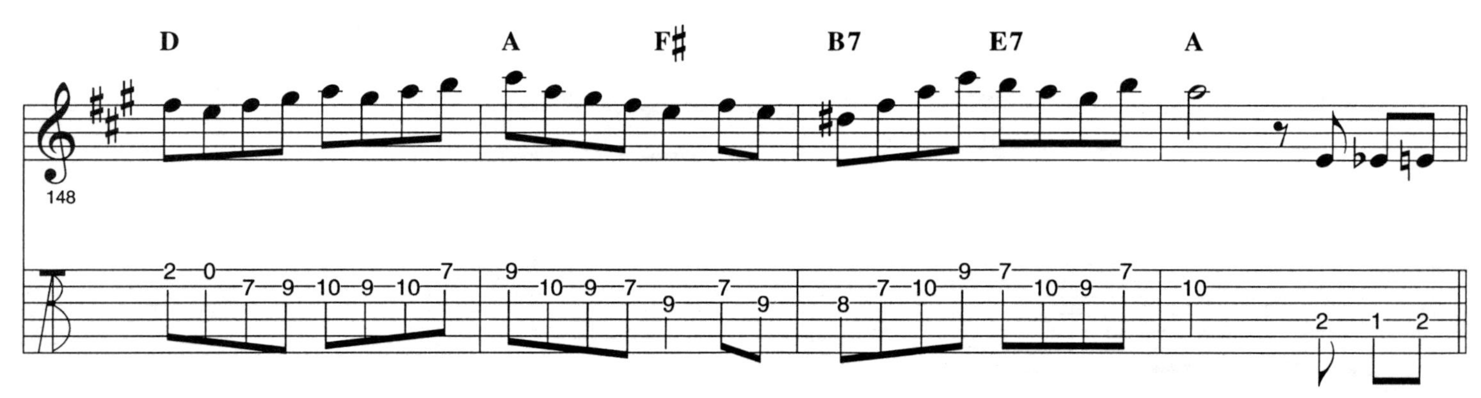
D
A
F♯
B7
E7
A
148

A
Am
E7
E7
Am
A7
152
[A] section variation

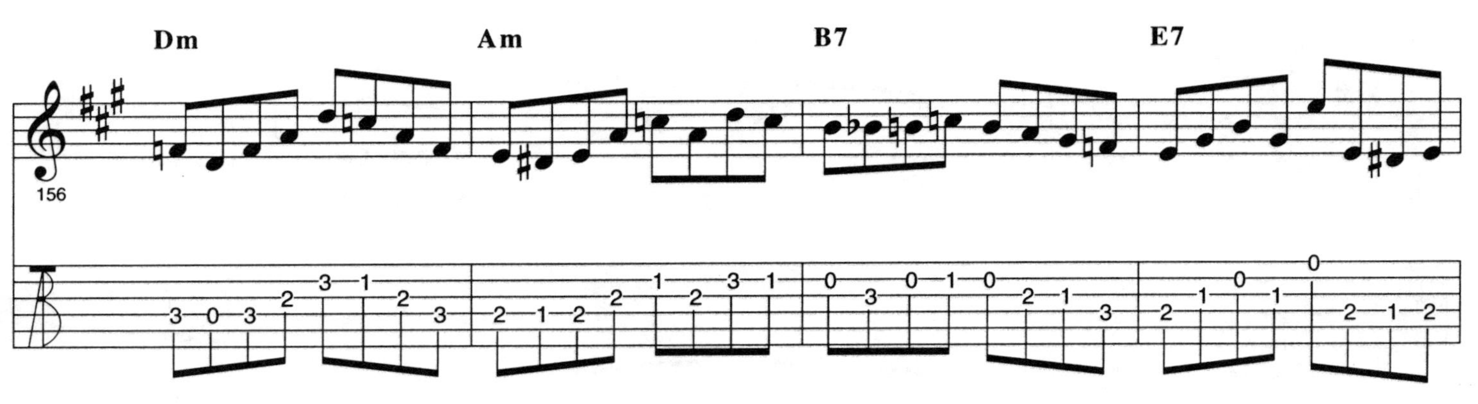
Dm
Am
B7
E7
156

Am
E7
E7
Am
A7
160

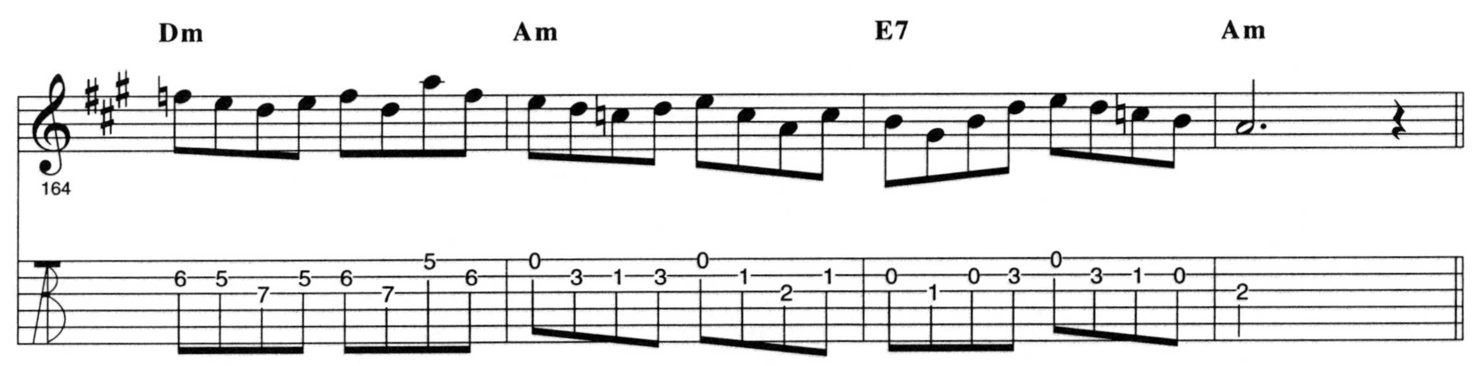
Dm
Am
E7
Am
164

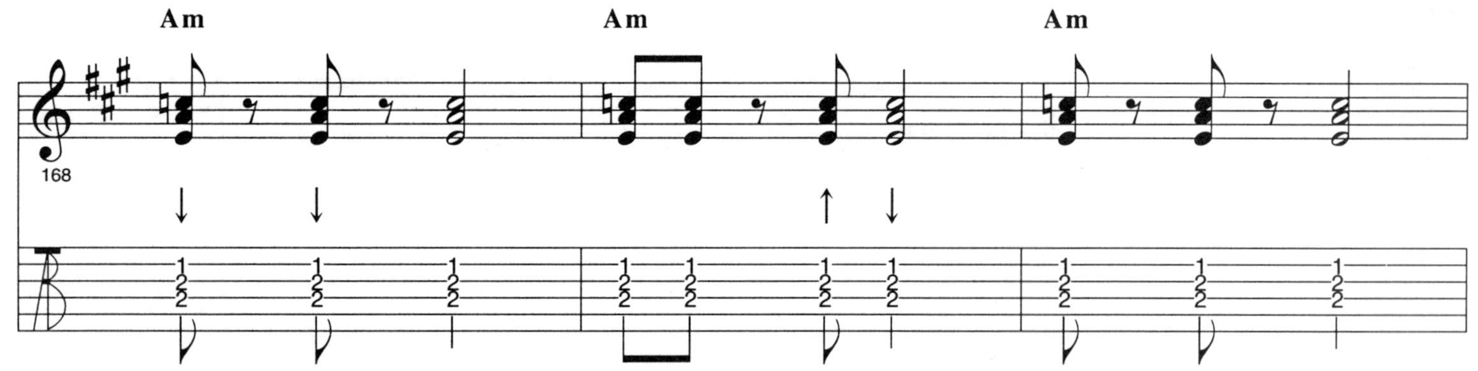
Am
Am
Am
168
1
2
2

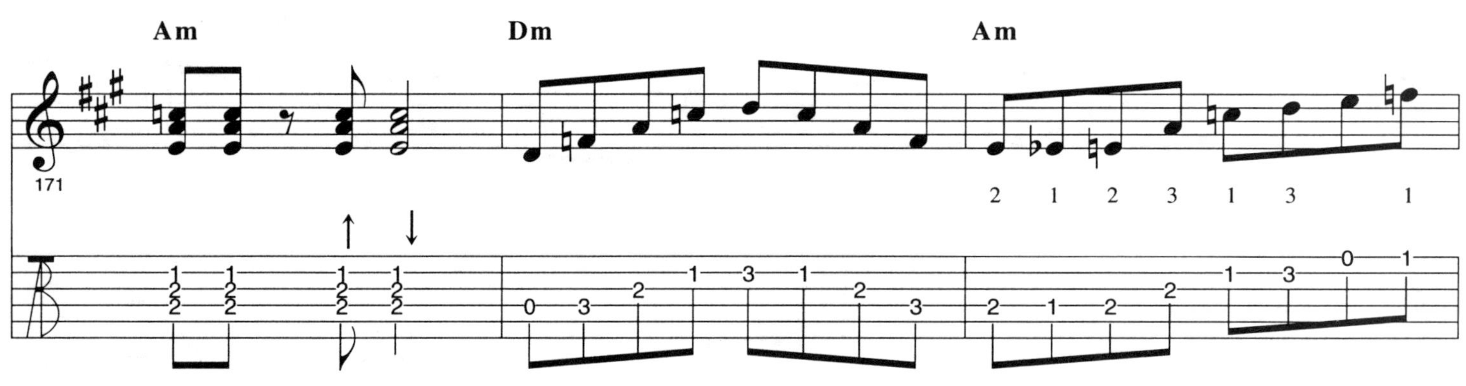
Am
Dm
Am
171
2 1 2 3 1 3 1

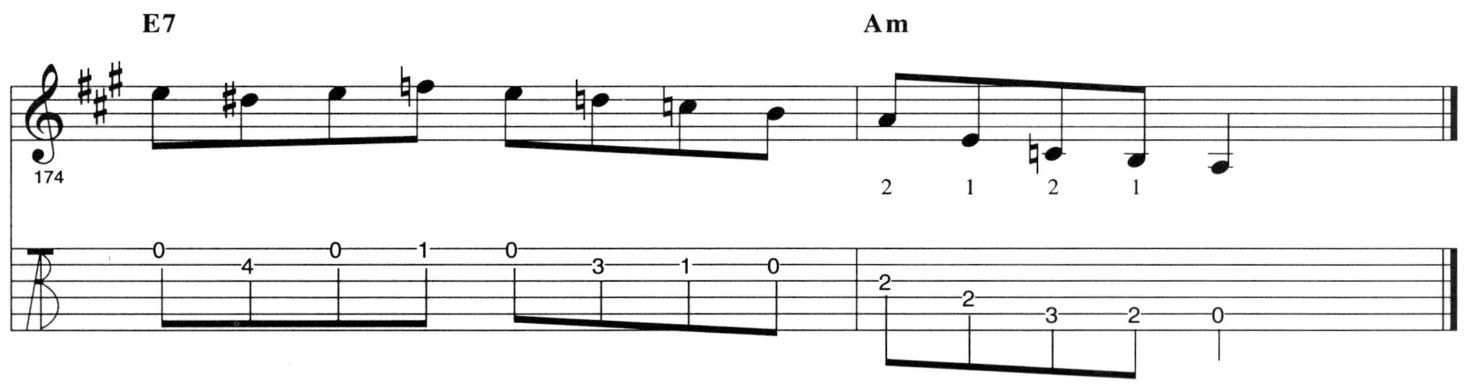
E7
Am
174
2 1 2 1

Bethena

Scott Joplin was termed the "King of Ragtime Composers." He had married a lady named Freddie Alexander of Little Rock, Arkansas in 1904. This was near the peak of his career. Young Freddie died after two months of marriage to Joplin and seems to be almost forgotten. None of Joplin's friends and acquaintances mention her when being interviewed for various biographies so very little is known about her.

Bethena was the first Joplin work published after the death of Freddie. The piece was dedicated to Mr. & Mrs. Dan Davenport. To quote Edward Berlin; "This is an unusual dedication. Davenport was not a prominent performer who could showcase Joplin's music. Nor was he a person of influence or wealth, one who could have helped Joplin's career or commissioned music. So why should Joplin dedicate this piece to Davenport or his wife?"

"The dedication may have had personal significance. Since this is Joplin's first copyrighted work (March 6, 1905) since Freddie's death. I think the Davenports might have helped Joplin through some difficult times, and the dedication was his way of showing appreciation. Supporting the idea that "Bethena" is connected with Freddie, or at least reflects Joplin's mood at the time, is that the music is sadly poignant. It is decidedly not a cheerful, merry waltz, and in this respect contrasts with all of Joplin's other waltzes."

"But then, what is the significance of the title? 'Bethena' is an unusual name. Was there a Bethena? If so, is she the beautiful woman pictured on the cover? Or is this a picture of Freddie." Bethena may have been Freddie's nickname. No one knows but all speculation aside, this is one of my favorite Scott Joplin waltzes and I hope to be yours soon as well.

Here we go. Almost every measure in this arrangement has two eighth notes tied together which will cause a double up or down with the pick hand. I have marked many places but not all. Get the hang of the sound of the tied eighths and it will start to come naturally.

Measure 4: the octaves – use the 1st and 4th finger to fret these notes and use the underbelly of the index finger to mute out the note between them – the 3rd string. The 1st and 4th fingers will slide up and down for the entire measure.

Measure 9 and 17 and the like: I use the 3rd and 2nd fingers for the low strings and use the 1st finger on the 3rd string. This way I can leave the bass ringing out throughout the measure.

Measure 10: 3rd finger on the 5th string, 1st finger gets the 3rd and 4th strings.

Measure 11: 2nd finger - 5th string, 3rd finger – 4th string and 1st finger 3rd string. This will allow the 4th finger to reach for and hopefully hit the "C" or 5th fret third string.

Remember – Maximum sustain with all the above measures.

B Section – the first note of measure 30 is the 4th finger the next grouping will look like an "F" position at the 6th fret.

Measure 31: Note the 8 or the "C" is held while the lower "C" is played on the 4th string.

Measures 41 – 52: Get familiar with the note groupings and see if you recognize them as an already learned chord form.

[C] Section – I see no real hard parts. There are many familiar chord forms in this section. You should try to get used to setting the entire measure's worth of notes down from the beginning.

[D] Section – Measure 115-116 and 123 - 124: Listen to the CD and notice the sustain in these two measures.

[E] Section: I've marked some of the timing areas to be aware of. Watch out.

Black and White Rag

This was the winning tune for me, as I mentioned in my introduction to this book. It is a rock solid arrangement to a classic tune.

Start off in **measure 2** with the first three notes held down.

In the measures like **measure 4** you will want to let the B♭ (3) ring a little but not too long over the second string open. They may clash a bit.

Measure 6, 22 and 38 have a slight gallop. Watch the arrows.

Measure 67: Hold down the "F" position "G" chord at the third fret and pick it through, watching out for the down/ups.

Measure 75–79: You will be building chords for the rolling right hand. Make sure to use the fingerings shown.

Clarinet Polka

The [A] Section doesn't get too tricky. Watch out for the fingerings for the [B] section. They get a bit tricky.

Measure 45: Use the first and second fingers for the double stops.

Measures 53–54: I try to crosspick these measures close to the bridge. It gives the sound a little more bite. Watch out for the down/ups.

Be sure to play this tune with a real bouncy feel.

East Tennessee Rag

Here's a real peppy one for you. There is no top speed for this one. The two parts are very similar but you may notice one slight change in the chord structure. The [B] section has one more "C" chord and one less "F." I was playing this tune with Doc Watson one day, and we must have ripped through it 20 times. When we were done he says something like "That was pretty good. But ya know, you were playing that wrong." He showed me the proper Doc Watson way to play East Tennessee Blues.

You shouldn't have much trouble with this one. Just be sure to play along with the CD. Get the timing right on the button, use the arrows and pick-direction markings or else someday when we play it together, I'll have to say: "That was good, but son, you were playing that wrong."

Jesse Polka

Here is one of my all time favorites to play (but then they all are). You have a lot of position shifts in this piece so get ready. I generally do my position changes with the use and aid of an open string (see measure two and three). Nothing else to say about the first part, except play with bounce and feeling and watch the arrow markings.

The [B] Section should breeze right along.

The [C] Section is not difficult in fingering, but the difficulty lies in playing across the strings at a fast pace. You will see what I mean when you get going on this part.

The [D] Section starts on a pickup note up swing – use the arrows. The notes on the third string need to ring and sustain, while the accent notes on the first and second strings should be short and quick. You will hear this on the recording. Use the fingerings as they are marked.

Measure 65: This is a neat trick that guitar great Fred Duggan showed me. The slide south and north (flat and sharp) is hit twice with a down/up, then you keep the pressure down and slide south (flat), and then bring the note back. Later in this piece you will have long passages of this type lick. It should sound like the notes are being sling shot and boomeranged right off of your guitar. Use the fingerings marked through this section and you will do fine.

The [E] Section changes abruptly into the key of D. Shift into second position throughout this section. You will notice there are no first-fret notes so in flatpicking second position, as opposed to classical II position, we use open strings, but shift so that the first finger will hit the second fret notes, second finger hits the third fret and so on.

The [A] Section variation is a higher version of the first [A] section. I have arranged it with a few more ornaments but for the most part it should be fairly easy.

Measure 106 is a little tricky. You will have to hit all the triplet notes as they are marked.

Measure 108: Use the first finger to hold the eighth frets, and the third finger to hammer onto the tenth fret. Note that it is a dotted eighth note and should be held out. Then the first and second fingers, hold the eighth and ninth fret and slide flat to seventh and eighth frets, then back to the eighth and ninth frets.

The [D] Section variation is the next tricky part. It has the slides that you had a taste of in the first [D] section, but now they are throughout the section. Good luck. Remember to hold and sustain the third string notes and chop off the higher notes.

The last obstacle is the ending. Use the fingerings marked and you should have no troubles.

Lady's Fancy

(Say Old Man Can You Play the Fiddle)

Here is another great five-section tune. It is more known as *Say Old Man,* though Flatpicking master Dan Crary made it famous as *Lady's Fancy.* This is a Texas fiddle tune and can be found on many recordings – Mark O'Conner, Benny Thomasson, Herman Johnson and many more.

An interesting point to make is that measures one, three and five are all interchangeable. The Texas fiddlers use both styles of the same phrase.

This arrangement has some nice twists and turns, but I don't see many real difficult areas areas that you wouldn't be able to figure out. Just be sure to use the arrows and fingerings as they are marked – they will make life easier. Have fun with this great tune.

The Lime Rock

This is another tune that I've learned years ago from guitarist Dan Crary. It is an extremely happy piece so don't make it drag.

The [A] Section: All of the 12th fret first string high "E"s can be hit either as a fretted note, or a harmonic note. Use the fingerings marked and be sure to make the hammer-on pull-offs snap and sound crisp.

The [B] Section has a few difficult areas. **Measures 19–20** are tricky so use the fingerings marked.

Measures 21 into 22 are tricky because you are sliding one note, and at some point in the slide it turns into two (or a double stop).

The [A] Section variation is next. I did something here that I feel is pretty neat. Notice the first of this part starts on the high E and does an arpeggiated run down the "A" scale. Four measures into this part it would repeat again, but instead what I did was to shift the first two notes to the left (or one beat early) to change the run. This is a neat trick and forces you to come up with something different to play. We shift the run to the left, but have to fix the shift or loss of one beat in the run at the end. Don't let it throw you.

The [C] Section should not be too much trouble, though it is all in closed position.

The next [A] variation is very similar to what you've already done. Remember that you can harmonic the high "E" notes.

The [D] Section is not difficult either. Just practice the position shift until it smoothes out. Now you are set and home free. Have fun with this great tune. If you want to hear Dan Crary and I play this one through together, you can find it on my *Doc's Jam* Video or DVD (see my discography).

Maple Leaf Rag

Here is the *Maple Leaf Rag* by Scott Joplin. Published in 1899, it was Joplin's second published ragtime piece. It became the first great instrumental sheet music hit in America. It sold approximately 75,000 copies in the first 6 months of publication and eventually topped the million mark. *Maple Leaf Rag* established Scott Joplin as the "King of the Ragtime Composers" and is unquestionably THE most popular ragtime piece ever written.

Scott Joplin (1868-1917) once lost to obscurity, has finally found his place in history and been issued his rightful position as one of the first truly great American composers. He was one of the nation's music pioneers, for he was the first to develop fully that piano form which could be considered the initial American art form, the piano rag. Although his peers respected Joplin as "The King of Ragtime Writers," the musical world refused to acknowledge his work as a bona fide means of musical expression.

There is only one other noted flatpicker that I have heard play this tune and that is National Flatpicking Champion Robin Kessinger. We recorded a CD together in 1998 called "Star of the County Down" which has grown to be a best seller.

I love this arrangement for *Maple Leaf Rag* and it quickly became one of my favorites to play around the house. It is a very tight arrangement and by that I mean there is a lot of movements and transitions but it is not too hard to play and all of the parts fit together very well.

The entire arrangement is laid out very well so as long as you watch your fingerings and arrow picking directions you should be in good shape.

Temptation Rag

This is the second Winfield arrangement for you. This arrangement came almost entirely from an original piano roll.

The introduction: When I have sets of triplets to perform, I try to arrange them so that the first two can be hammer-ons or pull-offs and then hit the last note. If played properly it will sound as if you hit all the notes. Down swing on the first note and up on the last.

The [A] Section should flow well. Watch out for the timing and the down/ups.

The [B] Section has very tricky first and second endings. These are some great diminished runs. Watch out for the fingerings.

The [A] Section variation has one real tricky run. Measures 50–51. Watch out for the double ups in a row and the fingerings.

Except for being a very long piece, you should not have any troubles throughout the rest that you hadn't encountered to this point. Good luck with it.

Tico Taco No Fuba

This is a very exciting tune, and somewhat of a challenge. Listen to the CD to get the feel of the eighth note rests in most of the measures [A] section.

All of the sections are clearly marked with the arrows and fingerings. Once the fingerings and picking hand techniques are mastered, you should fly through this piece. There are many places to watch out for, but they are all old hat to you if you've gone through all the songs and arrangements in this book. Good luck with this classic and let me know how this arrangement and all the others treat you.

Steve Kaufman's Instructional Materials – also at www. flatpik.com

Twin Pickin' Book with CD
The Legacy of Doc Watson Book
The Anthology of Norman Blake Book
Kaufman's Encyclopedia of Celtic Tunes for Flatpicking Guitar Book
Kaufman's Encyclopedia of Celtic Tunes for Mandolin Book
Bullet Train – The Book with Full CD
Kaufman's Collection of Traditional American Fiddle Tunes Book
Kaufman's Collection of Traditional American Fiddle Tunes 2 CD Set
Kaufman's Collection of Traditional American Fiddle Tunes Video
Flatpicking the Gospels – Video
Flatpicking the Gospels for Guitar – Book w/CD~Audio
Flatpicking the Gospels for Mandolin – Book w/CD~Audio
Flatpicking the Rags and Polkas plus other 3, 4 and 5 part tunes– Book w/2CDs
Championship Flatpicking – VHS Video Only
Championship Flatpicking – Book w/CD
You Can Teach Yourself Flatpicking Guitar – VHS Video Only
You Can Teach Yourself Flatpicking Guitar – w/CD
The Complete Flatpicking VHS Video Only
The Complete Flatpicking Book w/CD
Smokey Mountain Christmas for Guitar – Book with CD
Smokey Mountain Christmas for Mandolin – Book with CD
The Power Flatpicking Fingerboard Book CD~Audio
The Power Flatpicking Fingerboard Video VHS Only
Learn to Play Waltzes Flatpicking Style
4-Hour Celtic Workout Book with 4 CDs
Picking Up Speed – Video - Drills for Flatpicking Guitarists
Flatpicking Through the Holidays! – VHS Video Only
Lead Breaks to Bluegrass Songs Flatpicking Style – Video
20 Bluegrass Mandolin Solos That Every Parkling Lot Picker Should Know BK w/6 CDs
20 Bluegrass Guitar Solos That Every Parkling Lot Picker Should Know Vol. 1 BK w/6 CDs
20 Bluegrass Guitar Solos That Every Parkling Lot Picker Should Know Vol. 2 BK w/6 CDs
20 Bluegrass Guitar Solos That Every Parkling Lot Picker Should Know Vol. 3 BK w/6 CDs
20 Bluegrass Guitar Solos That Every Parkling Lot Picker Should Know Vol. 4 BK w/6 CDs
20 Swing Tunes That Every Parking Lot Picker Should Know Vol. 5 BK w/6 CDs
Flatpicking with Doc (and Steve) ~ Video
The Art of Crosspicking – Video
Learn to Flatpick 1 ~ "From the Beginning" ~ Video
Learn to Flatpick 2 ~ "Building Bluegrass Technique" ~ Video
Learn to Flatpick 3 ~ "Developing Speed and Style" ~ Video
Learn to Flatpick 1, 2, 3 ~ A 3 DVD Set with 3 Booklets

Easy Gospel Guitar – Video

Basic Bluegrass Rhythm Guitar – Video

4 Hr. Bluegrass Workout ~ Book w/4CDs

4 Hr. Bluegrass Workout for Banjo ~ Book w/4CDs

Steve Kaufman's Listening Materials – also at www. flatpik.com
CDs • Videos • Cassettes • DVDs

Back Home - CD with Two Time National Flatpicking Champ Robert Shafer

Circles – Solo Steve - CD - Over Critically Acclaimed!!!

Winfield Winners – 8 Champs in Concert! Live concert from Kamp – Video VHS Only

Steve Kaufman – *Flatpicking to the Next Level* – Live Show Video – Video VHS Only

Star of the County Down with Robin Kessinger – CD

Bullet Train – CD

The Arkansas Traveler – CD

Not Much Work for Saturday with Wayne Henderson CD

The Arkansas Traveler – CD

To the Lady – CD

Breaking Out – CD

Frost on the Window – Cass Only

Strange Company with Nancy Strange, Don Cassell & Will Byers – Cass. Only

An Evening with Steve Kaufman – Live Show Video – VHS Only

Doc's Guitar Jam – Recorded Live at Merlefest w/Steve Kaufman, T. Rice, D. Crary and more – VHS or DVD

The Best of the Camp Concert Series ~ Volume 1 and volume 2 combined on a Double CD package

The Best of the Kamp Concerts – Volume 3 - 2 CD set - Live from 2000

The Best of the Kamp Concerts – Volume 4 - 2 CD set - Live from 2001

The Best of the Kamp Concerts – Volume 5 - 2 CD set - Live from 2002

Some of Steve's Goodies

Steve Kaufman's Flatpicking Kamp Embroidered Denim Shirts

Steve Kaufman's Acoustic Camp Shirts

Steve Kaufman's Acoustic Camp Denim cap w/Suede Bill

Steve Kaufman's Yellow Picks – 10 to a pack

To receive Steve's newsletter, catalog or tour schedule call
800-FLATPIK in North America
Outside the North America +865-982-3808 voice / Fax

Steve Kaufman
P.O. Box 1020
Alcoa, TN 37001

Order on line and sign up for Steve's Email List at www. flatpik.com
Questions and Comments to: Steve@flatpik.com

About the Author

Steve Kaufman was born into a musical family in 1957. His father was a jazz piano player and his mother was a classically trained pianist. Music was always around. At age four, Steve started plinking at the piano, and did so for several years. At age ten, he moved on to the electric guitar, but put it away after a few years. Next came the cello for a few years, starting in the fifth grade. After this, Steve picked up the acoustic guitar and blazed right through a "Folk Guitar" method book. When finished, he thought *...if this is as hard as it gets, its not for him.* Then, his younger brother Will started playing the banjo, and Will's instructor told him he needed a rhythm guitar player to help with his timing. Steve picked up his guitar again, and got into the bluegrass rhythm. One day Will brought home a Flatt and Scruggs LP which featured Doc Watson on guitar, and Steve was hooked on flatpicking.

Steve practiced hard with his newfound love of music, sometimes up to eight hours a day. At age 18, he entered the National Flatpicking Championships in Winfield, Kansas, and made the top ten. The following year was a wash, but in 1977, Steve took second place to Mark O'Conner. In 1978 at age 21, he returned to win the championship. After being barred for five years, he returned on the sixth year to win the 1984 championships again. At the time, Winfield barred the winner for five years, but they could come back on the sixth year. In 1986 they decided to open up the contest to everyone and not bar the past years champs. Steve returned to win his goal. He became the winner and the first and (as of this writing) only three-time winner of the National Flatpicking Championships. He is also noted to have three consecutive wins in the nationals, because he was barred all the years he did not enter.

Steve continues to work hard in the world of music. He began producing books and videos in 1989 after teaching private lessons for close to 20 years. His catalog of instructional materials is close to 44 items and his listening CDs and videos number over 14. Steve began touring the world, conducting seminars, workshops, clinics and concerts in 1990. After five years, he and his wife Donna began *Steve Kaufman's Flatpicking Camp.* Every other year they have added more camps into their agenda, and now, under the title *Steve Kaufman's Acoustic Kamps,* they host a *Fingerpicking Kamp,* and an *Old Time Banjo, Bluegrass Banjo and Mandolin Kamp.* They have grown into the largest kamps of their kind in the world, with students traveling from around the world to Maryville, Tennessee. In 2002, Steve Kaufman received the Gold Award from a reader's poll in *Acoustic Guitar Magazine* for running the "Best Workshops, Seminars and Camps."

Steve stays busy being a husband and father, running his Kamps, tour schedule, writing books and recording videos and CDs. He also owns and operates the area's premier acoustic venue and espresso bar: *The Palace Theater* in downtown Maryville (see www.palacetheater.com). Also connected to the Palace Theater is a café and deli called *The Palace Café and Catering.*

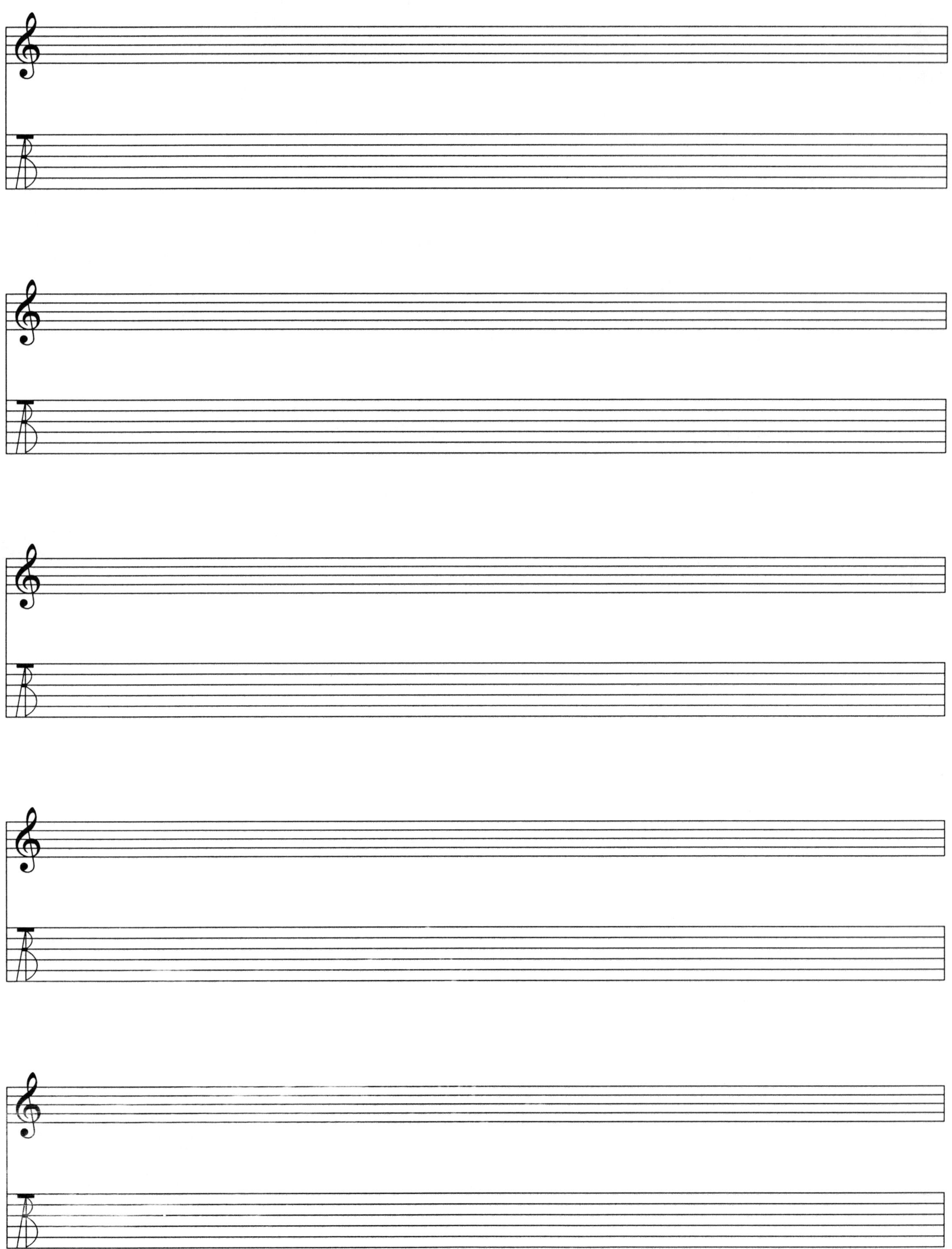

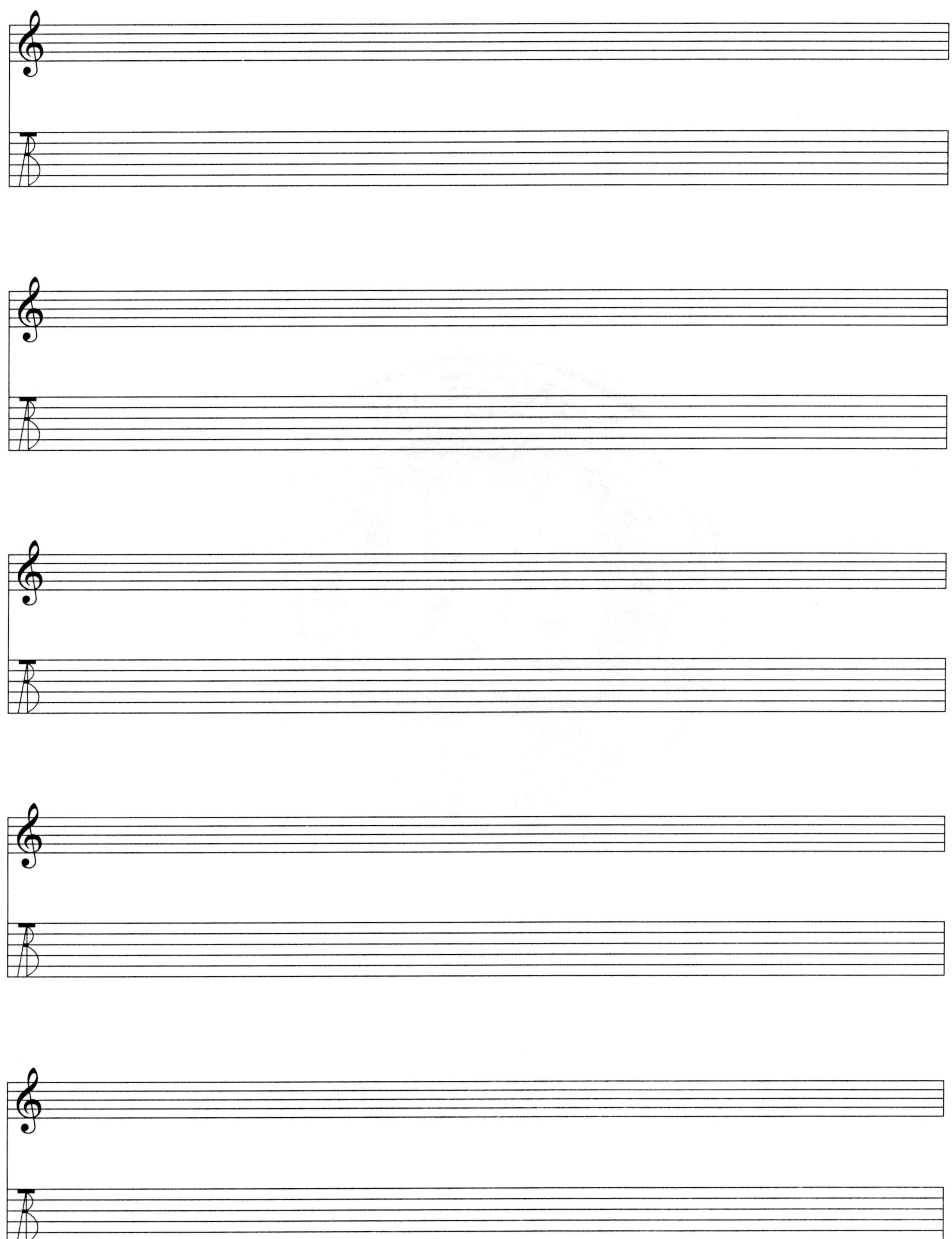

EXCELLENCE IN MUSIC
MEL BAY®
Since 1947